CINEMA OF PAIN

CINEMA OF PAIN
On Quebec's Nostalgic Screen

Liz Czach and André Loiselle,
editors

WILFRID LAURIER
UNIVERSITY PRESS

LAURIER
Inspiring Lives.

This book has been published with the help of a grant from the Canadian Federation for the Humanities and Social Sciences, through the Awards to Scholarly Publications Program, using funds provided by the Social Sciences and Humanities Research Council of Canada. Wilfrid Laurier University Press acknowledges the support of the Canada Council for the Arts for our publishing program. We acknowledge the financial support of the Government of Canada. This work was supported by the Research Support Fund.

Canada
Funded by the Government of Canada

Canada Council   Conseil des arts
for the Arts   du Canada

ONTARIO ARTS COUNCIL
CONSEIL DES ARTS DE L'ONTARIO
an Ontario government agency
un organisme du gouvernement de l'Ontario

Library and Archives Canada Cataloguing in Publication

Title: Cinema of pain : on Quebec's nostalgic screen / Liz Czach and André Loiselle, editors.

Names: Czach, Liz, [date] editor. | Loiselle, André, editor.

Description: Includes bibliographical references and index.

Identifiers: Canadiana (print) 20200153919 | Canadiana (ebook) 20200154613 | ISBN 9781771124331 (softcover) | ISBN 9781771124355 (EPUB) | ISBN 9781771124348 (PDF)

Subjects: LCSH: Motion pictures—Québec (Province)—History. | LCSH: Québec (Province)—In motion pictures. | LCSH: National characteristics, French-Canadian.

Classification: LCC PN1993.5.Q43 C56 2020 | DDC 791.4309714—dc23

Cover design by David Drummond.
Text design by Janette Thompson (Jansom).

© 2020 Wilfrid Laurier University Press
Waterloo, Ontario, Canada
www.wlupress.wlu.ca

This book is printed on FSC ® certified paper. It contains post-consumer fibre and other controlled sources, is processed chlorine free, and is manufactured using biogas energy.

MIX
Paper from
responsible sources
FSC® C103567

Printed in Canada

CONTENTS

SECTION IV—Métropole & Région

INTRODUCTION

Liz Czach and André Loiselle

In his 1993 book *Genèse de la société québécoise*, renowned Quebec sociologist Fernand Dumont contends that it is normal for a nation whose sense of identity is disappearing to want to return to its roots to better understand its current circumstances (Dumont 1993, 13–14). The sense of identity of the Québécois nation was seriously challenged as early as 1980, when the first referendum on sovereignty-association failed to fulfill the nationalist dream that had been the driving force behind the social progress and cultural effervescence of the 1960s and '70s. A couple of years after Dumont's remarks were published, a second referendum also failed to deliver on the nationalist promise of a *Québec libre*. At least since the failure of that second referendum in 1995, the loss of a cohesive nationalist mission in the province has precipitated Dumont's prognosis that the nation would yearn to revisit its ancestral origins to find some purpose in its present-day existence. This collection of original essays argues that this phenomenon has translated into a pervasive nostalgia in Quebec culture—including a peculiar reimagining of Catholicism—that is especially evident in the province's vibrant but deeply wistful cinema. As Jim Leach points out in the closing chapter, 1995 saw a poignant cinematic evocation of "the Catholic religious practices associated with Quebec's traditional cultural identity" in Robert Lepage's first feature film, *Le Confessionnal.*

In the current context, however, nostalgia does not simply denote a sentimental longing for the bucolic pleasures of bygone Catholic rituals. There is certainly some folkloric treatment of the past in Quebec's contemporary cinema, as is manifest in the films inspired by the tall tales of *raconteur extraordinaire* Fred Pellerin, such as Luc Picard's *Babine* (2008) and *Ésimésac* (2012), which superimpose fantastical folk tales upon the reality of the quaint village of St-Élie-de-Caxton. But Quebec's nostalgia is generally more tortured and much gloomier than the pastoral elegy to maple syrup delivered by Pellerin and legendary folksinger Gilles Vigneault in Francis Legault's documentary *Le Goût d'un pays* (2016). Our understanding of nostalgia in contemporary Quebec cinema is closer to the etymological sense of the term, which underscores the element of pain (*algos*) associated with the longing for a return home (*nostos*). This aching desire for "home" in Quebec films takes a wide range of forms: the struggle to reassert filial roots or mend broken relationships; explorations of reminiscent spaces; the regeneration of haunting stories and the unearthing of forgotten traumas. Whether it is in grandiloquent historical melodramas such as *Séraphin, un homme et son péché* (Binamé 2002), intimate realist dramas like *Tout ce que tu possèdes* (Émond 2012), charming art films like *C.R.A.Z.Y.* (Vallée 2005), earnest documentaries like *L'Empreinte* (Poliquin and Dubuc 2014), or even gory horror movies like *Sur le seuil* (Tessier 2003) and light-hearted comedies like *Filière 13* (Huard 2010), the contemporary Québécois screen projects an image of shared suffering that seems to unite the nation through a melancholy search for home.

In her 2008 book *The Future of Nostalgia*, Svetlana Boym offers a typology of nostalgia that divides the concept into two broad categories:

Two kinds of nostalgia are distinguished: the restorative and the reflective. Restorative nostalgia stresses *nostos* and attempts a transhistorical reconstruction of the lost home. Reflective nostalgia thrives in *algia*, the longing itself, and delays the homecoming—wistfully, ironically, desperately. Restorative nostalgia does not think of itself as nostalgia, but rather as truth and tradition. Reflective nostalgia dwells on the ambivalences of human longing and belonging and does not shy away from the contradictions of modernity. Restorative nostalgia protects the absolute truth, while reflective nostalgia calls it into doubt. Restorative nostalgia is at the core of recent national and religious revivals; it knows two main plots—the return to origins and the conspiracy. Reflective nostalgia does not follow a single plot but explores ways of inhabiting many places at once and imagining different time zones; it loves details, not symbols. At best, reflective nostalgia can present an ethical and creative challenge, not merely a pretext for midnight melancholias. This typology of nostalgia allows us to distinguish between national memory that is based on a single plot of national identity, and social memory, which consists of collective frameworks that mark but do not define the individual memory. (xviii)

While there are certainly instances of reflexive nostalgia in contemporary Quebec cinema, much of the corpus seems to be of the restorative kind, aiming to formally recapture an eluding sense of identity and, most importantly, not recognizing itself as nostalgia. This parallels a certain socio-political trend in the province, whereby conservative public intellectuals promote the crucial importance of keeping traditional values at the core of contemporary Quebec culture, while insisting that this has nothing to do with nostalgia (Bock-Côté 2016). Sociologist Mathieu Bock-Côté is perhaps the most vocal defender of the need for Quebec nationalism to remain solidly rooted in the province's long history. His brand of conservatism, which sees multiculturalism as the cause of a *dénationalisation tranquille*, "asserts that man [*sic*] needs anchors. It is his relationship to history that is at stake ... It responds to a vital need for man to inscribe himself in a specific historical continuity, which provides anthropological stability" (Bock-Côté 2015a; our translation). To a large extent, the anchor the Québécois must hold on to is his rural heritage. In an article defending *l'homme rural* against stereotypes of backwardness, Bock-Côté urges his contemporaries to "wonder if old virtues have not been lost with our entry into urban modernity. The virtue of being grounded; of transmitting one's heritage. And perhaps also, a certain realism, a sense of measured action. The prudence of rural people is not fatalism. It is a way of remembering that if we do not take care of our world, it will be degraded" (Bock-Côté 2015b; our translation). For Bock-Côté and other Quebec conservatives, the future of the Nation is irrevocably linked to a rural past that urbanites should neither disparage nor forget. "While this position relates to what could be called historical conservatism," he writes, "we must not see it as a nostalgia for an old world to which no one would want to return. Rather, it expresses the desire to find some solid foundation for the future" (Bock-Côté 2016; our translation).

Some of our readers might agree with Bock-Côté and flatly reject our premise that Quebec society and, more specifically, Quebec films are steeped in nostalgia. Nevertheless, this book asserts that contemporary Quebec cinema, in all its multifaceted richness, does exhibit strong nostalgic tendencies that cut across visual styles, narrative themes, and modes of address. To explore all the intricate variations on the theme of nostalgia in recent Quebec films, we have structured our anthology around four broad themes: (1) Indigenous Longings; (2) Yearning for a Pre-Modern Quebec; (3) Gendered Suffering; and (4) Métropole & Région.

Section I examines films that reflect a current impulse to reimagine contemporary Quebec as an Indigenized nation. Political science professor Marc Chevrier in his 2012 book *La République québécoise* argues that a sovereign Quebec should find inspiration in the history of New France, especially in the period when the colony was on the verge of achieving a kind of collectivism inspired by Indigenous forms of government. For Chevrier, the "Great Peace of Montreal" signed in 1701 is perhaps the most striking example of a consensual association among settlers and First Nations, a genuine confederation based on equality among independent but co-responsible peoples whose concerted actions could achieve common goals (Chevrier 2012, 160–67). A certain nostalgia for the *République néo-française* of the eighteenth century (Chevrier 2012, 107), where Indigenous and European civilizations intermingled in a culture of *liberté, égalité et fraternité*, seems to animate a number of Quebec filmmakers, who look at indigeneity as a model for a renewed sense of identity. Kester Dyer's Chapter 1, "Landscape, Trauma, and Identity: Simon Lavoie's *Le Torrent*," reads Simon Lavoie's 2012 period drama from a perspective that provides clues about the profound nature of relationships between Québécois and Indigenous peoples, at the same time as it offers tools for reconceptualizing intercultural relationships and non-Indigenous attitudes toward territory. Based on Anne Hébert's 1950 novella of the same title, *Le Torrent* recounts the violent childhood of François (Victor Andres Turgeon-Trelles), rendered deaf after a severe beating by his zealously Catholic mother. But the film departs from its literary source in ascribing an Innu identity to the enigmatic character of Amica, who comes to live with François after his mother's death. Furthermore, Lavoie fuses Indigenous and Québécois identities by casting Québécoise actress Laurence Leboeuf in the roles of both Amica and François's mother as a younger woman, forging a kind of cultural hybridization. Within this Oedipal framework, the film creates an ambiguous tension between the appropriation of Indigenous identity and the Québécois character's inability to fully own, or return home to, the land he associated with his past, which instead comes to haunt and possess him.

Modernity is a topic closely linked to the reactive emergence of nostalgic sentiments. As Geraldine Pratt and Rose Marie San Juan remind us in their book *Film and Urban Space* (2014), "a long line of political philosophers, from Kant, Hegel through Marx, Levinas to Fredric Jameson have condemned nostalgia for its reactionary effects of preserving the status quo ... [It is also] a reaction to the ruptures and displacements of modernity and globalization" (115). In the Quebec context, modernity is most often associated with the social changes brought about by the Quiet Revolution of the early 1960s.[1] Accordingly, nostalgic yearnings are often directed toward a pre–Quiet Revolution era where one can find refuge from the many ills and disorders of contemporary life. The chapters in Section II survey various cinematic expressions of this yearning for a pre-modern Quebec. In Chapter 2, "The Quebec Heritage Film," Liz Czach studies heritage biopics like *Ma vie en cinémascope* (Filiatrault 2004), *Maurice Richard* (Binamé 2005), and *Louis Cyr: The Strongest Man in the World* (Roby 2013) to highlight the peculiar brand of nostalgia these films exhibit. The heritage film emerged most prominently in Britain in the 1980s, at a time when the Brits needed to be reminded of the past glories of the now defunct empire. Quebec in the early twenty-first century is very far from Britain in the 1980s; that said, the heritage film genre in both these national film contexts evinces a nostalgic return to the past—although there is a stark difference in what they yearn for. If the British heritage films hearken back to an era of colonial rule and the lives of the upper class and aristocrats, then the Quebec heritage film looks back longingly to an era of pre–Quiet Revolution oppression when the Québécois populace lacked the means for self-determination. This return to an era of collective suffering thus inverses the usual operation of the genre by focusing on a humiliating and downtrodden past rather than a glorious one. Yet paradoxically, it serves the same purpose of stirring nationalist sentiments. Indeed, the heritage film reaffirms a past in which Quebec identity was cohesive, shared, and binding, a coherent past that in the face of an increasingly multicultural and multi-ethnic Quebec is reassuring.

While Quebec heritage films tend to be produced with relatively big budgets and feature local stars, the films of Bernard Émond, which are analyzed by a number of our contributors, are much smaller-scale and avoid the glamour of Quebec's thriving star system. However, Émond's oeuvre shares with the heritage film a deep longing for the lost values of pre-modern Quebec. As Alessandra Pires discusses in Chapter 3, "'La Nostalgie de la maison inconnue': The Ethics of Memory in Bernard Émond's Recent Work," the filmmaker is always concerned with the loss of a communal identity, with the disengagement from the environment and the denigration of manual labour that modernity brought about. As Pires notes, for Émond, *nostalgia* is not a longing for a specific moment in the past so much as a yearning for what has vanished over time. Speaking for all Québécois, he contends that "we miss familial and social solidarity, we miss dignity at work, we miss the rapport with nature, and we miss the sentiment of a common history and shared values. We would be wrong to reject these feelings as *passéist*. It seems possible to me to regain a part of what we lost in the consciousness of this very lack and these losses" (Émond 2016a, 50).

An inability to acknowledge this loss and thereby regain some of what is lacking leads to the condition experienced by Pierre (Patrick Drolet), the main character in Émond's film *Tout ce que tu possèdes* (2012). Pierre's difficulties in interacting with the outside world seem insurmountable to him, as he prefers to hide within his own self-destructive vertigo. Radically retreating from society into himself, Pierre exemplifies the modern isolationist version of the individual, a phenomenon that according to Émond belongs to a world in which the familial links of the past have dissolved and social relations have disintegrated.

Many Quebec films of the past twenty years focus on characters, like Pierre, whose belonging to the alienating ethos of modernity has completely isolated them from their surroundings. This is case for the character of Rémy (Rémy Girard) in Denys Arcand's *Les Invasions barbares* (2003), who, at the beginning of the film, finds himself withdrawn from society, dying in an overcrowded hospital room, estranged from his children and disconnected from his friends. As the film progresses, however, Rémy reconnects with his family and age-old companions. This narrative journey toward reconciliation infers a figurative (if not literal) return to a time when life and love were simpler. In Chapter 4, "Fingerless (Anti)Christ: A Reminiscence of the Church in 1966 in Denys Arcand's *Les Invasions barbares* and Éric Tessier's *Sur le seuil*," André Loiselle argues that this time is subtly identified in the film as the pre–Quiet Revolution—more specifically, pre-1966. In both *Les Invasions barbares* and Éric Tessier's contemporaneous horror film *Sur le seuil* (2003), aging priests single out 1966 as the year the Church lost its power, which caused modern Quebec to lose its way. In both Arcand's film and Tessier's, the collapse of Catholicism in the province appears as a painful loss of direction and meaning, symbolized by a fingerless figure: a damaged statue of Christ in the former and a novelist-cum-spawn-of-Satan in the latter. To understand the meaning of 1966, Loiselle offers a brief survey of the public discourse of the time and shows that this was a period characterized by profound anxiety and dread in the face of an uncertain future. Much of the fear associated with 1966 stemmed from the rise of the women's liberation movement and Second Wave feminism. Picking up on the symbol of the severed fingers, Loiselle concludes that both films mourn the castration of masculine religious power that resulted from the changes that came in 1966. Still affected today by this loss of power, many Québécois men suffer from a bad case of masculine nostalgia.

Section III further investigates the notion that nostalgia is, indeed, gendered. Gina Freitag in Chapter 5, "The *Dys*-Comforts of Home in Quebec Gothic Horror Cinema," proposes to read a handful of Quebec horror films through the lens of Gothic nostalgia. Gothic horror, a subgenre most often associated with feminine realms of domestic ruins and dark desires, lends itself perfectly to the examination of the unique ways in which female characters connect to their past to assert their agency. Within the particular idiom of horror films like Éric Falardeau's *Thanatomorphose* (2012), Maude Michaud's *Dys-* (2014) and Pascal Laugier's *Martyrs* (2008), this form of nostalgic self-exploration necessarily indulges in abjection, blood, and gore. Thus, the particular kind of nostalgia that can be labelled as Gothic is one that operates within an uncanny domestic space where a painful process of regression allows the female character, by digging deep into her traumatic origins and peeling away the layers of her objectified body, to free herself from the male gaze and transcend the constraints of Quebec patriarchy. This excruciating experience takes place within the confines of the home: a paradoxical space that is both a metaphor for the nostalgic desire to withdraw from a threatening world of men and hide in a female space of comfort, and an abject environment imbued with the disintegrated ego and rendered *unheimlich* through a rejection of the Symbolic realm of social responsibility. In other words, the home is at once the idealized domestic place to which the female character wishes to retreat to find herself, and the Gothic ruin that confronts her with the inevitable breakdown of a body that fails to personify the authentic self. As these films gruesomely demonstrate, this is a horrendous but worthwhile exercise.

Women seem able to emerge transformed from their nostalgic journeys through the agonies of Gothic suffering; men have a much harder time overcoming their sense of loss. Amy Ransom in Chapter 6, "Men in Pain: Home, Nostalgia, and Masculinity in Twenty-First Century Quebec Film," further develops Loiselle's argument, analyzing the recent corpus of "male melodramas," where a male protagonist struggles with more or less success to find his place in a transitional society that has begun to evolve away from traditional notions of home. Though the films Ransom studies belong to a variety of genres, they all exploit the melodramatic mode in their dual engagement: the family in crisis is coupled with male victimhood and aggression. By drawing on scholarship that realigns the melodrama with the traditionally male-oriented genres of the thriller, the detective film, and the action film, and shifting the focus of feminist scholarship on the melodrama from the female protagonist to the male, Ransom's chapter explores how these films deploy the spectacle of men in pain as symptomatic of masculine nostalgia, conceived as a longing for traditional notions of the patriarchal family, with its clear-cut and hierarchical gender roles as the basis of the nation. But as much as these films express nostalgia for an idealized simpler time when gender roles were more easily distinguishable, they also evoke a strong albeit unattainable desire to escape the strict rules of the conservative society dominated by Catholic edicts. Thus, the men in pain in these films appear sadly indicative of "ce passé qui ne passe pas" [this past that won't pass] in relation to the lingering hold of the French Canadian past on the Québécois present. By revealing the contradictions inherent in a contemporary Quebec society in transition, the male melodrama shows characters indulging in a conservative nostalgia they are paradoxically eager to evade.

A core contradiction in Quebec society today is the tension between the cosmopolitan, forward-looking multiculturalism of Montreal and the traditional, deeply francophone, and still surprisingly religious ethos of the rest of the province. As the chapters in Section IV, "Métropole & Région" discuss, many Quebec films pit the allure of the exciting, worldly metropole against the equally strong urge on the part of the nostalgic Québécois to return to the regions where their rural ancestors can still be found. In Chapter 7, "The Rural (Re)Turns of Young Protagonists in Contemporary Quebec Films," Miléna Santoro addresses the many ways in which the geographical return to Quebec's traditional countryside is problematized in films like Xavier Dolan's *Tom à la ferme* (2013), Catherine Martin's *Une jeune fille* (2013), Pascale Ferland's *Ressac* (2013), François Péloquin's *Le Bruit des arbres* (2015), and Sophie Deraspe's *Les Loups* (2014). The antinomic cliché would be for these films to show that while urbane hipsters seek refuge in the countryside, those who have grown up in the regions and experienced rural hardship would find the urban alternative quite appealing. But even though these films participate in nostalgia implicitly or explicitly through their setting in Quebec's hinterland, their young protagonists inject new life into the old cliché, for the decisions they make to stay in the regions or go to the metropole remain ambiguous and undetermined. The metropole does not offer a solution, but

neither do the regions. For Santoro, the rural context of these films constitutes a recasting of the landscape as a foundation for growth as well as a site
of memory, loss, and adversity.

In Chapter 8, "Return to Abitibi in Bernard Émond's *La Donation*,"
Katherine Anne Roberts interprets Émond's cinema as evoking both the
debt the Québécois owe to their ancestors with respect to what he calls "the
essence of French-Canadian culture," and the debt he personally owes as
a filmmaker to his predecessors. In setting *La Donation* (2009) in Abitibi,
Émond reflects on the difficult history of that remote region, while looking
back at the films that inspired him, such as l'abbé Maurice Proulx's *En pays
neufs* (1937) and *Ste-Anne-de-Roquemaure* (1942), Gilles Groulx's unsigned
Normétal (1960), and Pierre Perrault's "cycle abitibien," notably *Le Retour à
la terre* (1976). In Émond's film, a young urban doctor, Jeanne Dion (Élise
Guilbault), has come to the former mining village of Normétal to temporarily replace the aging Dr. Yves Rainville (Jacques Godin). When Dr. Rainville
passes away and bequeaths his practice to her in his will, she must decide
whether she will accept this gift and remain in the remote village or return
to Montreal. The final scene of the film shows Dr. Dion standing on a lonely
road holding an infant in the aftermath of a car accident that has killed the
baby's mother. Though the film ends without resolving whether Jeanne will
take over Dr. Rainville's medical practice, the final frame shows her as having
already decided to devote herself to others as Rainville had done throughout
his career. The story becomes a means for Émond to further explore the
themes of loss, debt, and cultural transmission, which dominate his oeuvre.

The final chapter of our book continues the reading of Émond's work,
this time putting it in dialogue with the films of Robert Lepage. In Chapter 9,
"Quebec–Montreal: Time, Space, and Memory in Robert Lepage's *Le
Confessionnal* and Bernard Émond's *La Neuvaine*," Jim Leach examines the
ambivalent ways in which the two filmmakers explore the threat to Quebec's
distinct culture in the age of globalization, and how it can survive the increasingly striking differences between Montreal's cosmopolitanism and the more
traditional culture of the rest of Quebec. Like *La Donation*, *La Neuvaine*
(2005) follows Dr. Jeanne Dion, but it precedes the events of the Abitibi
film. Having witnessed the brutal killings of a battered woman and her child
whom she had tried to help, Dr. Dion decides to abandon her practice. She
has lost her own child to an incurable disease and is now haunted by the
idea that her actions, the decision to get involved with a patient, contributed
to this act of violence. She leaves Montreal for a small village near Quebec

City, Ste-Anne-de-Beaupré, which is known for its Catholic basilica where the faithful come to obtain miracles from the saint. A chance encounter with a devout young man, François (Patrick Drolet), gradually allows her to come to terms with her grief by re-engaging with the traditions that fostered a collective identity grounded in the teachings of the Church. Lepage's *Le Confessionnal* (1995) interweaves 1952, when Alfred Hitchcock came to Quebec City to shoot *I Confess*, with 1989, when Pierre (Lothaire Bluteau) returns to Quebec City after a three-year stay in China to attend his father's funeral. At the funeral, Pierre is disturbed by the absence of his adoptive brother Marc (Patrick Goyette). When Pierre reconnects with Marc, he finds Marc troubled by the fact that he does not know who his real father was. Genuinely committed to helping his brother, Pierre agrees to try to solve the mystery of Marc's birth. This narratively connects 1989 to 1952, the year Marc was born. While very different in style and structure, the two films focus on the lasting heritage of the Catholic Church, and both invite audiences to reassess the past and the difficulty of defining a distinctive Québécois identity without returning to its roots in Catholicism. For Leach, the key question becomes how to define a culturally Catholic identity as distinct from the religious doctrines that imposed what Lepage calls the "yoke of religion." Neither film offers a cheery answer to this question, but through the depiction of Pierre and François as altruistic characters who exude a spirituality detached from the Church's dogma, Lepage and Émond similarly suggest that salvation for the Québécois may rest in a sense of responsibility and devotion to others. A similar argument could be made for a number of contemporary Quebec films, such as Léa Pool's *La Passion d'Augustine* (2014), where the Church's loss of ascendency leaves room for other forms of selfless dedication. In the case of Pool's film, a passion for music, and especially for the musical education of young women, drives the religious fervour of a small congregation of nuns at a time when Vatican II and the Quiet Revolution are changing the face of Catholicism.

Our anthology does not propose a single explanation for the recent emergence of nostalgia as a common theme in Quebec cinema. Nor do we claim that all contemporary Quebec cinema is nostalgic. However, it seems clear to us that, at a time of disconcerting uncertainty, many Québécois filmmakers are expressing a sense of aching loss and painful longing; a longing for the past, for the simplicity of country life, for the impression of strength and stability that the Church or patriarchy or cultural homogeneity used to provide; a longing for the authenticity and territorial legitimacy of Indigenous people; or just a longing for a safe place to call home. From our perspective, the sheer diversity of topics and approaches presented in this collection bears witness to this widespread tendency in early twenty-first-century Quebec cinema. However, while this anthology comprises the work of scholars from across North America, it does not include any contributions from colleagues affiliated with the francophone universities of Quebec. Our invitations to Québécois film historians and critics were met with a great deal of reluctance and even suspicion.

This might be due to the fact that the theoretical approaches used by our contributors differ significantly from the methodologies generally employed by francophone scholars. Indeed, the main objective of this collection is to interpret the theme of nostalgia in Quebec cinema within a "cultural studies" framework, which is quite unlike the practices common in francophone universities both in France and in Quebec. In fact, francophone academics often use the English term to refer to this approach, rather than a French term like "études culturelles," so as to stress that this is an anglophone concept operating outside of traditional francophone "sciences humaines." For example, in his 2013 article "Ce que les *cultural studies* font aux savoirs disciplinaires," Sorbonne professor Éric Maigret writes: "Les *cultural studies* sont le révélateur de phénomènes culturels nouveaux, difficilement analysables par les sciences humaines qui ont été institutionnalisées il y a un siècle" ["Cultural Studies examines new cultural phenomena that are difficult to analyze using the human sciences that have been institutionalized for a century"] (Maigret 2013, 145).

While Canadian film studies functions implicitly as a form of cultural studies, providing largely interdisciplinary readings of films as a set of more or less obvious metaphors for Canadian culture, *études cinématographiques québécoises* has tended to adopt methodologies that are closer to sociology, attempting to explicate and quantify cinema as a social phenomenon. From Christiane Tremblay-Daviault's *Un cinéma orphelin. Structures mentales et sociales du cinéma québécois (1942–1953)* (1981) and Yvan Lamonde and Pierre-François Hébert's *Le Cinéma au Québec. Essai de statistique historique, 1896 à nos jours* (1981), through André Gaudrault and colleagues' *Le Cinéma en histoire. Institutions cinématographiques, réception filmique et reconstitution historique* (1999), to Gilles Marsolais's *Cinéma québécois. De l'artisanat à l'industrie* (2011), Marc-André Robert's *Dans la caméra de l'abbé Proulx. La société agricole et rurale de Duplessis* (2013), and Bruno Cornellier's *La «chose indienne.» Cinéma et politiques de la représentation autochtone au Québec et au*

Canada (2015), *études cinématographiques québécoises* over the past forty years, at least, has focused on historiography, statistics, intitutions, and politics, and has spent little time on cultural interpretation. As such, our cultural studies approach to nostalgia is unlikely to resonate with the kind of scholarly research being done in francophone Québec.

Another reason for the reluctance of our francophone colleagues to contribute to this anthology might be that it is difficult for Québécois intellectuals to recognize and accept the centrality of nostalgia as a trope in contemporary Quebec cultural practices. After all, "restorative nostalgia does not think of itself as nostalgia, but rather as truth and tradition" (Boym 2008, xviii). Conversely, perhaps those of us who choose to look at Quebec cinema from outside the province are woefully mistaken in our interpretation of what is going on in the province. But clearly what we see as a crucial phenomenon in contemporary francophone cinema in this country has, to this point, not gathered much interest from those closest to it.

Note

1   It should be noted, however, that a direct correlation between modernity and the Quiet Revolution needs to be nuanced. Some have argued that modernity began long before 1960; others believe that modernity took longer to be fully established than is usually accepted. In the words of Olivier Marcil, "en 1960, l'avènement de la Révolution tranquille, par ses bouleversements majeurs, donne l'impression que le Québec fait enfin son entrée dans la modernité" [In 1960, the beginning of the Quiet Revolution, with all the changes that it brought about, *gives the impression* that Quebec had finally entered modernity] (Marcil 2002, 223).

SECTION I

Indigenous Longings

1

LANDSCAPE, TRAUMA, AND IDENTITY:
Simon Lavoie's *Le Torrent*

Kester Dyer

Simon Lavoie's 2012 period drama *Le Torrent* displays evident reverence for the Anne Hébert story from which it is adapted. This tale recounts the violent childhood of François, rendered deaf after a severe beating by his zealously Catholic mother, an injury that paradoxically attunes him to the sound of a powerful stream. But *Le Torrent* departs from its literary source in one striking way. Lavoie ascribes an Innu identity to the mysterious Amica, who comes to live with François after his mother's death. Furthermore, Lavoie fuses Indigenous and Québécois identities by casting Laurence Leboeuf in the roles both of Amica and of François's mother as a younger woman. Thus, within this Oedipal framework, the film creates an ambiguous tension between the appropriation of Indigenous identity and the Québécois character's inability to fully own, or "return home," to the land he associates with his past, which instead comes to haunt and possess him.

Arguably, *Le Torrent* oscillates between what Svetlana Boym (2001) sees as the contradictory manifestations or reflexive and restorative forms of nostalgia, the longing or empathy of *algia* and the return home of *nostos*. This chapter therefore explores this film's deployment of nostalgia and seeks to ascertain whether this feature obscures colonial relationships or points to Quebec's necessary reconfiguration of nationhood. To be sure, Lavoie's portrayal of Amica recalls Boym's description of historically romantic nostalgia, where "[a] young and beautiful girl … buried somewhere in the native soil; blond and meek or dark and wild," embodies nature (13). At the same time, *Le Torrent* mirrors Anthony Vidler's (1996) observation that "the uncanny has been interpreted as a dominant constituent of modern nostalgia," which Freud linked to "the impossible desire to return to the womb" (x). The womb is central to *Le Torrent*'s metaphorical discourse. Indeed, the landscape epitomized by the stream in *Le Torrent* becomes associated with François's birth, while his mother's double is nominally Indigenized. As such, given Quebec's status as a settler-colonial society that was in turn colonized, and one whose impossible return to France was marked by a painful and "tenacious nostalgia for origins" (Dumont 1996, 332),[1] Lavoie here appears to imagine an Indigenous presence that potentially inhibits Quebec's totalizing reappropriation of territory and instead generates a more reflective longing.

In parallel, other films help elucidate Quebec cinema's propensity to foreground nostalgia for the period in which *Le Torrent* is set as well as Quebec's relationship with Indigenous peoples. For instance, the infamous Quebec postwar melodrama *La Petite Aurore, l'enfant martyre* (Bigras 1952) highlights themes that overlap with Lavoie's film and, most importantly, offers a tangible temporal path across the Quiet Revolution as a significant point of demarcation in modern Quebec history. Indeed, many recent cinematic portrayals of Quebec before the Quiet Revolution, though often lingering on the hardship and marginalization experienced by French Canadians (as Liz Czach argues in her chapter), tend paradoxically to romanticize pre-1960s Quebec and implicitly emblematize the Quiet Revolution as a point of rupture. This cinematic propensity illuminates how nostalgia operates in Quebec. In addition, the work of Jeff Barnaby, a Mi'kmaq filmmaker from Listuguj, also looks to the past and stresses concerns about assimilation and colonialism, while emphasizing violence against children, a theme that underpins both *Le Torrent* and *La Petite Aurore*. Through bodily mutilations and inscriptions, Barnaby's work evokes Indigenous world views that see humans as morally determined by language and the land as a sentient being (Basso 2000, 41–42; Sable and Francis 2012, 42). Moreover, just as *Le Torrent* complicates chronology by conflating past and present, Barnaby deploys speculative genre tropes to explore historical trauma. Thus, while *Le Torrent* depicts the struggle to grasp memory and territory, Barnaby portrays post-apocalyptic suffering and enforced alienation from past, present, and future notions of home.

In light of these examples, I here propose an analysis of *Le Torrent* that takes a partly comparative approach. I focus primarily on Lavoie's text, its various expressions of nostalgia, and its representation of Indigenous characters. I consider *Le Torrent* vis-à-vis other nostalgic representations of pre–Quiet Revolution Québec and other contemporary cinematic examples that engage with the collision between Indigenous and Québécois cultures. I also contemplate this film's relationship to *Laurentie* (2011), another feature that exhibits a crushing sense of sadness and loss, which Lavoie developed (and co-directed with Mathieu Denis) in parallel with *Le Torrent*. Finally, I juxtapose these analyses with Barnaby's oeuvre in order to highlight views of *algios* and *nostos* that are either convergent or irreconcilable with Indigenous understandings of homeland. By grasping how representations of suffering in Barnaby's work either accord or clash with Quebec's painful longing for home, I hope to unpack the multiple functions of nostalgia in *Le Torrent*. To frame this research, I draw primarily on Boym's theorization of this concept, complementing her perspective with further theoretical work on melancholia, a theme that is also pervasive in Quebec cinema (Bellemare 1992; Poirier 2004, 69–78; Weinmann 1997) and that Boym understands as constituent of nostalgia (2001, 55). Elements ascribed to nostalgia potentially implicate Quebec ethically, and seemingly resonate with postcolonial approaches to loss, which I attempt to untangle here. In addition, I draw on Indigenous scholarship, including Mi'kmaq history and thought, conceptions of time, and studies on historical trauma. Overall, this chapter seeks to shed light on how representations of pain in Quebec cinema intersect with cultural and geopolitical identities, provide clues about the profound nature of relationships between Québécois and Indigenous peoples, and supply tools for reconceptualizing intercultural relationships and non-Indigenous attitudes toward territory.

Le Torrent: Nostalgia or Melancholia?

Set in 1920s rural Quebec, *Le Torrent* tells the story of François, a young man brought up on an isolated farm by Claudine, his abusive and obsessively religious mother. After Claudine is trampled to death by an unruly horse that François admires and with which he identifies, François pieces together the years of abuse he has endured at the hands of his mother, completely cut off from the world. While reconstructing his life and attempting to understand the reasons for his mistreatment through his own memories and the clues he finds in his mother's possessions, he meets and begins to live with Amica, the daughter of a peddler whom he catches trespassing on his land. From memory-images accompanied by internal monologue, we learn that François became deaf after his mother struck him for finally standing up to her, after he refused to complete her lifelong plan for him to become a priest. Paradoxically, François's deafness sensitizes him to the land and especially to a powerful stream into which the young Claudine, an unmarried mother exiled from her community, had once contemplated throwing him as an infant. Thus, François's origins are intimately tied to the land that surrounds him, but they are also intertwined with an original "sin" that haunts and defines both his life and that of his mother. Complicating these events and bringing them to the surface is the presence of Amica, whom François demands from the peddler in exchange for money and as compensation for squatting on his land. Unlike in the Anne Hébert novella on which the film is based, Amica and her father are here portrayed as Indigenous (Innu) people. This explicit insertion of an Indigenous element comes to significantly inflect the film's main themes of longing for a lost childhood and (in)ability to connect fully with the spirit of the land.

In his introduction to a symposium on nostalgia and colonial melancholia, Rob McQueen asserts that nostalgia can act as a framework for colonialism. Indeed, nostalgia appears to persist in settler states' contemporary longing for a past uncomplicated by Indigenous demands. In this respect, McQueen's understanding of nostalgia correlates with Paul Gilroy's notion of post-imperial melancholia. In Gilroy's telling, nations that had hitherto enjoyed the prestige and other benefits of ruling over vast empires find themselves confronted with a loss of both empire and its attendant prestige in contemporary postcolonial contexts where such histories have become utterly discreditable (Gilroy 2005). McQueen's discussion of Gilroy's work in the context of a symposium focused on nostalgia accords with Boym's suggestion that a correlation exists between these two concepts (McQueen 2011, 5). At the same time, Boym's concern with the forward-looking orientation and ethical potential of nostalgia echoes Ranjana Khanna's take on melancholia, for whom this sentiment acts an ethical imperative toward the future (Khanna 2003, 25). Thus, given my own contention that Quebec's persistent struggles with its particular post-imperial melancholic disavowal have resulted in an overemphasis, in Quebec national cinema, on its status as a colonized nation rather than as a colonizing one (Dyer 2017), the similarities and differences between manifestations of melancholia and those of nostalgia help nuance the way in which important preoccupations confronting the Quebec collective imaginary are represented in *Le Torrent*.

For Boym, nostalgia differs from melancholia insofar as it is a collective phenomenon. She states that "unlike melancholia, which confines itself to the planes of individual consciousness, nostalgia is about the relationship between individual biography and the biography of groups or nations, between personal and collective memory" (xvi). This claim's exclusion of melancholia as a sentiment capable of generating collective meaning contradicts observations by scholars such as Khanna, Gilroy, and Cheng (2000), who employ melancholia as a framework precisely for the purpose of probing deeply entrenched national loss and anxiety. Where Boym sees nostalgia as more democratic, these scholars' compelling mobilization of melancholia as a conceptual key for helping to grasp the anxieties of national groups prompts a closer scrutiny of nostalgia's specifically collective appeal. In fact, while Boym sees melancholic loss as linked only to personal history, it seems probable that boundaries between personal and collective loss are fluid. Indeed, it appears more likely that nostalgia's propensity for populism gives it merely an aura of democracy and inclusiveness rather than a more fundamentally egalitarian basis.

My skepticism about nostalgia's democratic credentials is consistent with Boym's own outline of its double-edged nature. Seeing nostalgia as made up of two components, one restorative and one reflective, Boym proposes that the former "attempts a transhistorical reconstruction of the lost home," adding that it "does not think of itself as nostalgia, but rather as truth and tradition," and that "restorative nostalgia is at the core of recent national and religious revivals; it knows two main plots—the return to origins and the conspiracy" (xviii). This reactionary aspect of nostalgia, because it stifles critical thinking about the underlying processes of democracy, vested interests, and imbalances of power, cannot be said to truly align itself with democratic principles insofar as these imply autonomy, equality, and self-rule. Instead, restorative nostalgia superficially exploits the mechanisms of democracy. In contrast, Boym describes reflective nostalgia as longing itself, as a delayed homecoming that "dwells on the ambivalences of human longing and belonging and does not shy away from the contradictions of modernity" (xviii). "At best," she adds, "reflective nostalgia can present an ethical and creative challenge, not merely a pretext for midnight melancholias" (xviii). In fact, the appeal of such open-endedness is also found in Khanna's theorization of melancholia despite Boym's intimation that nostalgia is superior due to its capacity to transcend the usual justifications for melancholic symptoms.

Boym characterizes modern nostalgia as a longing for a past world marked by absolutes that never existed and to which one cannot return (8). In this respect, the reified vision of pre–Quiet Revolution Quebec conjures images of francophones as more clearly defined by their colonized status. Although contemporary Quebec undoubtedly still exhibits the aftershocks of its historically marginalized status, it cannot realistically "hope" to return to the perceived pre–Quiet Revolution absolutes that label it as a colonized society. Furthermore, following Boym's definition, one can suppose that the "absolute" nature of Quebec's colonized status—even during the post-conquest period of marked disenfranchisement that lasted at least up until the 1960s—though founded on unquestionably significant inequalities that characterize colonial structures, remains a profoundly relative, impure condition. Indeed, the historical origins of francophone culture in North America necessarily imply that an unavoidable element of Quebec identity is constituted by its lost and then underplayed role as a colonizer. Thus, as Boym reminds us, melancholia is linked to the loss of an unidentifiable ideal, whereas nostalgia mourns for something that can be identified as an imaginary and idealized past, albeit one that never existed. Given its hyperbolic and unconcealed nature, nostalgia flirts with an admission of the impossibility of its idealized object. By the same token, it serves to remind us what that ideal actually was and how it feasibly coincides with the lost ideal of melancholia, which, in contrast, remains concealed. In this respect, nostalgia and melancholia can be posited as acting dialogically, with nostalgic sentiments pointing to and thereby sharpening the melancholic's ethical engagement with their lost ideal. Such an ideal might intuitively correspond to a nation, but for Khanna, in postcolonial contexts it relates to the formerly colonized nation's espousal of the nation-state as a model. Meanwhile, for Gilroy, melancholia exhibits a pain at the loss of empire and the loss of the prestige of being a colonizer. Given its complex colonial history, it seems apparent that Quebec may attribute its own melancholia to an entangled combination of these factors. Working in dialogue, however, melancholia and nostalgia may help provide clarification. Indeed, citing Kant's positive assessment of the synergy between the two concepts, Boym admits that this thinker sees "in the combination of melancholy, nostalgia and self-awareness a unique aesthetic sense that did not objectify the past but rather heightened one's sensitivity to the dilemmas of life and moral freedom" (13).

Nostalgia for *La Petite Aurore*

As Czach explains, the contemporary Quebec film industry has tended to look back nostalgically to the pre–Quiet Revolution period through what she identifies as Quebec's own particular form of heritage film. In a presentation delivered at the Society for Cinema and Media Studies (SCMS) annual conference in 2016, Julie Ravary makes note of these same productions, which she refers to as "historical" epics. Ravary points to "an unprecedented wave" of these films during the early 2000s, noting the release of three similarly structured "blockbusters" in less than four years: *Séraphin : Un homme et son péché* (Binamé 2001), *Nouvelle-France* (Beaudin 2004), and *Le Survenant* (Canuel 2005). Although these films yielded dramatically different box office results, Ravary notes comparable narrative elements that include nationally specific themes such as "Quebec's colonial past, the control of the Catholic church on the social and sexual emancipation of women, and the poor economic conditions of the French Canadian colonies" (Ravary 2016, n.p.). One salient example of this type of commercially oriented, nostalgic, historical and/or literary film appearing in the last two decades is Luc Dionne's remake of the postwar *La Petite Aurore*, retitled simply *Aurore* (2005). As Czach aptly stresses, *Aurore* garnered spectacular earnings at the Quebec box office. With its focus on sustained and relentless parental violence directed toward a young child, *La Petite Aurore* is a strange and revealing object for a remake, and its renewed success thus highlights the appeal of coupling the theme of violence toward children with nostalgia for Quebec's period of historical oppression, a combination foregrounded again in *Le Torrent*.

Indeed, Heinz Weinmann (1990) has highlighted the significance of *La Petite Aurore* as an indicator of Quebec's deep-rooted preoccupations and includes this disturbing film in his delineation of Québécois identity across a selection of other key texts. Weinmann reads *La Petite Aurore* as an aborted attempt to assert Quebec independence, and sees this impulse revived more successfully in Francis Mankiewicz's *Les Bons Débarras* (1980), which he dubs "the revenge of Aurore" (for another example of the contemporary reworking of the Aurore trope, see Czach's reading of Daniel Roby's 2013 biopic *Louis Cyr* in this volume). For Weinmann, *Les Bons Débarras* constitutes the first (ultimately foiled) culmination of a process whereby the nation finally rejects its family romance complex where the colonizing stepmother in *La Petite Aurore* stands in for England and Aurore herself represents the scapegoat that French Canada sacrifices in order for Quebec to "germinate" into a subsequent post–Quiet Revolution incarnation (43).[2] Although Weinmann argues his point "rather contortedly" (Marshall 2001, 110), viewing *La Petite Aurore* as a futile attempt to trouble Quebec's postwar hegemony is undoubtedly plausible. Without question, the stifling clerical nationalism and neo-colonial dependence of Quebec's "great darkness" transpires in this film. Indeed, as Czach reminds us, Scott MacKenzie (2005) has strikingly described the self-sacrificial masochism and helplessness at the heart of this film, while Loiselle (2007) pointedly associates the abuse portrayed in *La Petite Aurore* with Quebec's oppression as a linguistically marginalized group. Likewise, Christiane Tremblay-Daviault's sociologically inflected history of postwar Québec cinema appears to support the premises underpinning *La Petite Aurore* as a foiled attempt at resistance. Tremblay-Daviault highlights the failure of family, rural community, and clergy to intervene on behalf of Aurore—thereby exacerbating her agony instead of relieving it—and describes *La Petite Aurore* as encapsulating an environment of silencing duplicity, self-destructive sadomasochistic interdiction, sexual repression, and brutally oppressive injustice (Tremblay-Daviault 1981, 213–18).

Given its historical setting, *Le Torrent* inevitably depicts the yoke of religious oppression, which indeed is one of its central themes. Yet as an auteur film, *Le Torrent* expresses a more nuanced, less Manichaean, and more ambiguous relationship with the past than the clearly nostalgic and overtly sentimental "blockbuster" melodramas highlighted by Ravary. Indeed, Lavoie's film refuses to offer the "retreat to a knowable identity and stable past" that Czach fittingly associates with the heritage film genre in Quebec. Nevertheless, *Le Torrent* echoes the violent abuse meted out to a young child (male this time) that *La Petite Aurore* dwells on so memorably. The persistence of this motif and its association with pre–Quiet Revolution Quebec is unmistakable. Boym suggests that the vivid portrayal of pain is linked to the fixation in *nostos* on a perfect imagined past that never existed. This aspect of nostalgia, she claims, "is not merely a lost Eden but a place of sacrifice and glory, of past suffering" (15). Although *nostos* partly accounts for the interest in violence against children in both *La Petite Aurore* and *Le Torrent*, it does not fully explain the persistence of this theme across texts with such fundamentally different commercial and artistic objectives. If *nostos* adequately corresponds to the populism of Quebec heritage films, the undeniable precedence of artistic imperatives in *Le Torrent* points to a more complex manifestation of nostalgia, one that is collective, but not merely populist, one that perhaps converges with melancholia.

In contrast with Lavoie's efforts to faithfully transpose Hébert's novella, the decision to depict Amica as an Indigenous woman departs markedly from the original literary text, and thus cannot fail to echo contemporary anxieties about Quebec's colonial relationship with Indigenous peoples. In addition, this divergence engenders another, potentially more problematic one. Indeed, the film's amalgamation of Amica and Claudine via Laurence Leboeuf, a non-Indigenous actress who takes on the role of both these women, strikes one uncomfortably as identity appropriation.[3] At first glance, we might perceive in *Le Torrent* the recurrence of a fetishized view of *métissage*, which underpins the recent Quebec documentaries *Québékoisie* (Mélanie Carrier and Olivier Higgins, 2013) and *L'Empreinte* (Yvan Dubuc and Carole Poliquin, 2015). Indeed, without denying the historical basis or productive possibilities of cultural exchange we can nevertheless assert that both documentaries, to varying degrees, deploy and rely upon the idea of biological and cultural hybridity as a means of solving historical antagonisms and of encouraging the parallel resolution of current socio-political discord. In spite of their uncritical approach to *métissage* and the attendant danger of identity appropriation, as well as the reassuring conclusions of both these films, it should be acknowledged that *Québékoisie* in particular ventures into some unsettling subject areas that take considerable steps toward confronting Quebec's colonial past. *L'empreinte*, however, relies more heavily on *métissage* as a defining characteristic of contemporary Québécois identity, casting Quebec as fundamentally different (and more progressive) than other settler societies. It thus reveals the existence in Quebec of nostalgia not only for pre–Quiet Revolution hardship but also for an idealized hybridity with First Nations that stems from Quebec's distant origins. In parallel, despite its casting of Laurence Leboeuf as an Indigenous Amica, *Le Torrent* engages with nostalgia in such a way as to complicate the impact of this sentiment by introducing the appropriation of Indigenous identity, not simply as a "solution" that reassuringly resolves Quebec anxieties about its colonial history, but as a troubling representation of Quebec's relationship to Otherness.[4] Consequently, Lavoie's film comments on the process of Quebec cinema's deployment of Indigenous figures to depict a haunting outcome that continues to impede and challenge the protagonist's ability to seize the land wholeheartedly.

For Boym, national awareness comes from outside the community. The romantic traveller brings this perspective. She writes: "The nostalgic is never a native but a displaced person who mediates between the local and the universal" (12). This perspective occurs in *Québékoisie*, where the film-makers recount their experience of foreign travel and its role in prompting a recognition of their ignorance about First Nations in Quebec. This young couple then travels "outside" mainstream society to visit several First Nations communities in Quebec. Outsider status also applies to François and Claudine, who are exiled from their French Canadian community. At the same time, Amica and her father have also been displaced from Indigenous land, and François's violent attempt to eject them from his property vividly reminds us of this situation. In this respect, Laurence Leboeuf's hybridized role as Amica/Claudine highlights the point of tension between insider and outsider and recommends her as an especially keen observer of the community/nation. Her sympathetic portrayal contrasts markedly with the older Claudine's, a dissimilarity paradoxically emphasized by pitching these characters as alter egos. Such tropes seem to indicate the film's desire to introduce into its nostalgic framework the idea that Indigenous presence productively informs us about the nature of Quebec's malaise. Thus, although we may discern in *Le Torrent* another apparent attempt to validate a Québécois occupation of Indigenous land by calling on Quebec's mythical Indigenous origins, the film's gaze toward the past differs from a manifest manoeuvre of this kind insofar as it remains open-ended and ambiguous. Both the past and the future as proposed in *Le Torrent* fail to translate into comfortable optimism, and this important nuance partly aligns it with Boym's account of *algia* or reflective nostalgia.

Incompleteness and Delayed Homecoming: Beyond the Quiet Revolution

Bill Marshall describes Quebec's modernization during the Quiet Revolution as a "destabilizing," "uneven," and "incomplete" process "closely bound up with an identity to be built and fought over." This highlights a central particularity of this period of rapid social, economic, and political change, which coincides intimately with important and lasting formations in Quebec national identity (2001, 49). Indeed, correlations between the Quiet Revolution and Québécois identity obscure perceptions of the past beyond this moment, and the consequent vagueness of pre–Quiet Revolution Quebec in the popular imagination renders it favourable to the mechanisms of nostalgia. Tellingly, the periodization of Marshall's book-length study on Quebec national cinema situates what the author describes as "Foundational Fictions" at the beginning of the

1960s, thereby reinforcing the commonplace exclusion of the dozen or so clerical-conservative melodramas of the postwar era, while recognizing nonetheless that "the most significant films of that epoch, such as *La Petite Aurore l'enfant martyre,* directed by Jean-Yves Bigras in 1951, form part of Quebec's film memory" (18). As such, Marshall's larger corpus is consistent with his position that the Quiet Revolution constitutes not only an important period of change, but also a national myth that further complicates the effects of modernization. In parallel, Boym's notion of reflective nostalgia as a longing that "delays homecoming" appears to converge with the "incompleteness" that Marshall attributes to the constant reimagining of Quebec identity through cinema. Just as Boym sees reflective nostalgia as the positive aspect of this concept, the "incompleteness" of Quebec nationhood that Marshall alludes to also surfaces as a site of opportunity rather than as an obstacle, despite the intuitive response to see incompleteness as something to be overcome. Boym's notion of delayed homecoming implies an ongoing movement toward home, the outcome of which has been deferred. As such, *algia* or longing itself is not static, but continuously open-ended and interrogative. Marshall, however, sees the Quiet Revolution not only as modernizing but also as originating. As such, although permeable and contestable, the myth of modern Quebec nationhood and of modern Quebec cinema's emergence during this period constitutes a formidable temporal boundary nonetheless.

Stressing a heterogeneity that belies the founding myth of the Quiet Revolution as a unified experience, Marshall proposes a constantly fluid identity that is also compatible with Homi Bhabha's view of the nation, which relies paradoxically on the discourse of its inherent modernity and at the same time on that of its distant origins, even as the two can never be reconciled temporally into the national narrative (Bhabha 1994, 203). Notably, Bhabha states that the nation must be told in "double-time," that of a nationalist pedagogy centred on the past, and that of living performative contemporaneity. Telling the nation, for Bhabha, is thus simultaneously accumulative and recursive (208–9). Going beyond an external search for identity on the basis of the "otherness of other nations," Bhabha posits an internal splitting of identity provoked by the heterogeneous people of the nation. As such, Bhabha's model mirrors Boym's splitting of nostalgia into its restorative (*nostos*) and reflective (*algia*) counterparts, its retrospective and prospective capacities (xvi). Moreover, Bhabha calls upon Ernest Renan's notion of "will" or "daily plebiscite" to bind his iterative grasp of national narrative (229–30), a move that overlaps with Boym's understanding of the *nostos* of a nation, where "individual longing is transformed into a collective belonging that relies on past sufferings that transcend individual memories" (15). Meanwhile, even though Marshall describes 1960s Quebec identity, represented emblematically in Gilles Groulx's *Le Chat dans le sac* (1964), as "ungraspable" because "in the throes of contradiction, emergence, and elaboration," he nevertheless deems that it successfully proposes a model for a future hegemony that coincides with viewer identification while rejecting state technocracy and violence (55–56). However, the recurrence of ungraspable identity in a brutal form in Lavoie's work throws the absolute rejection of violence into doubt. Indeed, his second feature, *Laurentie*, released only one year before *Le Torrent*, depicts a protagonist whose unstable national identity leads to a sense of belonging limited to white, male, francophone homosociality. In light of Marshall's assertion about the identity parameters taking shape in 1960s Quebec, *Laurentie* either presents us with shocking residual elements of phallocentric national priorities or points to a more profound malaise than anticipated in Marshall's analysis. Bhabha's suggestion that the time of the nation's representation is both double and split offers a way of understanding this anomaly. As Bhabha points out, Frantz Fanon warns against the reification of the nation-state while maintaining a struggle for national culture (218). Meanwhile, Marshall observes the emergence of a new nationalist hegemony in 1960s Quebec cinema, yet *Laurentie* depicts a protagonist unsatisfied with the perpetual incompleteness of this identity. Thus, Lavoie's second feature portrays a reification of the nation-state and a disparaged abandonment of political struggle—precisely the opposite of the outcome prescribed by Fanon in *Les Damnés de la terre* ([1961]2002). The protagonist of *Laurentie* is literally split according to the temporalities of nationalist pedagogy and performance. On the one hand he exhibits violent frustration toward anglophones and fetishizes canonical Québécois authors, including Anne Hébert. At the same time, he desires the urbane cosmopolitanism and self-confident worldly identity of his English-speaking neighbour. The protagonist of *Laurentie* rejects the underlying oscillation between "then" and "now" that Bhabha exposes in the nation's storyline, and this psychic refusal becomes violently unhinged.

Bhabha's emphases on loss and on non-homogenous temporality also echo Khanna's view of melancholia. Indeed, on one level, *Laurentie*'s combination of a violent fear of the Other with inexplicable and insufferable melancholia suggests a link between this condition and an unclear, insecure identity, the result of the unassimilated loss of nationhood, a failure to attain national completeness. Khanna posits that a haunting associated with melancholia frames the temporality of postcolonial nations and provokes an ethical demand on the future (15). This haunting provocation results from the contradictory adoption of (or aspiration to) the very nation-state structure that such decolonizing entities had once resisted (25). Considering this, the excessive melancholia of *Laurentie*'s protagonist points not to incomplete nation-statehood, but rather the lost/incomplete decolonizing ideals of the Quiet Revolution. *Laurentie*'s confrontation of Quebec's residual malaise also uncovers a bridge between pre–Quiet Revolution nationalism and its contemporary reiterations, which undermines the popular conflation of the latter with 1960s liberation ideals. The film thereby enables incursions into the past, pointing logically to French colonialism, inadvertently highlighting an Indigenous presence omitted from its rationale, and insisting on an investigation of past trauma. Continuing this reflection on Otherness in *Le Torrent*, Lavoie sought to cinematically render the figures of Amica and of the peddler. Perceiving these characters as romanticized Romani-like outsiders in the Anne Hébert novella, and attributing this trope to European literary influences, Lavoie deemed their close reproduction to be incongruous in a contemporary Québécois film narrative calling for socio-cultural and historical plausibility. As such, the director explains his choice to recast Amica and the peddler as Indigenous characters as one aimed at capturing the marginalized status of the figures in the literary source as closely as possible (personal interview with author). As a result, this deviation from the original story introduces Indigenous presence into *Le Torrent*, an element that is utterly lacking in *Laurentie*'s critique of xenophobia.

Implicating Quebec: Historical Trauma and the Films of Jeff Barnaby

In light of the difficulty posed in looking past the Quiet Revolution as constitutive of modern Québécois identity, Adam Lowenstein's book *Shocking Representations* (2005) provides useful theoretical tools for investigating national historical trauma. Meanwhile, the work of Mi'kmaq filmmaker Jeff Barnaby also helps elucidate the nature of Quebec nostalgia through themes common to Indigenous and non-Indigenous filmmakers in Quebec. Indeed, Lowenstein's focus on horror cinema converges with Barnaby's own predilection for this genre. Exploring the relation between horror cinema and historical trauma, Lowenstein challenges trends in trauma studies that preclude the representation of traumatic events in national history. For Lowenstein, this interdiction, though based in caution and respect, silences victims' experience of trauma. He aims to shatter this unproductive impasse by valuing what he terms the "allegorical moment." Drawing on Benjamin's Messianic Time, Lowenstein understands allegory as an instance of cinematic representation that unites the spectator with the historical event in a "shocking collision" that fuses experiences across time and space and brings past and present together (2005, 2). Interestingly, Lowenstein's analysis of Georges Franju's work stresses a "brutality ... characterized by a rage aimed at 'breaking all that stifles'" (20), a description evocative of both the brutality present in *La Petite Aurore* and the constriction of the *Duplessiste* era in which it was produced. The propensity to shock in *La Petite Aurore*, and its correspondence with Lowenstein's focus on representations of transitional, transformational states, can be considered in conversation with more contemporary provocations looking onto past trauma, such as those portrayed in *Le Torrent* and in Jeff Barnaby's work.

Each chapter in Lowenstein's book focuses on the national trauma of a colonial power or settler-colonial nation, stressing the determining effect of such wounds on national identity. Indeed, Lowenstein's glib phrase, "I am traumatized, therefore I am" (10), which encapsulates the contemporary fascination with horror, also echoes the iconic phrase in Groulx's *Le Chat*, where the protagonist summarizes the incomplete transformation of Quiet Revolution Quebec by declaring, "I am French Canadian, therefore I am searching for myself." Paradoxically cementing Quebec's identification with the Quiet Revolution, Groulx's existential call to explore trauma encourages a glance back into history and beyond the boundary that symbolically separates *la grande noirceur* from the 1960s. Applied to Quebec, Lowenstein's model reveals other layers of complexity arising from Quebec's ambiguous history as both colonizer and colonized. Indeed, an emergent Indigenous cinema expresses historical trauma most powerfully, particularly in light of Indian Residential School abuses. In this respect, Barnaby's *Rhymes for Young Ghouls* (2013) deploys the motifs of horror, abjectness, and violence inflicted upon children, motifs that correlate with the kind of risk-taking but rousing cinematic texts Lowenstein proposes. Without straightforwardly superimposing Lowenstein's Western framework onto an Indigenous text, his model, applied to *La Petite Aurore* anachronistically and in response to the themes brought forward, not only in *Le Torrent* but also by *Rhymes*, reveals surprising correlations that inevitably entangle the Québécois viewer.

These juxtapositions interrogate the selective amnesia, or "strange forgetting," of the violent means employed in founding the nation, which Bhabha reminds us is linked to Renan's "will" (229). Ironically, "remembering to forget" inhibits unsettling recollection beyond the barrier of the Quiet Revolution, a proscription ambiguously contradicted by Quebec's national motto *Je me souviens*, the visibility of which was promoted by the first Parti Québécois government in the 1970s. Thus, Renan's "remembering to forget" can be likened to nostalgia insofar as the latter represents a skewed remembering or idealizing of Quebec's tragic past. Lowenstein's approach, applied to a somewhat distant and disturbing text like *La Petite Aurore*, opens up Quebec's cinematic past for critical scrutiny and validates Weinmann's intent to connect films to one another that are temporally situated on either side of the Quiet Revolution. *La Petite Aurore*'s theme of an abused child returns in *Le Torrent* and associates this motif with Quebec before the Quiet Revolution. However, Barnaby's *Rhymes for Young Ghouls*, which portrays the genocidal Indian Residential School trauma, and which indirectly implies Quebec's participation in this federally implemented system, counterpoints Weinmann's tendentious reading of Aurore as the victim of colonial injustice.

In spite of Barnaby's hard-hitting, iconoclastic style, his oeuvre displays a marked absence of overt criticism of Quebec's colonial aspirations. In contrast, his personal interview comments on the subject of language are more scathing:

> This is what kind of blows my mind about growing up in Quebec ... We have the language laws here, and everything that they're saying—we want to preserve our culture, we want to preserve our language, we want to protect our land—is exactly what Native people have been saying for the past ... well since the French got here. And for the life of me I just don't understand why it is that they maintain a kind of ethnocentric view of the culture in Quebec rather than ... embrace and maybe even work together with the Native people. (Barnaby 2012)

Barnaby's public presence, then, seems to form the first site of implication. Unlike his celebrated Abenaki precursor, Alanis Obomsawin, Barnaby's work doesn't exhibit politically explosive events such as Restigouche and Oka, which opposed Indigenous and settler forces in Quebec. Instead, Barnaby allegorizes the pervasiveness of colonial processes designed to carry out linguistic and cultural effacement. Indeed, Barnaby's style could not be in starker contrast to Obomsawin's NFB documentary realism, drawing as it does on horror, fantasy and dystopian fiction. Barnaby's engagement with cinema nevertheless bears a significant link to Obomsawin via her 1984 film *Incident at Restigouche*, which documents Quebec police raids on his home reserve of Listuguj, and which he credits with instigating his own career (Barnaby 2013).

As Jerry White compellingly argues, Obomsawin's work cannot be reduced to an indictment of Quebec sovereigntist hypocrisy in the face of Indigenous claims. White aptly points out that Obomsawin's *Kanehsatake: 270 Years of Resistance* (1993) primarily condemns federalist political forces, even if this filmmaker has not shied away from also critiquing sovereigntist politicians, most notably in *Incident at Restigouche*, about an event that occurred during a Parti Québécois mandate (White 2002, 373). Nevertheless, in spite of their denunciation of federalist leaders, Obomsawin's Oka films cannot fail to implicate Quebec as well. As I have suggested previously (Dyer 2017), in *Kanehsatake*, Obomsawin activates and archives a sense of Québécois postcolonial melancholia, which, calling upon shared aspirations, acts as an ethical imperative toward the future. Given the history of relations between French Canadians and Mi'kmaq, this affirmation perhaps carries even more weight with regard to *Incident at Restigouche*, which pits the Quebec government against the Mi'kmaq, an Indigenous nation whose century-long alliance with French-speaking Acadians was, according to Mi'kmaw historian Daniel N. Paul, "based on mutual admiration and respect for each other's culture and friendship" (2006, 73). Thus, by acknowledging Obomsawin's influence, Barnaby rekindles the memory of her vivid on-screen confrontation with the Quebec Minister for Recreation, Hunting and Fishing, Lucien Lessard, and his denial of Mi'kmaq sovereignty on the grounds that "to have sovereignty, one must have one's own culture, language and land." This evocation not only questions Quebec's claim to comparatively good relations with Indigenous peoples but also stimulates its postcolonial melancholia for the political loss of Acadia and New France, the loss of integrity in the treatment of its Mi'kmaq allies, and a similar loss present in Quebec's failure to follow through with the decolonization project of the Quiet Revolution by fully applying its ideals to all nations.[5] Thus, despite his radically different style, Barnaby builds cumulatively on Obomsawin's presence in Quebec film history, and complements her twofold approach by stirring Québécois empathy concerning the consequences of assimilation while implicitly bringing to attention Quebec's non-Indigenous, settler status and historical responsibilities.

These two contrasting ways of implicating Quebec generate discomfort and self-reflection but also possibility. Indeed, both Obomsawin and Barnaby appear to reach out to Quebec, subtly highlighting opportunities for solidarity. These opportunities are facilitated by overlaps between Indigenous and certain Western conceptions of time that have different rapports with melancholia and nostalgia. Khanna establishes the temporal nature of melancholia by associating it with Benjamin's Messianic Time, where the present freezes into a constellation with a historical moment, thus forming a unity and presenting a revolutionary opportunity (Khanna 2003, 15; Benjamin [1940]2003, 396). For Québécois, such pairings conceivably include the coupling of outrage at Lord Durham's 1840 report explicitly recommending francophone assimilation with twentieth-century Québécois struggles to address linguistic and cultural preservation. Similarly, the latent power of Obomsawin's intervention in Listuguj as a catalyst for Barnaby's emergent career decades later suggests that analogous conceptions of time, historical trauma, and resistance manifest themselves in Indigenous art and culture in ways that can be placed in parallel with Messianic Time. Indeed, the notion of Indigenous narrative achronicity described by Paula Gunn Allen (1986, 148), in which characters enter a past that has strong bearing on the present, displays similarities with the temporal aspect of melancholia and reveals key differences with Boym's view of restorative nostalgia, or *nostos*.

Significantly, these sorts of non-linear narrative patterns occur in Barnaby's *From Cherry English* (2004). In this short film, an Indigenous protagonist named Traylor, after a sexual encounter with Lilith, a mysterious white woman, not only literally loses his tongue but also is then pulled into a scene in which he meets figures from his past, his deceased grandmother and uncle. This scene's blending of different time periods corresponds to Allen's Indigenous achronicity and shares with Messianic Time an incompatibility with the temporal regime that governs *nostos*. Indeed, for Boym, the illusion of *nostos* is shattered when two temporal moments are brought together. As Boym determines at the outset of her book: "Nostalgic love can only survive in a long-distance relationship. A cinematic image of nostalgia is a double-exposure, or a superimposition of two images—of home and abroad, past and present, dream and everyday life. The moment we try to force it into a single image, it breaks the frame or burns the surface" (xiii–xiv). *From Cherry English* opposes the illusion of *nostos*, undermining Traylor's superficial display of Indigenous symbols precisely by combining two moments into one.

Similarly, the narrative of *Le Torrent* shatters François's illusion about his past. Lavoie deploys a non-linear chronology that minimizes the visibility of its movements between three stages in its protagonist's life—that is to say, François as a young man, a young boy, and a newborn baby. In this respect, the film's flashbacks are signalled by the adult François observing himself at a younger age, but appear within the same scene or shot. In the first encounter with his past, François sees himself as a young boy entering the frame with no cuts or transitions to help distinguish between the moments in which two of his selves appear. The scene simply shifts temporality without cutting, continuing the plot in an earlier epoch. Consistently treating time in this way, the film promotes a feeling that different temporal moments meld into one, fused together by memory and locale in a manner consistent with Messianic Time and compatible with Allen's achronicity. As François goes through his deceased mother's belongings, he pieces together not just memories of her violent cruelty toward him but also her own tortured hopes for him to become a priest as a means of redeeming her illegitimate pregnancy and consequent exile. The seamless flashbacks pointing to François's painful origins and childhood are accentuated formally by graphic matches, by sound bridges, and by the doubling up of actors to play different roles across generations. A subtle use of this device features Victor Trelles Turgeon playing both François and the priest who fathers him, but a more obvious amalgamation is the aforementioned portrayal by Laurence Leboeuf of both Amica and Claudine as a young woman.

Aside from its relationship to time, Boym's assertion about nostalgia precludes the combination of home and abroad, and also of the dream world and everyday life. In further contrast with *nostos*, the dream motif in *From Cherry English* becomes difficult to distinguish from the everyday. For Bonnie and Eduardo Duran, whose work combines Jungian principles with traditional Indigenous world views, dreams are an important vehicle for "healing and the integration of world cosmologies" (Duran and Duran 1995, 45) and enable the freer discussion of inhibitive issues (150). Cinema, particularly in the allegorical form espoused by Barnaby, also offers a vector for intercultural communication. In *From Cherry English*, Traylor's grandmother speaks to him in Mi'kmaq as she proceeds to sew back his dislodged tongue, but since her dialogue is not subtitled, non-Indigenous viewers find themselves in the same position as Traylor, unable to decipher her advice. Traylor is left instead with the words of his uncle, who blurts out, "You wanna speak Indian? Get drunk and speak bad English." *From Cherry English* ends with

Traylor reaching for a glass of alcohol after he wakes. His failure to heed his grandmother's instructions thus underpins the connection between dreams and the Mi'kmaw language as vehicles for understanding and healing, and his incapacity is extended to non-Indigenous viewers, who also realize their inability to grasp the language or its cultural and epistemological possibilities. Barnaby thus highlights the irony that non-Indigenous Quebec cannot understand the language of the Indigenous society that initially welcomed it, thereby signalling Quebec's own failure to properly integrate to the language of previous occupiers, precisely the commitment that Quebec expects from immigrants.

Barnaby's film thus prods an underlying source of linguistic anxiety and contradiction at the heart of Quebec's ongoing identity debates. This provocation is further stressed by the analogous effects of the punchline of Barnaby's film and the ironic denunciation of colonial linguistic marginalization found in Michèle Lalonde's emblematic 1968 poem "Speak White," which alludes to the 1840 Durham Report. Notably, contemporary nostalgia for this poem was recently channelled for the Quebec stage by Robert Lepage in his 2016 play *887*, which looks back on Lepage's youth in Quebec City. By making Lalonde's poem "Speak White" and its appropriation of non-White colonized identity its central motif, Lepage's play, like the wave of Quebec period films mentioned earlier in this essay, betrays an ongoing nostalgia for a lost time when Québécois could credibly assert their colonized status as a means of anti-colonial rebellion and righteousness. Indeed, as David Austin points out, Black identity appropriation in subversive texts like Lalonde's poem or, more famously perhaps, Pierre Vallières's *Nègres blancs d'Amérique* (1968), have their roots in the genuinely comparable socio-economic situations of African Americans and French Canadians in the early 1960s (Austin 2013, 51). The repurposing of racial epithets into such expressions as *nègres blancs* and *negritude blanche* to describe the struggle of francophone Québécois even prompted such figures as Édouard Glissant to draw comparisons between the two groups (Austin 2013, 58–59). However, while its goal, like Lalonde's, was one of alignment and solidarity with decolonization movements, the simultaneous elision of Black presence in Quebec history seriously undermines its effect. As Austin highlights, Quebec possesses an unacknowledged history of Black enslavement by the French. Moreover, the ongoing redeployment of 1960s texts through contemporary productions like Lepage's, at a moment when the power dynamics for francophone Québécois have changed greatly, but when Black presence and marginalization remain largely unacknowledged, inevitably warps the impetus of such moves, leaving only their more problematic implications.[6]

In parallel, while Barnaby's films tend to implicitly stress the implications regarding Quebec's settler status, they directly target English as the colonizing language, thereby fostering empathy between Québécois and Indigenous struggles. Indeed, some commentators cite the relative superiority within Canada of Quebec's record on certain Indigenous issues, including language preservation (Morse, Axtell, Dickason, and Delâge, cited in Marshall 2000, 239–241; Beavon and Cooke, cited in Salée 2003, 117–18). However, such relative merits do not adequately address the roots of the Québécois malaise as probed directly or indirectly by Indigenous artists such as Obomsawin and Barnaby, and cannot therefore put to rest contradictions inherent in Quebec's national aspirations without the fundamental reconceptualization of such objectives. In this respect, Barnaby's *Rhymes for Young Ghouls*, which tackles the subject of Indian residential schools, again targets English-speaking agents and Canadian policy, but cannot fail to evoke collective responsibility for similar abuses committed in Quebec, nor the assimilation of Indigenous children into francophone culture. So if Barnaby's films echo the linguistic concerns of Québécois, they simultaneously undermine the principles upon which contemporary mainstream Québécois nationalism is founded, notably through candid portrayals of the destruction of Indigenous bodies, which ultimately constitute visceral attacks on settler colonialism. Indeed, Barnaby's films denounce the processes that ensure the integration of colonial brutality against Indigenous communities by consistently subjecting the Indigenous body to violence whether as sadomasochism in *From Cherry English*, as self-amputation in *The Colony* (2007), or through the "voluntary" skin graft operation of *File Under Miscellaneous* (2010). The associations between linguistic assimilation, epistemic violence, and bodily torture, sexual or otherwise, are repeatedly emphasized in Barnaby's work. This concurs with the Mi'kmaq perspective on the inseparability of language and world view and with Duran and Duran's parallel contention that in Indigenous thought, "mind, spirit and body do not function separately, but are seen as a totality" (15). The sexualized infliction of pain also links language to the land as a sentient being via the inscription of hieroglyphs on the protagonists' bodies. As such, the protagonist's body in *File Under Miscellaneous* evokes the land being carved up with scientific precision, thus mirroring the dissection of the political map according to the ideal of nation-statehood to which Québécois nationalism yet adheres and aspires.

Conclusion

The violent tropes examined in this chapter coincide with themes in Québécois cinema that express real or imagined consequences of a dark national history, perhaps resulting from colonial marginalization or the distressing failure to genuinely decolonize Quebec for all peoples. Most notoriously, the sadistic treatment of the body in *La Petite Aurore* recounts the disturbing torture of a young girl by her stepmother under the impotent gaze of the clergy, but *Le Torrent* exemplifies the irrepressible nature of this legacy and goes so far as to boldly intertwine the identities of Indigenous and Québécois characters, while also complicating chronology by confounding past and present. The protagonist's deafness, caused by severe physical abuse in the name of Catholic zeal, paradoxically attunes him to the landscape's power over him and creates an ambiguous tension between the appropriation of Indigenous identity and the inability of Québécois characters to fully possess the land, which instead comes to haunt them and seemingly overrides Western religious imperatives. This echo of the Indigenous world view that human behaviour is morally determined by the interdependence of language and landscape (Basso 2000, 41–42; Sable and Francis 2012, 42) also suggests the ethical demand of melancholia put forward by Khanna complemented by *algia*'s critical potential for "narrat[ing] the relationship between past, present and future" (Boym 2001, 50). And such interlocking concepts provide a glimpse of intercommunicative cinematic propensities in Quebec.

Lavoie's decision to make Amica Indigenous and then to amalgamate her with Claudine is unquestionably a controversial move, but one that surprisingly does not satisfy the common purpose of appropriating Indigenous identity, that is to say of providing "comfort" or "relief" to the settler for the wrongdoing perpetrated through colonialism. Instead, the film points to the ongoing discomfort, unresolved tensions, and impasses set up by colonialism. Viewed in light of Barnaby's overlapping thematic concerns, *Le Torrent* rather reveals and highlights the contradictions at play in Quebec's relationship to the land and to Indigenous peoples. For François, the sound of the powerful stream that clarifies his surroundings "is like the blood raging in [his] veins." This blood, according to the convoluted familial representations in the film, suggests both identity appropriation and *métissage*. Thus, Indigenous presence seemingly holds the key to understanding François's and by extension Quebec's relationship to the land. Indeed, in spite of the film's amalgamation of Indigenous and Québécois identities, Indigenous presence ultimately still influences this relationship and cannot be effaced. As François observes, he is like "a child dispossessed of the world, ruled by a will *before* his own" (my emphasis). These thoughts might refer in Hébert to the legacy of the *Duplessiste* era, and in Lavoie to the consequences of decisions taken to bring Quebec out of this period and into modernity, decisions that perhaps include a loss of solidarity with First Nations. Additionally, although they may be seen as an echo of tropes that situate Indigenous peoples as anachronistic or in a fixed past, these thoughts may also intimate the persistence of a will that precedes settler presence, a will that constrains Quebec's ability to move forward until it is suitably satisfied. Certainly, Barnaby's work draws centrally on the presence of deceased family members to drive its narratives and indirectly challenges Quebec's deep-rooted anxieties and contradictions by provoking fundamental questions in terms of its position as a colonizing and colonized nation. Linguistic assimilation, so central a preoccupation in Quebec, is repeatedly foregrounded in Barnaby's work, especially in *From Cherry English*. As an Indigenous filmmaker originating from the territory now known as Quebec, and through his treatment of time, of the distinction between the real and the imaginary, and of the body, Barnaby not only creates a space for mutual empathy but also insistently recalls the nature of relationships between Indigenous and Québécois peoples, thereby serving to demystify dominant conceptions of nationhood.

Notes

1   Unless otherwise indicated, all translations from the French are my own.
2   Note that in his interpretation of the Quebec family romance, Weinmann refers to England, and not Britain, as the adoptive parental figure.
3   In contrast, Amica's father, the peddler, is played by Innu actor, Marco Bacon.
4   Questioned on this topic, Lavoie expresses doubts regarding facile claims to *métissage* and, in contrast, stresses the historical introspectiveness and insularity of Québécois society. He explains his intention of presenting Amica, not as an Indigenous character played straightforwardly by a non-Indigenous actress, but rather as an obvious construct formed in the protagonist's mind, a vision of his mother as a young woman conflated with an idea of Otherness. Lavoie describes *Le Torrent* as partly seeking to tackle Quebec's troubled relationship to Otherness and as engaging with Quebec's collective imaginary, collective neuroses and with the long-standing references that are present in its historical consciousness (personal interview with author).
5   The sequence of events and comments made by government actors provides a few insights into René Lévesque's personal convictions concerning the

contradictions of the Listuguj attacks by a government defending its own sovereign rights. Two raids took place in Listuguj, on 12 and 20 June 1981. Most Quebec newspaper reports of the period highlight Lucien Lessard as the main government figure involved in events. Lessard gave an ultimatum to the Mi'kmaq and ordered the eventual raids on the Listuguj community. An article in *La Presse* on 23 June highlights Lessard's incompetence in this case and in two other important dossiers under his control. The same article acknowledges, however, that Marc-André Bédard, as Minister of Justice, should be held accountable for the excessive use of force during police raids. Lévesque's first pronouncement on the matter came on 23 June. Quoted in *Le Soleil*, Lévesque reacts to the involvement of federal Minister for Indian Affairs, John Munro, who had suggested that Ottawa reclaim jurisdiction over negotiations with the Mi'kmaq, by stating that Munro should "stay home and shut up" ("Munro" 1981). In the same article, Lévesque deplores the arrests of eleven Mi'kmaq during the raids but also reaffirms the government's intention to limit their fishing activities and does not rule out another raid. On 24 June, Lessard quits the case after a final disappointing (i.e., failed) negotiation with Mi'kmaq leaders, leaving the dossier in Lévesque's hands ("Rencontre infructueuse"; "Rencontre avec Lessard" 1981). On 25 June, Lévesque promises that the provincial police will not re-enter the Listuguj community and describes the use of massive force as "a very debatable decision" by police officials ("QPF" 1981). A piece in *Le Devoir* on June 26, elaborates on Lévesque's comments. In this report, Lévesque calls on the Mi'kmaq to negotiate, adds that the media have dramatized the situation, and responds to criticism by saying that Quebec's government is the only one in Canada to have signed a territorial agreement (James Bay) with First Nations and the only one not to differentiate between Status and Non-Status Indians. He argues that the fact that Quebec is negotiating special agreements confirms its recognition of First Nations as distinct peoples as well as their historic and hereditary Indigenous rights ("Restigouche" 1981).

6   The recent controversy surrounding Robert Lepage's 2018 theatre production, *SLĀV*, and the aborted development of another project, *Kanata*, perhaps represents the culmination of this tendency in Lepage's work. *SLĀV* repurposes the songs of African American slaves, sung in this production by a group composed mainly of white performers. The show was eventually stopped by the Montreal International Jazz Festival in response to public protests. Meanwhile, *Kanata* purported to deal with the history of relations between Indigenous peoples and European settlers in Canada, but featured only European artists. The show was cancelled following the withdrawal of funding from co-producers after Indigenous artists, community leaders, and activists published an open letter in *Le Devoir* criticizing the production for the absence of Indigenous participants. Lepage subsequently announced that the production of *Kanata*

would go ahead in late 2018, following an arrangement struck with le Théâtre du Soleil for which he accepted to waive his own artist's fee. A new version of the show renamed *Kanata — Épisode I : La Controverse* finally opened in December 2018 in Paris. Writer Maya Cousineau Mollen (Innu) and filmmaker Kim O'Bomsawin (Abenaki), both signatories of the open letter criticizing the *Kanata* project, as well as sociologist Guy Sioui Durand (Wendat), attended the play's opening, and all three reacted unfavourably to it in various media. Standing by the need for an Indigenous perspective, especially with regard to the disturbing portrayal of violence against Indigenous women, these Indigenous commentators also decry the insertion of a plotline that positions Lepage as a victim of censorship as well as the deployment of a "white saviour" character in the play, which celebrates the heroic integrity of a French artist representing the plight of Indigenous peoples.

SECTION II

Yearning for a
Pre-Modern Quebec

2

THE QUEBEC HERITAGE FILM

Liz Czach

In a 2013 special issue of the *American Review of Canadian Studies* devoted to Quebec cinema, the editors enthusiastically declared: "Quebec cinema has arrived." One robust indicator of Quebec cinema's arrival is its presence on an international stage—beyond the borders of the province, Quebec's cinema has been increasingly gathering attention and accolades. First there was Denys Arcand's Best Foreign Language Oscar for *Barbarian Invasions* in 2003 and, more recently, the nomination of a film from Quebec for that same prize three years running—Denis Villeneuve's *Incendies* in 2011, Philippe Falardeau's *Monsieur Lazhar* in 2012, and Kim Nguyen's *Rebelle* in 2013. On the film festival circuit, Quebec filmmakers such as Denis Coté and Rafaël Ouellett have picked up prizes at prestigious European film festivals while Xavier Dolan has become the critical darling of the Cannes Film Festival, sharing the jury prize for *Mommy* in 2014 and winning the Grand Prix for *Juste la fin du monde* in 2016. In addition to the Oscar nominations and festival accolades, there are other indicators that attest to the relatively healthy state of Quebec filmmaking within the borders of the province, including a consolidation of the industry, a robust star system, audience appeal, box office success, and the proliferation of film genres. Since the turn of the millennium, Quebec filmmaking has shown an unprecedented diversity and vitality that has moved beyond both the long-standing practice of auteur filmmaking and the well-established tradition of the lowbrow comedy (the prominence of which dates back to the 1970s) to embrace genre filmmaking that now includes horror flicks, psychological thrillers, romantic comedies, and buddy cop films, among others. Many of these genre films have found receptive audiences, and accordingly there has been a steady flow of commercially successfully films produced in the province. By all indications, Quebec's cinema has indeed arrived.

One of the most notable trends in Quebec's expanded field of film production is the box office success of three films released in the early 2000s: *Séraphin, un homme est son péché* (Charles Binamé, 2002), *Aurore* (Luc Dionne, 2005) and *Le Survenant* (Érik Canuel, 2005). *Séraphin*, for example, took in $6,749,187 at the domestic box office, whereas *Aurore* recorded a stunning $971,582 on its opening weekend and went on to garner $3.5 million at the box office.[1] Set in the not-so-distant past and based on literary works or historical events, this trio of films firmly inaugurated Quebec cinema's entry into the production of the heritage film. While the heritage film as a discernible genre emerged most prominently in 1980s Britain, it has steadily proliferated around the globe and now is prevalent in innumerable national contexts and guises. Genres, as Steve Neale (1999) has elaborated, obey the rules of repetition and difference, and the heritage film, despite its response to various national and sub-national contexts, has quite consistently retained a set of basic components. Andrew Higson (2006) and Bélen Vidal (2012), among others, have outlined the predominant characteristics of heritage films, noting that they are usually costume dramas or have a period setting, are typically adaptations, are visually lush with a stress on spectacle, and focus on the upper-class and aristocratic elites. Furthermore, heritage films frequently cast stars to increase the film's broad appeal, often perform well on the festival circuit, and are prestige pictures situated between art cinema and genre filmmaking (Higson 92–95). Of course, the appeal of genre films lies in their ability to adhere to audience expectations while infusing changes that will differentiate a particular film from its predecessors and competitors. In the case of the heritage film, national and subnational contexts often provide just enough regional specificity to provide this distinguishing feature. With their emphasis on literary works and on the past, the national context of heritage films becomes one of their defining attributes. Particularly pertinent to this chapter is the degree to which the heritage film "has become a supple term to refer to the ways in which national cinemas turn to the past at different moments in their histories in search of their foundational myths" (Vidal 3). Thus, the heritage film's investment in a nation's foundational myths takes on specific resonances depending on which nation and what past is under scrutiny. The rise of the heritage film in Quebec at the beginning of the new millennium presents an ideal opportunity to interrogate the relationship of Quebec's present era to its past. But what has led to the proliferation of the heritage film and its subgenres at this particular historical juncture? What are the industrial and socio-political conditions that have given rise to the heritage film's prominent arrival in Quebec at the beginning of the new millennium? And furthermore, how is the heritage film symptomatic of the debates and concerns regarding Quebec's status as a nation in the twenty-first century? The emergence of the heritage film in Quebec at the beginning of the twenty-first is the result of the alignment of a number of factors: Quebec's cinema's broader nostalgic turn, changes in film funding priorities, and socio-cultural concerns that have shifted the spotlight back onto fundamental questions of what it means to be Québécois.

For a few decades, Quebec cinema has shown a preoccupation with the past that has, with increasingly more frequency, manifested itself as a nostalgic impulse. As André Loiselle (2007) has noted:

> Nostalgia and a fixation on ancestral roots … became the dominant ethos of Quebec in the nineties and early in the new century. Signs of nostalgia can be seen throughout the spectrum of cultural production. That some of the most commercially successful films ever made in Quebec— *Séraphin, un homme est son péché* (2002, Charles Binamé), *La Grande Séduction* (2003, Jean François Pouliot), *Les Invasions Barbares* (2003, Denys Arcand), *C.R.A.Z.Y.* (2005, Jean-Marc Vallée), *Aurore* (2005, Luc Dionne), *Le Survenant* (2005, Éric Canuel), and *Maurice Richard* (2006, Binamé)—are drenched in nostalgia is only the most obvious indication of this phenomenon. (153)

Each of the films Loiselle mentions does indeed make use of the past, but what qualifies as nostalgic varies across this spectrum of films. As Loiselle's brief list makes evident, the use of nostalgia cuts across a swath of genres from the auteurist art film through to the comedy, biopic, and costume drama. Yet how nostalgia is deployed in these films is open to a wide range of valid readings. Furthermore, not all recent Quebec films set in the past exhibit an overt nostalgia. For example, Léa Pool's *Maman est chez le coiffeur* (2008), set in 1966, depicts the traumatic aftermath on familial dynamics when a father's homosexual relationship is revealed. Morgan Charles argues that *Maman*, as well as Philippe Falardeau's *C'est pas moi, je le jure* (also from 2008), point to a resurgence of Quebec's "cinéma orphelin" (Charles 1). These films, she contends, "speak to the contemporary ambivalence around the project of national memory" (5–6). However, such an ambivalence, I contend, is not evident in the majority of Quebec heritage films, in which the past is a conduit to a specific type of national memory—one of oppressed victim. The success of these heritage films at the box office has ensured that funding agencies look favourably upon this film genre. In what follows I first turn to how the popularity of this cycle of films accords with the current mandates of funding agencies before considering their ideological repercussions.

The heritage film is a predictable response to funding exigencies and the new realities of Canadian film financing. Neoliberalism has put government agencies such as Telefilm and SODEC (Société de développement des entreprises culturelles) under increased pressure to see a return on what are described as funding investments rather than grants. Funding agencies have long privileged auteur-driven art films as the preferred means to lend credibility and prestige to the project of building a national cinema. These expenditures have been justified in the name of creating art—particularly if that art reflects Quebec identity and culture. Auteur films that win prizes on the international festival circuit bestow cultural prestige on Quebec filmmaking even when that success does not necessarily translate into box office numbers. The logic of cultural capital of festival awards, to invoke Pierre Bourdieu's (1987) well-known formulation, increasingly brushes up against the forces of economic capital—the cold hard cash of box office receipts that will ensure a return on the investment of the cultural agency. However, an eye solely on box office receipts can jeopardize the rationale for a funding agency's raison d'être. Providing government money for films that are overtly commercial genre films potentially raises questions about wasting taxpayer dollars supporting so-called lowbrow shlock that does not reflect Quebec values, culture, or identity. Additionally, if a film is an identifiably marketable and commercially driven genre film, why does it need financial aid? For funding agencies that are caught in the double bind of losing money on unprofitable art films and being unable to invest in apparently culturally valueless genre films, the heritage film provides an ideal, middlebrow, middle-of-the-road compromise. With its period settings, high production values, attentiveness to picturesque *mise en scène*, and literary or historical allegiances, the heritage film leaves an impression of high culture in a way that slasher horror films, psychological thrillers, and raunchy sex comedies do not. The heritage film fulfills the mandate of funding agencies to produce respectable cultural products that reflect Quebec's values while also making good on the neoliberal imperative to see a return on investment. Producers looking to make profitable films have turned to the genre's broad appeal as one strategy for pursuing commercial hits, while funding bodies attain the elusive goal of ostensibly supporting artistic productions of cultural value that are also popular.

The inclination of government agencies to fund heritage film productions has been bolstered by the genre's meteoric ascent in Quebec. As noted earlier, Quebec's cycle of heritage films was no doubt ushered in by the phenomenal commercial success of *Séraphin, un homme est son péché, Aurore,* and *Le Survenant.* But why did the heritage film emerge with such prominence in Quebec only at the turn of the twenty-first century when it had been identified as a genre in Britain as early as the 1980s and '90s? Higson's account of the rise of British heritage film holds some clues as to what transpired in Quebec some twenty-five years later. Higson was among the first film scholars to identify and analyze the heritage impulse in films, identifying a cycle of quality costume dramas made in Britain in the 1980s and early '90s, including *A Room with a View* (James Ivory, 1985), *A Passage to India* (David Lean, 1984), and *Howard's End* (James Ivory, 1992). Higson writes:

> The heritage cycle and its particular representation of the national past is in many ways symptomatic of the cultural developments in Thatcherite Britain. The Thatcher years, of course, coincided with an international capitalist recession that accelerated Britain's decline as a world economic power, but that also saw the growth of multinational enterprises, including the European Community. Inevitably, these processes disturbed traditional notions of national identity, which were further upset by the recognition that British society was increasingly multiracial and multicultural. (93)

Higson argues that the heritage film is a means to avoid speaking directly to contemporary issues by regressing to an idealized and less problematic past. Of course, there are equally pertinent readings of these films that do not interpret them as ideologically conservative, but Higson's characterization of how they confront the shifting dynamics of a politicized and polarized British society is a pertinent point of comparison. These film productions, as he points out, retreated from dealing with social upheaval, such as the aftermath of the Brixton riots, and returned to a seemingly less troubled past. He writes: "By turning their backs on the industrialised, chaotic present, they nostalgically re-construct an imperialist and upper-class Britain" (93). The British heritage film thus presented an "apparently more settled and visually splendid manifestations of an essentially pastoral national identity and authentic culture: 'Englishness' as an ancient and natural inheritance" (93). In sum, Higson, and others, read the British heritage film as arising from a reactionary impulse in the face of immigration and multiculturalism and the forces of transnationalism.[2]

Similar forces of internationalization and globalization have been felt around the globe, and perhaps nowhere are they more pronounced than in Western Europe and North America. Quebec has likewise not been immune to the effects of the global flow of people and goods, and the past twenty years have witnessed a shift toward a more globalized Quebec society that is increasingly multicultural and multiracial as a growing number of immigrants make Quebec home. Furthermore, a generation of younger Quebecers is as comfortable communicating in English as in French and often thinks globally rather than locally. Challenges from Indigenous peoples and the continually diminishing role of the Catholic Church, among other factors, have contributed to Quebec's weakening claims to a shared national identity, culture, language, and collective memory. In his contribution to this anthology, Loiselle further explores early twenty-first-century expressions of nostalgia as responses to the radical decline of the Church's traditional patriarchal ascendancy in the province. Perhaps the strongest evidence of the demonstrable anxiety in Quebec over the province's future was the Bouchard–Taylor Commission (2007–8), which was struck to investigate the public discontent over reasonable accommodation practices as they related to cultural differences. The Bouchard-Taylor Commission was a watershed moment in articulating the fear that Quebec's claim to a shared national identity, language, and collective memory was waning. The perceived decline of that shared identity has driven many conservative commentators in the province to sound increasingly alarmist bells about this state of affairs. In the face of such anxiety, the heritage film positions itself as a retreat to a seemingly more stable identity and more knowable past. As Jim Leach (2010) asserts, the "idea of heritage is, of course, a response to the disorientation of an increasingly global society in which the experience of both nature and of distinctive cultures (and the links between them) is being eroded" (279). The forces that gave rise to the heritage film phenomenon in Britain have found a striking parallel in the socio-political landscape of Quebec at the beginning of the twenty-first century.

Britain in the 1980s, however, is not synonymous with Quebec twenty-five years later, and while the heritage genre in both these national film contexts evinces a nostalgic return to the past, there is a stark difference in what they yearn for. The British heritage films hearken back to an era of colonial rule, British imperial power, and aristocratic luxury; Quebec's history has no such imperial legacy to look fondly back upon. Somewhat paradoxically, the Quebec heritage film does not yearn for an era of colonial privilege but rather returns the viewer to a time when the Québécois were a colonized people beholden to Anglo-Canadian and American commercial powers, ultraconservative premier Maurice Duplessis, and the Catholic Church. The Quebec heritage film, unlike its British counterpart, does not exhibit nostalgia for a time of power and privilege, but looks back longingly to an era of pre–Quiet Revolution oppression when the Québécois lacked the means for self-determination. This return, via the heritage film, to an era of dispossession turns the usual operation of the genre on its head, focusing as it does on a humiliating and downtrodden rather than glorious past. Québécois culture is steeped in the memory of this ignoble past—of having been conquered and suffering. Martin Patriquin (2018) traces this narrative back to the 1759 Battle of the Plains of Abraham and the French defeat at the hands of the British. *La Conquête*, Patriquin writes, "birthed the narrative of the Québécois as a conquered people, living in virtual enslavement under a foreign power." He continues: "If the more than 250 years since *La Conquête* has shown anything, it's Quebec's collective will to keep its own folklore intact." Similarly, historian Jocelyn Létourneau (2006) has argued that the history of the Québécois is indebted to the "mythistoires des losers," where the *loser* "revient comme un leitmotiv pour encadrer la très grande majorité des situations dans lesquelles se retrouvent le Québécois d'héritage canadien-français" (159).[3] The heritage film thus offers a venue in which the *mythistoire* of the Quebecois as losers, rather than winners, can reassert itself.

So why, at the turn of the millennium, did the return to such a depiction of the past find favour with film agencies, producers, directors, and audiences? Put bluntly, the Quebec heritage film reaffirms a past in which Quebec identity was cohesive, shared, and binding. These films present a coherent past that in the face of an increasingly multicultural and multi-ethnic Quebec is reassuring. It could be argued that there no longer exists a unified vision of what it means to be Québécois, and the heritage film, with its depiction of a dispossessed era, reaffirms the continued status of the Québécois as a colonized people *in the present* by representing their colonized and oppressed past. Put another way, despite the massive economic, cultural, and societal changes that Quebec has undergone over the past fifty years, the Québécois today are reluctant to let go of the status of a dispossessed minority even when, today, other minorities (Indigenous peoples, immigrants, refugees) might more justifiably claim that position. Indeed, conservative critics like Mathieu Bock-Côté (2018) have gained prominence in the province by arguing that the majoritarian Québécois "live in a world subjected to the emotional tyranny of certain whining minorities who make an art of always playing the victim."[4] Critiques like these reveal the political stakes regarding who gets to claim victim status in Quebec (Bock-Côté 2018). Relatedly, Gérard Bouchard (2015) suggests that the process of decolonization is incomplete; despite the global and international forces at play in their province, Québécers continue to be, he argues, a linguistic and cultural minority in an anglophone sea and thus still occupy a weakened position. "Accordingly," he contends, "there is in the francophone majority a very strong historical consciousness—we could say a memory under tension. It is a memory that is fueled largely by the feeling that the francophone majority still has an account to settle with its colonial past and with its present" (12). The heritage film, I would argue, provides one avenue for settling these accounts. Working with this "memory under tension," the heritage film reaffirms a hold on a past that provides a strong Québécois identity formed under the conditions of colonization and oppression. Immigrants, and Quebecers who are unfamiliar with their province's history, alongside a younger post-referendum generation, long removed from the era of Duplessis and the power of the Catholic Church, may be unconvinced by arguments for sovereignty or see decolonization as an unfinished project.[5] The heritage film sets out to remind viewers of this history and reawakens decolonization as a goal. In the project of creating a unified Québécois society, "there will always be a need for a symbolic cement[,] an identity component made up of a sense of belonging, memory, values, and collective projects" (Bouchard 14). The heritage film works to reaffirm, for older Québécois, or create, for newcomers and younger generations, a collective shared memory of a colonized past (and, by inference, present). As Bélen Vidal has succinctly put it: "The heritage film debate connects the period film to a network of cultural and industrial practices that relate to the construction of a collective cultural memory" (2). In Quebec, the heritage film constructs a collective cultural memory in which the suffering of the Québécois people is a foundational myth of the nation.

The heritage films that emerged in Quebec with such prominence at the turn of the new millennium were not the first films to portray suffering as a foundation for collective imagining. Indeed, the foundational text of Quebec victimhood on film is undoubtedly Jean-Yves Bigras's 1952 melodrama *La Petite Aurore, l'enfant martyre*. Based on the true story of Aurore Gagnon, a young girl brutally abused to the point of death by her stepmother and father in 1920, the film depicts in graphic detail the victimization of Aurore and the physical abuse she suffers. Scott Mackenzie (2005) vividly describes the film as

> one of the most sadistic, masochistic, and guilt-ridden films ever to be produced, anywhere ... Aurore is denied her food, has her hair cut off and is burnt on the stove, has her tongue scorched with a hot iron, is thrown down a stairwell, is whipped, struck with the handle of an axe, has her hands burnt, is locked in an attic, and has the picture of her dead mother torn up in her face, all by her father's new wife. The viewer is placed in a highly masochistic positions as she watches atrocity after atrocity performed on the girl with absolutely no one intervening. (178)

The masochistic position of the viewer is reinforced by the general helplessness that pervades the film and by Aurore's appalling death. Neither the state, nor the Church, nor the neighbours intervene effectively enough to prevent her death. Yet despite the morbid nature of film and its portrayal of a helpless victim, *La Petite Aurore, l'enfant martyre* struck a chord with Quebec audiences and was a commercial success. The film resonated with audiences that read Aurore as an allegory for their own suffering. As André Loiselle (2007) suggests:

> At one level, little Aurore, who has lost her mother and is tortured by an evil stepmother and an emasculated father, can be seen as an allegory for francophone Quebec. Abandoned by the *mère patrie* (France), and controlled by an evil tyrant (Britain) and complicit patriarch (Duplessis), Aurore suffers such tortures as having her tongue burnt. The correlation between the child and [the] subjugated French Canadian is made clear when the evil stepmother points a hot iron toward the camera standing in for Aurore, as she says, "Je vais te brûler la langue" [I am going to burn your tongue]. That *langue* means at once "tongue" and "language" cements the reading of *Aurore* as allegory of a linguistic minority feeling oppressed by the assimilatory forces of federalism. (22)

It should be noted that the 1952 version of *Aurore* was not set in the past, but told as a contemporary version of the story. Consequently, the film spoke to the existing historical situation of the audience and encouraged their identification with Aurore. The 2005 remake, however, returns to the time of the original events (the late 1910s), and this version presents a nostalgic portrayal of the suffering of the French Canadian populace as a means to produce collective memory and identity. Key to the millennial heritage film is the melodramatic display of physical hardship, oppression, and general dispossession of the people of Quebec.

In thinking through how collective suffering is at the root of the foundational myths propagated in the Quebec heritage film, it is useful to return to the etymological meaning of nostalgia. Formed by the Greek word *nostos*, meaning "to return home," and *alge*, which refers to "pain" or "suffering," this long-forgotten definition of nostalgia refers to the suffering caused by the desire to return home.[6] Drawing upon this etymological understating of nostalgia, the Quebec heritage film expresses a longing for the past that is neither pastoral nor reflective of a pre-lapsarian ideal, but rather one that is steeped in pain and suffering. Éric Bédard (2007–8) has analyzed the portrayal of this suffering and pain—particularly the representation of the role of religion during *la grande noirceur* ("the Great Darkness," as the Duplessis era is often referred to)—in the three breakout heritage films of the new millennium: *Séraphin, Le Survenant,* and *Aurore.* Yet equally prominent is the emergence of a subgenre of the heritage film, the heritage bio-pic, and a trio of films that were released around the same time: *Ma vie en cinémascope* (Denise Filiatrault 2004), about popular Quebec chanteuse Alys Robi; Charles Binamé's film about Montreal Canadiens hockey legend *Maurice Richard* (2005); and Daniel Roby's *Louis Cyr: The Strongest Man in the World* (2013), which followed slightly later. The heritage biopic is a particularly robust site upon which to construct a collective memory. As Raphaëlle Moine (2014) has noted in a discussion of French heritage biopics: "Heritage fiction and biopics share a common commemorative function by revitalizing sites of memory in the course of revisiting them. Both serve to evoke and put forward a collective past, construing it as a common good in which spectators recognize themselves" (56). The evocation of a collective past via the biopic is strengthened through the appeal to actual personages and real historical events. In this trio of films, the titular characters, Alys Robi, Maurice Richard, and Louis Cyr, are promoted as national heroes upon whom a collective memory and identity can be built. It is key, however, that the heroes (and heroine) of these films, and their role as fathers (and mother) of the Quebec nation, be seen as suffering. The anguish of the titular characters in these heritage biopics can be read as metonymic for the collective memory of the Québécois experience of the past as painful. In the Quebec heritage biopic, the "common good," as Moine puts it, is to reaffirm and bolster the foundational myth of the pain and suffering that characterizes the Quebec nation's coming into being. In what follows I look briefly at each film and at how each titular character's subjugation, physical hardship, and pain serves to bolster the foundational myth of Quebec's suffering and, in turn, the role each played as a national(ist) icon. In each of these heritage biopics, the torment of the Quebec people is symbolized by the suffering of an emblematic Quebec icon.

Ma vie en cinémascope (2004)

Denise Filiatrault's *Ma vie en cinémascope* (2004) charts the rise and fall—in characteristic artist biopic fashion—of one of Quebec's best-known singers, Alys Robi (1923–2011). The Celine Dion of her time, Robi became a popular singer in Quebec before establishing an international career that peaked in the 1940s. Following a car accident in 1948, she suffered depression that spiralled into a nervous breakdown, and she ended up in a psychiatric institution, where she underwent a lobotomy without her consent. *Ma vie en cinémascope* follows the well-worn rags-to-riches-to-rags biopic formula. The film begins with Robi at her lowest point—her confinement and operation—before flashing back to her early life to depict her climb to fame. The film ends with a return to the hospital, where Robi is shown being released into her father's care. Robi was one of Quebec's first international stars, and her success abroad and the idea that one could rise above the status of second-class citizen to take the world by storm was pivotal to her status as one of Quebec's founding figures. Equally important, however, is the tragedy of her decline in mental health, confinement, and eventual lobotomy. The building of a collective memory of disenfranchisement requires our heroes and heroines to suffer, and *Ma vie en cinémascope* delivers this with melodramatic aplomb.

Ma vie en cinémascope's opening credit sequence begins with a shot that follows a male figure, clad in fedora and overcoat, as he strides toward an imposing building. A caption informs us this is St-Michel Archange Psychiatric Institute, Quebec City, 1952. The date and location clearly position us within the depths of *la grande noirceur*, inside a Catholic-run hospital. As Bédard has noted, evoking the Catholic Church in the Duplessis era has increasingly come to serve as a shorthand means of conveying impending brutality. The soundtrack bears this out—it begins with an ominous base chord followed by a rushed and pulsing drumbeat that matches the pace of the figure on screen as he strides toward the building. Even before he enters, we hear the stylized non-diegetic screams of patients echoing on the sound-track—their screams function as both a form of acoustical memory and a forewarning of the abuse and pain that is meted out in the hospital. The grey building, the wails on the soundtrack, and the ominous musical chords, along with the audience's collective memory of the Duplessis era, together establish the cruelty associated with institutions run by religious orders. The next shot shows feet, enveloped in a habit, hurrying along a corridor. A brief medium shot of a nun shows her face almost completely obscured by her habit, but what we can make out shows her stern, impassive expression. The succeeding shot shows an orderly wheeling an empty gurney, and both arrive at the room where Robi is being kept. The orderly throws open the door and coolly but quickly sets about preparing her for her operation. Robi, portrayed by Quebec star Pascale Bussières, recoils to the corner of her bed, screaming for them to leave and resisting as they strap her down to the gurney and cut off her hair, wisps of it falling to floor. She sobs and screams that they don't have the right and that she isn't crazy. "I don't want to go" and "Daddy," she plaintively sobs as she's wheeled down the corridor. The opening credit sequence's final image is of an elevator door closing as she cries, "No!"

Ma vie en cinémascope portrays Robi as a woman ahead of her time. The Robi of Filiatrault's film is a modern, ambitious woman whose aspirations and love affairs, with married men, run counter to the prevailing morality of the time. What is pertinent to my discussion here, however, is how the film stresses her body's defilement and employs a melodramatic style that empha-sizes her pain and suffering. In her classic essay "Film Bodies: Gender, Genre, Excess," Linda Williams (1991) charts how certain film genres portray and affect a bodily sensation. The horror film, melodrama, and pornography—all three are "body genres"—both portray and evoke tears, fear, and arousal. She writes: "What seems to bracket these particular genres from others is an apparent lack of proper esthetic distance, a sense of over-involvement in sen-sation and emotion" (5). Undisputedly, *Ma vie en cinémascope* uses a highly wrought, excessive style that seeks to engage the viewer's sensations and emotions. The melodramatic conventions it employs, however, are not used solely to provoke tears, but also to reproduce the pain in an audience that rec-ognizes and identifies with the pain inflicted on Robi's body. Robi's writhing and screaming body as she is wheeled away for her lobotomy works as both a literal and metaphorical inscription of pain. The film aligns Robi's suffering with the suffering of the French Canadian populace during the Duplessis era. *Ma vie en cinémascope* produces the past as a site of collective traumatic memory to be recalled and relived by contemporary audiences. That the structuring event of *Ma vie en cinémascope* is Robi's lobotomy underscores her status as an icon of national suffering. Her pain and the neglect she suffers engage viewer sympathies, and her despairing cry of "No" reverberating down the corridors of the asylum sets the stage for her failed resistance and her position as a victim of the Duplessis era. "No," for a contemporary Quebec audience, can be, as Robert Lepage has shown in his film *Nô* (1998), suggestive of many meanings: it can signify resistance to the Duplessis era and to the abusive powers of Catholic-run institutions, or it can be a rallying cry of the dispossessed against those forces. It can also evoke the successful "No" vote in the two referendums in 1980 and 1995 that failed to bring sovereignty to Quebec. Once Roby's cry of "No!" subsides, the pulsating soundtrack fades out, the opening credits end, and the lobotomy sequence begins. There is an overhead shot of Robi dressed in a white hospital gown on an operating table surrounded by doctors and nurses—all indistinguishably dressed in white operating gowns. She prays to herself in urgent, hushed tones. Yet neither her prayers, nor the Church, nor her father will save her—she has been forsaken. The overhead operating lamp is turned on, bathing her in a soft white light, and as the anesthetic takes hold, she gives herself over to the procedure—a resignation that has religious overtones reminiscent of Joan of Arc accepting her death at the stake. Robi's shorn head is also a reminder of the women whose heads were shaved at the end of the Second World War to mark them as having collaborated with the enemy. Here, Robi is being shamed for having the audacity to pursue a career and seek pleasure from married men. Robi (Pascale Bussières) is a beautiful and angelic, albeit tragic, victim. As Amy Ransom (2014a) has noted, in a discussion of recent musical biopics produced in Quebec, "these films feed the less than laudable national taste for victims." Likewise, the heritage biopic not only represents its protagonists as victims but portrays their suffering as a precondition for becoming a true Québécois and a national icon.

Maurice Richard (2005)

When hockey legend Maurice Richard died in 2000, he became the first non-politician to be granted a state funeral. He had long been a national icon in Quebec, having led the Montreal Canadiens to eight Stanley Cup Championships. Long before his death he had been mythologized in, for example, Sheldon Cohen's classic National Film Board of Canada animated film *The Hockey Sweater* (1979), based on Roch Carrier's short story. In that story, Carrier recounts how every young boy growing up during the era of Richard's hockey stardom emulated him. Charles Binamé's 2005 biopic *Maurice Richard* brings this larger-than-life legend to screen, and does so by ... well ... making him larger than life. In her study of the importance of hockey in Quebec, *Hockey, PQ*, Amy Ransom (2014b) examines how the film "reinscribed Richard as a national hero" (22). Indeed, it is difficult not to view *Maurice Richard* as a hagiography, one that recounts how the hockey legend seemingly single-handedly started the Quiet Revolution—particularly in the film's use of the Richard Riot as a key element in the plot. Much like *Ma vie en cinémascope, Maurice Richard* begins with the classic biopic set-up: it starts with a defining moment and then flashes back to retrace the events that led up to it. Rather than focus on Richard's hockey achievements and his role in helping the Montreal Canadiens win five straight Stanley Cup championships between 1955 and 1960, the film begins with the Richard Riot, when fans took to the streets in March 1955 to demonstrate their anger at Richard's suspension for the remainder of the '54–'55 season by the English-speaking president of the NHL, Clarence Campbell. The reprimand was viewed as unfairly harsh and as motivated by anti-French bias in the NHL. The use of this event to bookend the film suggests that the riot was more than a culminating point in Richard's career—it also marked the birth of Quebec nationalism. As Benoît Melançon (2009) has pointed out, the Richard Riot has reached mythic proportions as a supposedly catalyzing event for the Quiet Revolution (114–15). The film perpetuates this perception and reaffirms the mythic status of the man and the event.

Released in 2005, but set during the years 1937 to 1955, *Maurice Richard* is firmly placed in the Duplessis era—again, hearkening back nostalgically to an era of disempowerment for Québécois. After the opening credit sequence establishes the Richard Riots as the film's framing device, a black-and-white flashback of an industrial-looking Montreal establishes the time and place with the caption "Montréal 1937, La grande noirceur." This one shot situates the viewer in a milieu that has become, through historical revision and cinematic tropes, synonymous with grim oppression. The film charts Richard's rise to the position of national hero—again like Robi. *Maurice Richard* accentuates the bodily pain and physical hardship Richard must endure to attain his status as an icon of Quebec identity—again like Robi. As Amy

Ransom (2014b) has pointed out, precisely "by focusing on the blood, sweat, and tears of Maurice Richard, Binamé's film reinscribes the hockey player's status as a French Canadian *lieu de mémoire*" (38). Indeed, the film uses Richard as an vehicle for building collective memory and identity, and it does so through the brutalization of his body. Ransom links this portrayal of Richard's physical hardship to Catholic imagery, particularly the Passion of the Christ, and to his role as a "redemptive, sacrificial hero for a modern, secularized Quebec-in-the-making" (38–39). I would extend this argument to suggest that the pain Richard is portrayed as enduring is represented to remind viewers of a shared experience of victimhood—to reaffirm in the contemporary moment the persistence of this underdog status. To do so, the film stresses the bodily duress to which Richard is subjected.

Maurice Richard was legendary for his physical strength and endurance. A Historica Canada heritage moment recounts the story of Richard (played by Roy Dupuis, who reprises this role in the feature film) being called in to play a game when he had asked for the night off. After spending the day single-handedly moving his family's furniture, he hits the ice and scores eight points (five goals and three assists). This episode is portrayed in *Maurice Richard*, affirming his legendary indefatigability. But it is his bruised and battered body—a body in pain—that is the precondition for his status as an icon of nationalism. Repeatedly, Richard is shown brutally body-checked, slammed, intentionally tripped, hit from behind, and so on. The most graphic display of the melodramatic convention of the pained body takes place during the second period of a game against the Boston Bruins at the Montreal Forum. The Boston coach tells his player to "Watch number 9—don't let him go by," thus setting up the obstacle that Richard will encounter. Soon enough, an advancing Richard is bodychecked by a Boston player and hits the ice head-first. Richard is down. The sound mutes, and the ensuing action is depicted in slow motion. The bloodstained ice indicates that Richard is badly hurt. He is rolled over and carried off the ice, blood dripping down his face. The next shot, reminiscent of Robi on the operating table for her lobotomy, is an overhead of Richard on a gurney. A close-up depicts the graphic stitching together of the gash above his eye. This is not, however, the end of the scene. With the blood still running down his face from his wound and streaked down his jersey, Richard returns to the ice to score a triumphant breakaway goal in painstaking slow motion. The blood on his face and jersey is left as a marker of the pain he and the Quebec people have endured.

Louis Cyr (2013)

Released in 2013, Daniel Roby's *Louis Cyr: The Strongest Man in the World* (2013) emerges a little later in this cycle of heritage biopics. It depicts the life of Louis Cyr, a nineteenth-century strongman, from his teens until his death in 1912 at the age of forty-nine from chronic nephritis. Cyr died before the coming of *la grande noirceur*, and the film depicts the hardscrabble existence of French Canadians of an earlier era, one of limited economic opportunities and general poverty. In this way, the film reflects the myth of a nation produced through pain and suffering. The Cyrs are economic refugees, who in 1878 relocate to the United States in search of better economic opportunities. In Lowell, Massachussetts, Louis forsakes attendance at school to help support his parents and nine siblings, and his resulting illiteracy becomes a subplot of the film, in that it limits his job choices and motivates him to insist on an education for his own daughter, whatever the cost. Given his lack of schooling, Cyr's brute strength becomes his sole means of escaping crushing poverty, although he initially does not display any aspiration to take advantage of his gift other than to accept the wage raise his boss gives him because he does the work of three men. However, when his sister dies of typhoid and the family can't afford anything better than a wicker casket too small for her body, Louis, the only viable breadwinner in the family, decides to capitalize on his formidable strength.

Roby, like Filiatrault and Binamé (see above), employs a flashback device to organize *Louis Cyr*. Cyr's life is recounted through a series of stories told to his estranged daughter, Lili, by his lifelong assistant and friend, Horace Barré. Lili, we will learn, yearns to follow in her father's footsteps and become a strongwoman performer, but Cyr, wanting a better life for his daughter, forbids it and sends her off to a religious boarding school to be educated. Lili can't forgive this betrayal and resists interpreting her father's actions as well intentioned. In the end, of course, *Louis Cyr* follows the conventions of melodrama: Lili returns home to reconcile with the ailing patriarch. The father–daughter relationship at the heart of Louis Cyr can be seen as a reversal of the Aurore incident, in that Cyr makes every effort to spare his daughter any hardship, particularly the physical suffering she would undoubtedly be subjected to if she were allowed to pursue her ambition of being a circus strongwoman. Instead, it is Cyr who must shoulder the burden of pain.

Initially, Cyr's displays of strength are depicted as wondrous, but as the film progresses we see the physical exertion take its toll on him until he collapses in visible agony in the film's most graphic scene. An aging and ailing

Cyr cannot accept the claims of his rivals that they are stronger than him. To reaffirm his status as the world's strongest man, Cyr performs a feat in which he attempts to restrain four horses, two on each arm, as they literally attempt to pull him apart. Cyr is shown straining as the horses struggle to move forward, and he is, at first, successful in keeping them in place. But as the scene progress, in slow motion no less, it becomes evident that the physical toll of this display of strength is excruciating. As the sound mutes, we witness reaction shots of the horrified audience and notice that blood is beginning to splatter across the front of his white shirt—he is bleeding from his ears. As the horses come crashing down, Cyr collapses as well, and an overhead shot shows him falling to the ground on his back with his arms extended, so that he momentarily resembles a crucified figure. A cut to a medium close-up side view of his head further accentuates his bleeding ears. The scene ends with a close-up of an apparently unconscious Cyr—his body, having been pushed to the limit, has succumbed. *Louis Cyr*, like its aforementioned biopic predecessors, positions the pained and bleeding body as a necessary condition for national mythmaking. The film functions as a reminder of a suffering national figure, an *aide-mémoire*, to reaffirm the hardship that is, and by extension continues to be, the condition of the Québécois people.

Conclusion

At the dawn of the new millennium, Jocelyn Létourneau published a collection of essays, *Passer à l'avenir* (2000), in which he interrogated the role of history and memory in Quebec and Canada. Translated into English in 2004 as *A History of the Future*, Létourneau suggests that thinking is "what allows man to resist the forces of the infinite past and indefinable future by opening up, in the interval of the present moment where he stands, *a breach that liberates him from heritage* and expectations without breaking his solidary with the cause of the ancestors or that of the descendants" (xiii, emphasis added). Létourneau powerfully evokes the stranglehold that heritage—and, as I have argued, its alignment with nostalgia and suffering—continue to have on the Quebec people. In cinema, a compelling counter-argument to this nostalgia of pain is articulated in the 2016 film *Ceux qui font le révolutions à moitié n'ont fait que se creuser un tombeau* [Those Who Make Revolution Halfway Only Dig Their Own Graves] (Mathieu Denis and Simon Lavoie), a work that is keenly aware of Quebec's history and politics but firmly set in the present. The film depicts the lives of a splinter group of student revolutionaries five years after the 2012 *carré rouge* protests against tuition hikes in Quebec. In one scene, we see one of the students, Tumulto (Laurent Bélanger), watching footage of the 1943 NFB documentary *Terre de nos aïeux* (dir. Jane Marsh), about a Quebec rural family working their farm. Shortly thereafter, he appears naked in front of his seemingly disinterested housemates/political allies to repent his apparent lapse into nostalgia. He declares:

> I'm accusing myself today, before you, of being guilty of the crime of nostalgia. I'm guilty of having let myself be lulled by the comforting and numbing sweetness of my past, while I swore before you to live only in the moment, in the present. Looking back is to feel gratified by something gone. To feel gratified by your own death, your own insignificance. The only way to stop dying, is to refuse all forms of gratification that do not come from concrete, tangible, present action. By miring myself in nostalgia like a pig rolling in its own shit, I betrayed a fundamental principle of our brotherhood. I can promise you now, that I will not slip again into this deathly nostalgia.

As self-professed revolutionaries, the film's main characters are prone to such hyperbolic declarations, but the substance of Tumulto's speech and his insistence on looking critically at nostalgia cannot be so easily dismissed. The film calls for a radical liberation from the past, nostalgia, and heritage to counteract the filmmakers, film funders, and audiences that have turned to the Quebec heritage film in a move that retrenches national identity and memory in the nostalgic albeit painful past. These heritage films disclose Quebec's nostalgic preoccupation with survival (*la survivance*) and pain (*la souffrance*) as coterminous, indissoluble, and necessary for a shared sense of identity.

Notes

1   http://www.ledevoir.com/culture/cinema/87103/en-bref-aurore-recolte -plus-de-3-5-millions, accessed 4 February 2017.

2   The forces of globalization, internationalization, and immigration have accelerated and amplified in the intervening decades, with the Brexit vote being another response to these changes.

3   The *mythistoire* "recurs like a leitmotif to frame the vast majority of situations in which the Québécois of French Canadian heritage find themselves."

4   "Nous vivons dans un monde soumis à la tyrannie émotionnelle de certaines minorités braillardes, qui ont l'art de se victimizer en toutes circonstances."

5   This operation of memory may be akin to what Marianne Hirsch has characterized as "post-memory" in that it "strives to *reactivate* and *reembody* more

distant social/national and archival/culture memorial structures by reinvesting the with resonant individual and familiar forms of mediation and aesthetic expression." See Marianne Hirsch, "The Generation of Postmemory," *Poetics Today* 29, no. 1 (Spring 2008): 111.

6   Only in the nineteenth century did the definition take on a temporal dimension and "returning home" transmute into a return to the past.

3

"LA NOSTALGIE DE LA MAISON INCONNUE":
The Ethics of Memory in Bernard Émond's Recent Work

Alessandra M. Pires

C'est ici que la littérature et le meilleur cinéma nous donnent une leçon :
il vaut mieux ne pas tout dire, ne pas tout montrer, ne pas tout expliquer.
Le hors-texte, le hors-champ sont essentiels, car les mots et les images
n'épuisent pas le réel : très souvent, ils le réduisent. [It is here that literature and the best films give us a lesson; it is better not to say everything,
not to show everything, not to explain everything. What is outside the
text (hors-texte), what is offscreen (hors-champ) is essential, because
words and images do not represent reality completely; quite often, they
reduce it.]

— Bernard Émond, "Elle pleure," 2016, 50[1]

Qui peut avec le moins peut avec le plus. Qui peut avec le plus ne peut
pas forcément avec le moins. [Someone who can work with the minimum
can work with the most. One who can work with the most cannot, inevitably, with the minimum.]

— Robert Bresson 1975, 43[2]

Introduction

This chapter explores configurations of memory and mourning in recent essays and films of Québécois filmmaker Bernard Émond, in particular, his films *Tout ce que tu possèdes* (2012, *All That You Possess*) and *Le Journal d'un vieil homme* (2015, *Diary of an Old Man*), based on a short story by Chekhov, one of his main literary sources of inspiration ("Vitupérer l'époque," 2011).[3] Both films contemplate notions of pain, nostalgia, loss, and mourning, core concepts in Émond's cinematic and literary works. Émond has repeatedly highlighted the impactful role that literature has played in his intellectual and creative development (Émond and Galiero 2009, 19–20).[4] But he has also written on the crucial impact the visual arts have had on his sober filmmaking style. In his essay "Images" (Émond 2011), Émond elaborates on his own *art poétique*. Art, the author suggests in this essay, begins and ends with humility. Émond, recalling a visit to Rome, argues that works of art such as the ones found at the Vatican Museum and the Basilica di Roma may crush the soul of the viewer by their magnitude. However, he reminisces, as he walked through Rome and the Vatican Museum, including the Sistine Chapel, the works of art that appealed most to his senses and affection, and that remain with him after his Rome visit, are four paintings by the Italian painter Giorgio Morandi (1890–1964). In the Vatican Museum, Émond discovered and admired Morandi's paintings,[5] which exude, if anything, sobriety, a quality that also informs Émond's filmmaking and writing (Émond 2011, 95). To fully understand the unique character of Émond's nostalgic cinema—if one can call it that—we must remain mindful of these influences, which shape his cinematic vision of Quebec and the Québécois identity. Accordingly, the analysis below will sometimes take brief detours, bifurcating away from cinema and extending beyond the Quebec context as a means to elucidate the filmmaker's intricate perspective on his own nation.

Unlike *Le Journal d'un vieil homme*, *Tout ce que tu possèdes* is not strictly speaking an adaptation of a literary work. It does, however, refer explicitly to literature, as it includes immersive meditations on the works of a Polish writer, Edward Stachura (1937–1979), whose brief stay in Quebec left its mark on Pierre Leduc (Patrick Drolet), the film's main character.[6] Historic reality and fiction mingle to give birth to a film in which not only the past but also the present and the future become the source of nostalgic longing. In *Tout ce que tu possèdes*, as well as in *Le Journal d'un vieil homme*, nostalgia blurs temporal boundaries and looks to the future while simultaneously immersing the characters and the audience in the past and the present. Taking his cue from the fluid dimension evoked by the Greek etymology of the word nostalgia, *nostos* (return home, travel, journey), and *algos* (pain, grief, sorrow), Émond does not stage static painful moments embedded in an immutable past. Rather it is the flow of the ever elusive return that informs his vision. His films thus turn markedly away from the nostalgic spectacles of pain displayed in the heritage biopics discussed by Liz Czach in this anthology, in which nostalgia is attached to a specific historical period. In Émond's films, the concept of nostalgia rather evokes an affective multilayering of temporal experiences, where the feeling of loss is rooted in the fleeting present as much as in the unknown past or the ambiguous future. To use an Émondian metaphor, nostalgia enacts the movement of the ocean, the to-and-fro of the foam that the tides ceaselessly bring in and wash away as the sea murmurs its back-and-forth lullaby of life.

Having embarked on a long journey toward understanding foreignness and otherness during a research trip to Poland as a student, Pierre, the protagonist of *Tout ce que tu possèdes*, eventually quits his academic job and rejects the identity that has been forged for him by external social forces. Breaking free from all institutions, Pierre becomes not only destitute but also increasingly self-destructive. He embraces a minimalistic way of life, both mentally and physically, within the bare space he inhabits. We see him walking back and forth to the nearby bookstore to sell his last material possessions, his books that he forsakes, along with his career. Pierre's new minimalist life is disrupted when he receives news from his estranged father and his former (or forgotten) girlfriend comes back to haunt his plans of *éloignement* (turning away) from societal roles. At first, his dying father informs Pierre that he would like him to take over his corporate empire. Pierre resolutely rejects the offer because he believes that his father built his business success with dirty money.[7] However, Émond does not present Pierre as an altruistic character guided by principles of social justice and equality. Rather, he is an isolated individual who can't face his father and ailing mother, and who abandoned a pregnant girlfriend and gave up on his job. His efforts to achieve uncompromising freedom betray in fact a deeply egocentric persona who prefers to retreat into the safe prison of the self. His inability to interact with the outside world seems insurmountable to him, as he prefers to hide in his own self-destructive vertigo. Radically retreating from society into himself, Pierre exemplifies the modern isolationist version of the individual, a phenomenon that according to Émond belongs to a world where familial links have dissolved and social rapports have disintegrated (Émond 2012, 12). Only the appearance of his daughter, Adèle (Willia Ferland-Tanguay), will take Pierre out of his narcissistic solipsism, however temporarily, and make him understand his profound nostalgia for the home he hardly ever knew—"la maison inconnue."

The works and life of Edward Stachura, whose poems Pierre translates, represent and reinforce his own desires and depression. However, Stachura's poems also contribute to a possible recovery at the end of the film with the letter the protagonist writes to Adèle. In spite of hints at Pierre's possible change at the end of *Tout ce que tu possèdes*, from gloomily rejecting everyone who tries to reach out to him to beginning to embrace his role as an accepting father, Émond leaves the viewer with enough ambiguity to allow for their own interpretation of the main character's future. In the final scene, the nomadically inclined Pierre leaves his daughter in the house that his own father bequeathed him. This open-ended gesture precludes any one-dimensional certainty about Pierre's sense of responsibility for familial continuity. The film intricately negotiates correlations between the ethics of memory and those of familial belonging, a cultural and moral nexus that Émond perceives as having been shattered by globalization.[8] Are we to be nostalgic for the traditional model? Would we be able to return to the old model and become less nomadic and more sedentary even if we wanted to? These are some of the questions that pervade viewers' senses and that seem designed by the filmmaker to elicit a broader critical thinking in his audience.

Mourning Memories

Je pense qu'il faut sortir de soi pour être capable de faire une œuvre, qu'il faut aller rencontrer les autres, ou ce qui est autre. [I think that one must step outside of oneself in order to create a work of art. One must encounter others, or that which is other.]

— Émond and Galiero 2009, 42

Les souvenirs [...] Peu nous importe qu'ils soient ou non des fictions, tant ils nous sont précieux. Ils sont la preuve de notre singularité : à chacun ces souvenirs, ils ne se partagent pas. [Memories ... It does not matter whether they are fictitious or not, as long as they are precious to us. They are the proof of our singularity: to each their own memories; they are not to be shared.]

— Pontalis 2012, 28

As mentioned earlier, Émond's protagonist embraces a life of utmost simplicity, and he dedicates his days entirely to the translation of Polish poet Edward Stachura's works. Stachura was the focus of Pierre's academic research and the reason for his research trip to Poland as a student. During his transitioning process, he begins to translate, an act that serves as a metaphor for the shift in his life. Convincingly represented by the composed, quasi-mute acting of Patrick Drolet, Pierre finds solace in Stachura's poems. Stachura's home country, Poland, metonymically replaces the home and comfort for which Pierre is longing. Through the labour of the translation process, Pierre travels daily to a paradoxical semi-well-known place. For Pierre, Stachura's final book, *Fabula Rasa*,[9] provides a translation of his own angst and pessimistic *Weltanschauung*. His translation work becomes his single obsession, until the appearance of his daughter. In the final letter Pierre writes to Adèle, in which he bequeaths her his father's house, he realizes that it is time to come to terms with a long, painful path that had already manifested itself when he abandoned his academic career and that led him to reject his father's inheritance.

A key element in Émond's oeuvre is the recurring *topos* of the house in his films and writings (Émond 2012–13, 65).[10] As discussed by Katherine Ann Roberts in her contribution to this book, "Return to Abiti in Bernard Émond's *La Donation*," places shape Émond's work: "The importance of place is … crucial to the analysis of the trilogy [*La Donation, La Neuvaine, Contre toute espérance*]," and at the core of Émond's "ideas about recuperating the positive essence of so-called French Canadian culture." This premise permeates *all* of Bernard Émond's oeuvre, not just in the quoted trilogy, and proves central to the essence of his work.

At this point, it will be instructive to examine some of Émond's recent essays, in which he develops the social and cultural ideas that constitute his cinematic views. Some of these texts were published in his book *Il y a trop d'images* (Émond 2011). Other essays appeared in various venues, including the montréalais journal *Revue Relations*, to which Émond has regularly contributed. Yet other essays are still unpublished and have been graciously shared with me by Émond in our private correspondence, with his permission to use them for this study.

In a conversation with the filmmaker published in their book *La Perte et le Lien* (2009), Simon Galiero mentions the recurrence of symbolic places in his films, to which Émond responds: "Vous mettez le doigt sur quelque chose qui est fondamental dans la façon dont je travaille [...] Il ne s'agit pas d'écrire une histoire et de trouver un lieu où elle va pouvoir s'incarner. C'est le lieu qui suscite l'histoire" [You are pointing out something that is fundamental to the way I work … It is not about writing a story and then finding a place where it should take place. It is the place that incites the story] (Émond and Galiero 2009, 75). In another article, Émond confirms that decisive inspirations for his films were triggered by the houses in which he lived or that he visited and that he was deeply attracted to along his life's journey. The spatial dynamics of houses are core components of Émond's works. The protagonists' lives and the memories that their families have built revolve around their dwelling places. According to Émond, his characters suffer a loss of place, anonymity, foreignness, and nomadic conditions:[11] "Dans tous mes films, ils y a des maisons brûlées, détruites, ou abandonnées. Et dans tous mes longs métrages de fiction, le personnage principal est quelqu'un qui perd sa maison ou qui la quitte" [In almost all my films, there are burnt houses, destroyed, or abandoned houses. And in all my feature fiction films, the main characters either lose or abandon their home] (Émond 2012–13, 65). In his recent essay "De la nostalgie" (2016a), an uncanny text with Proustian notes in which the author explores the political and cultural status quo of our times, Émond introduces the notion of what I suggest we call nostalgia for the unknown home, or, as the author himself puts it in French, "la nostalgie de la maison inconnue" (Émond 2016a, 50). In this text, Émond highlights once more the relevance of houses for his oeuvre, this time his grandfather's house. He discusses his grandfather's attachment to the place in Verchères, Quebec, where he had lived in the 1920s, and how that attachment played a role in their lives, including in Émond's own psyche:

> Cette ferme, je ne l'ai jamais vue, et la nostalgie que j'éprouve découle probablement de celle de ma parenté, de mes oncles, mes tantes et mes grands-parents eux-mêmes pour cette belle terre en bordure du fleuve où ils étaient les maîtres. […] Ce lieu mythique qui évoque pour moi la beauté de la tradition, la dignité du travail, la solidarité familiale et villageoise, […] n'a probablement rien à voir avec la ferme réelle où ont vécu mes grands-parents [This farm, I never saw it, and the nostalgia that I feel for it probably results from the one that my relatives feel, the nostalgia that my uncles, my aunts, and my grandparents themselves have for this beautiful land on the shores of the St. Lawrence river, where they were the masters. To me, this mythical land evokes beauty and tradition, the dignity of labor, familial solidarity and the villagers' solidarity … but it has probably nothing to do with the real farm where my grandparents lived]. (Émond 2016a, 50)

Despite Pierre's rejection of his father's patrimony in *Tout ce que tu possèdes*, the house that his father wants him to inherit kindles his desire to accept the paternal legacy. The family house resonates in his recollections of his childhood and begins to outline the future lineage of the family embodied in his daughter Adèle: "C'est qu'il y a une sorte d'inscription humaine profonde, indélébile dans les lieux. Ce n'est pas quelque chose qui passe par le discours, mais on en sent parfois très fortement le sens" [There is a kind of profound and indelible imprinting in places. It is not something that can be expressed through words. But one can still strongly feel its meaning at times] (Émond and Galiero 2009, 75). Throughout his career, Émond has insisted on the responsibility that each individual must assume with regard to society and future generations. Through the voice of Pierre, Émond expresses the main theme of the film and addresses the relationship the character develops with the house, not as a mere object, but as a subject of his memories, of his past. The house embodies a quasi-character that has an autonomous existence in Émond's psyche: "J'ai dormi parterre dans la maison de nos ancêtres" [I slept on the floor of our ancestors' house] (Émond 2012, 14).[12]

By ending *Tout ce que tu possèdes* with Pierre's letter to his daughter Adèle, in which he entrusts her with his childhood home, Émond indicates via his main character that all facts rely on the individual's sense of responsibility toward the next generation. In her essay "Héritage et Patrimoine" (2012), Mélissa Thériault explains how Pierre realizes the need to accept the inheritance and to pass it on to his daughter: "Pierre constatera en effet que 'sans liens humains, la vie n'a aucun sens' et que les repères peuvent être retrouvés" [Pierre realizes that indeed "life without human relations has no meaning," and that the lost relationships can be found once again] (Thériault 2012, 132). Émond creates a cinema that entails a mental and physical *via crucis* both for his characters and for his viewers. And although the filmmaker emphasizes that he is moving toward a cinema whose paradigm unveils the necessity of human rapport rather than demonstrating its unattainability, in most of his films, including the two recent releases discussed in this essay, the lack or questioning of human connections defines his main characters[13] (Coulombe and Jean 2006, 240–42): "Qu'une vie, c'est forcément une série de pertes, une série de défaites. C'est sûr que ça se reflète dans mon cinéma" [Life is a series of losses, a series of defeats. This is certainly reflected in my cinema] (Émond and Galiero 2009, 30–31). Regarding the definition of nostalgia, the core concept in Émond's works, the filmmaker maintains that it cannot be grasped easily ("De la nostalgie"). He suggests that one should look back, and gather and respect the values of the past and the morality of *how things used to be*. The present, Émond argues, must be honoured in ways that enable us to celebrate it as an autonomous place, neither as an entrapment, nor as a *hic et nunc* to which one were to surrender one's sentiments and values. According to Émond, looking back at one's life serves as a *tour de force* for the future despite the impact of the past that fuels dissatisfaction with things undone.

In the final scene of *Tout ce que tu possèdes*, Pierre, having left the family home to his daughter, disappears from the screen, walking across the railway. It is up to the viewer to decide whether he had initiated a fresh path by vanishing from our eyes with no direction, thus creating the essence of his own new ethics, or whether he has chosen to eliminate himself out of disgust or nostalgia for what he could never really accomplish, and/or for what he is ultimately unable to do: to live fully in the present tense, or to lead a life free of guilt. As such, the final scene perhaps evokes a sense of nostalgia for the present. The ambiguous potentiality of the character's movement, at once full of promise and deeply nihilistic, creates a sense of hope that vanishes as quickly as it materializes. In the process, this concluding image interweaves aspirations, faith, disillusionment, abnegation, and self-denial. By accepting the family house as an inheritance from his father, Pierre accomplishes his one responsibility. He did not deny the family legacy altogether. On the other hand, Pierre has still denied most of his inheritance: he has kept *only* the family country house for the next generation, that is, his only daughter, Adèle, who becomes the sole inheritor of her father's and his ancestors' house. Pierre's responsibility finally finds closure. According to his logic, he can leave with his mind focused only on his own future. Yet from Adèle's perspective, Pierre's departure renders her a fatherless child who will be faced with a deep sense of loss, and as a result, the future may also become a source of nostalgia. The responsibility of a father never ends as long as the child is alive in this world. Pierre leaves believing that he has fulfilled his duties. In refusing to compromise his freedom in order to take care of another human being, Pierre remains a selfish character. But is judging the main character this decisively not in itself an act of *mauvaise foi*, and just as self-serving as the *mauvaise conscience* with which the protagonist stages his own disappearance at the end of Émond's film?

In a chapter titled "Kant," in his recent book *Critique du jugement* (Quignard 2015), French writer Pascal Quignard describes what the concept of *mauvaise conscience* unveils: "Qu'est-ce que la mauvaise conscience? L'impresssion de ne pas avoir fait comme il fallait. / Avoir peur de perdre la protection, la nourriture, l'amour des autres; la crainte sociale d'être rejeté par le groupe et le Père du groupe" [The impression of not having acted as one should have. Being afraid of losing the protection, the nourishment, the love of others; the social fear of being rejected by the group and by the Father of the group] (Quignard 2015, 71). From a Quignardian perspective, then, Pierre never lived up to his responsibility toward his daughter, and even less toward his mother, whom he could not face during a visit to her assisted living facility. He also fails to fulfill his responsibility toward his former fiancée, whom he had forsaken when he left for Poland as a student while she was pregnant. Pierre neglected them through indifference, and left them for a second time, abandoning his dying mother and leaving his former fiancée to raise their child. Pierre denies and refuses any human relationship. His acts are motivated solely by self-interest, and he appears to lack a sense of guilt, even though the viewer suspects that a complete absence of guilt is unattainable. Pierre's remaining cognitive responsiveness and sense of responsibility are dedicated solely to his daughter. He convinces himself that once he leaves the house to her, his conscience will allow him to navigate freely through the world, and she will have a sense of having had a father. To a child, the implications and wounds left by the absence of the father are continuously in development, regardless of whether paternal belongings are being passed on.

To summarize, Bernard Émond remains an existentialist in his own unique way. An ethical thinker who chooses to experience the pain of imagining an optimistic dimension to his despondent thoughts. Émond ends his article "De la nostalgie" by quoting the writer Gaston Miron: "L'avenir est aux sources" [The future is in the sources], a seemingly comforting postulate that merges past and future into a creative palimpsest.

Nostalgic Memories

> C'est drôle parce qu'il y a une dizaine d'années, je me suis dit, en regardant ce que je faisais, qu'au fond je ne parlais que de la perte, et je n'ai pas cessé de parler de la perte. Mais ce que je sais, c'est que dans mes derniers films, je parle de plus en plus de la nécessité du lien. [It is funny because about ten years ago, I told myself, watching what I was doing, that ultimately I only ever talked about loss, and I have never stopped talking about loss. But what I know now, it is that in my more recent films I talk more and more about the need for connections.]
>
> — Émond and Galiero 2009, 163

Mon lieu de l'archive est ma mémoire. [My archives are my memories.]

— Pontalis 2012, 12

In one of his recent essays, titled "Gratitude" (2015), Bernard Émond explores the concept stated in the title. The premise of this uplifting essay is linked to the etymological root of gratitude; the word is derived from the Latin *gratus* and its English translations "loved, dear"[14] (Lewis 1889). This immediately strikes the reader as a comforting notion. However, Émond's essay takes the reader into the realm of pain. Émond delves into the world of gratitude by reflecting on a loving and mourning writer immersed in nostalgia for his lost wife after years of a shared life. He refers to the oeuvre of the French writer Marc Bernard, whose later works memorialized his relationship with his wife, who died of cancer at the age of sixty-six.[15]

In an unexpected way, Marc Bernard emerges as a kindred spirit to Bernard Émond; both of them wrote trilogies that explored similar themes.[16] In Bernard's ode to the *bien-aimée*, the writer exalts their shared life and plunges deeply into a state of melancholia from which, according to his writings—or more precisely to Émond's readings of the texts—he never recovered. Émond comments, "Je ne connais rien de plus beau sur le deuil que ces trois livres, où la douleur de la perte et la gratitude d'avoir vécu et aimé sont intimement mêlées" [I don't know anything written on mourning that is more beautiful than these three books in which the pain of loss and the gratitude of having lived and loved are intimately interwoven] (Émond 2015, 10).

In "De la Nostalgie," Émond elaborates on what the word *nostalgia* means to him. In his interpretation, *nostalgia* indicates a sign of a certain lack rather than a longing for the past. At least in the context of the Québécois workers who lived in the fields and who observed the disintegration of families caused by changing times: "Cette nostalgie ne serait donc pas l'indice d'un désir de revenir en arrière, mais bien plutôt le signe d'un manque" [This nostalgia, then, does not translate (into) a desire to go back, but is rather the sign of a lack] (Émond 2016a, 50). Émond also insists that what the term nostalgia reveals is tied to a "sign of a real lack":

La nostalgie que nous éprouvons d'un lieu ou d'une époque mythiques est le signe d'un manque réel. La solidarité familiale et sociale nous manque; la dignité du travail nous manque; le lien avec la nature nous manque; le sentiment d'une histoire commune et de valeurs partagées nous manque. Nous aurions tort de rejeter ces sentiments comme *passéistes* : dans la conscience de ce manque et de ces pertes, il me semble y avoir la possibilité de regagner une partie de ce que nous avons perdu.

[The nostalgia we feel (for) a place or a mythical era is the sign of a real lack. We miss familial and social solidarity, we miss dignity at work, we miss the rapport with nature, and we miss the sentiment of a common history and shared values. We would be wrong to reject these feelings as *passéist*. It seems possible to me to regain a part of what we lost in the consciousness of this very lack and these losses]. (Émond 2016a, 50)

Le Journal d'un vieil homme (2015), a film based on Chekhov's novella "A Dreary Story" (1889) and shot with the poignant sobriety of Morandi, presents a dying man in a perennial state of mourning. According to French authors Bacqué and Hanus in their book *Le Deuil* (here freely translated as *Mourning*), the English lexicon serves to illustrate the unique French term *deuil*, which provides subtle semantic differentiations that are germane to the realm of this kind of suffering. English renderings of *deuil* can include "bereavement," "grief," and "mourning," each of them referring to a certain time and social sphere in which those who bear the pain find themselves encapsulated (Bacqué and Hanus 2010, 20–21).

Nicolas (Paul Savoie), the main character of *Le Journal d'un vieil homme*, inhabits a world of grief. Professionally, he is (like the protagonist in Émond's previous film), an academic, a science professor, who, unlike Pierre in *Tout ce que tu possèdes*, loves his profession to such an extreme degree that he is blinded by it. Nicolas is unable to see the changes that the academic world and the students' desire to learn are undergoing. In Émond's film, Nicolas is a widower who has remarried and now has a daughter who is fifteen years old. At the point where the viewer enters his story, Nicolas is the only one who knows that he is dying. He can no longer understand the life choices that he has made. His second wife, Barbara (Marie-Thérèse Fortin), and their daughter Anna (Ariane Legault) show no interest at all in sharing their lives with him, and Nicolas considers them frivolous and tedious. His true passion, his first wife, died young, and her daughter from her first marriage, Katia (Marie-Ève Pelletier), he adopted when she was also fifteen. Now in her forties, Katia is Nicolas's kindred spirit. His life revolves around the eldest daughter, the memories of his adored first wife, and his work.

Nicolas's uneventful life is structured around his work, including his short daily walks to his office. The town's sights on his way to work brighten his day and elicit the pleasure he derives from trivial moments. He also enjoys the contemplation of nature every time the family leaves for their country house. The sober composition of the images showing his tranquil environment, revealing the "essence of the landscape,"[17] is reminiscent of Morandi's economical illustrations of the Italian countryside, where the understated materiality of the surroundings alludes to a bittersweet peacefulness and earthy melancholia. As for his teaching, Nicolas mentions that "il a honte de ne pas céder sa place à un autre, quoique malade" [he is ashamed of not leaving his position to someone else, even if he is terminally ill]. Perhaps the dullness of his life and the affliction of not having his loved ones next to him increase his agony during his final days. Insomnia becomes his main companion. In fact, Nicolas declares insomnia the main trait of his existence, and he defines himself as a man without much certainty in life. Considering it a "déformation professionnelle" [professional hazard], Nicolas blames his lack of certainty on the fact that he is a researcher. He also focuses his angst on his fear of death, and throughout the film he often repeats that his lack of faith in any god or in any transcendental or mystical ideology puts him in constant waiting mode, making him more vulnerable to the reality of death: "il n'y a rien d'autre à faire qu'à attendre" [there is nothing else to do than wait]; "toutes les nuits je pense que la mort me prendra" [every night, I think that death will take me]. Nicolas's state of mind is akin to what French psychoanalyst J.-B. Pontalis defines as *Sehnsucht*, adopting the term from German Romanticism in order to describe a kind of nostalgia that relates not only to the past, but also to the frustration stemming from the discrepancy between one's idealized future in a longed-for lost homeland and the factual homeland that awaits the returning migrant (Pontalis 2012, 63).[18]

At the end of his life, Nicolas finds his only solace in contemplating nature and in the company of Katia. Katia, on the other hand, has premonitions of her adopted father's death, and the viewer notices her significant distance from her beloved Nicolas. Love has supported them so far; however, her longing for his company cannot endure watching him dying. Katia, an actress who abandoned her career a decade earlier, is not unlike Pierre in *Tout ce que tu possèdes*. She finds herself inept at facing society and its demands. Performing has become impossible for her. She sees herself as a failure, an actress without any talent. Depression and melancholy have taken over her life.

When Nicolas finally has the courage to confess to Katia that he does not have much longer to live, in a final scene shot during the winter in what seems to be a rural Québécois area, Katia tells Nicolas that she will not stay with him (she had purchased a country home next to her father's) and that she is leaving for Europe. She leaves Nicolas perplexed and alone, and she does not indicate any concrete plans for her life in Europe. She leaves him speechless, weak, and fearful in the midst of a snowstorm. Like Pierre in *Tout ce que tu possèdes*, Katia lacks meaningful connections to other human beings. The only person she loved, her adopted father, is about to die and will leave her completely alone. The viewer is left with the impression that Katia has no strength to live without Nicolas. Again, Émond offers an open ending and leaves it up to the viewer to speculate as to whether Nicolas will die at this moment, or whether he will meet Katia again; whether she will take her own life as a consequence of her deep depression, and/or whether Nicolas's family will find him stranded but alive in the midst of the storm. As in *Tout ce que tu possèdes*, there emerges a sense of nostalgia for the elusive potentiality of the future. The following philosophical comment from an unpublished text by Émond echoes the Chekhovian filmscript he had adapted to the twenty-first century:

> Nous vivons dans un monde désenchanté, incertain, oublieux, inquiet, et voilà que nous est offert le souvenir, érigé dans la pierre, des croyances et de l'espérance de ceux qui nous ont précédés. Nous aurions tort de rejeter la nostalgie que nous ressentons. Cette nostalgie est l'indice d'un manque, et dans la conscience de ce manque il y a la possibilité de regagner une partie de ce que nous avons perdu. Car comment vivre sans passé? [We live in a disenchanted, uncertain, forgetful, restless world; but there is the memory of the beliefs and hopes set in stone by those who came before us. We would be wrong in rejecting the nostalgia that we feel. This nostalgia is the consciousness of a lack, and in the consciousness of this lack, it is possible to make up for what we have lost. Because how could one live without the past?] (Émond "Entrer dans une église" [unpublished])

Conclusion

> Mon indignation me lasse : elle ressemble trop à de la bonne conscience, elle se prend trop pour de la vertu et, au bout du compte, elle me donne trop facilement l'impression d'être *au-dessus* des choses. Or nous ne sommes jamais au-dessus de quoi que ce soit : nous sommes *dedans*, et dedans jusqu'au cou. [My indignation wears me out; it feels too much like self-righteousness. It pretends to be virtue and it ultimately gives me the impression that I am *above* things. Now, we are never above anything; we are rather in things; and in things up to our necks.] (Émond 2018)

> Moi, je suis un partisan de l'exigence parce que l'exigence nous fait sortir de nous-mêmes. [Me, I am a supporter of rigour, because being rigorous makes one less self-centred.] (Émond and Galiero 2009, 12)

Exposing oneself to Bernard Émond's cinematic works and essays, one never loses sight of his passion for his subjects. As mentioned earlier, the filmmaker approaches his subjects through a close rapport with the people involved in his projects. Émond's passion for the oppressed also appears in the options he pursues, the readings he chooses, and the perspective on everyday life he embraces. In his essay "S'exprimer, pour quoi faire?" (2011), he offers a self-analysis as a citizen of his home city, Montreal, while observing a musician at a large farmers' market, the Marché Jean-Talon. Reflecting on the artists' long path toward learning their craft, Émond defines once again his own *art poétique:*

> Connaître et pratiquer un art, c'est avant tout sortir de soi pour aller à la rencontre de ce qui est l'autre; c'est arriver à force de travail et d'étude à pouvoir s'approcher des grandes œuvres et de ce qu'elles portent de sens et d'ouverture au monde. C'est à ce prix qu'on devient capable d'offrir. [In order to understand and practice an art, it is essential to step out of oneself and to reach out to the other; it requires hard work to get close to the great masterpieces and appreciate their meaning and openness to the world. This is the price an artist must pay to be able to give.] (Émond 2011, 86)

Throughout his works, Émond emanates the core idea that not only the artist, but anyone implicated in living and sharing in a society, must be a demanding and harsh judge of his own work and expertise. In other words, one must be an ethical thinker, grounded in the facts that shape society. For the filmmaker and writer, this sense of responsibility is deeply rooted in the cultural traditions of the people, families, and friends. In this context, far from implying any form of escapism, Émond's creative advocacy for nostalgia focuses on honouring the memories of one's own group while reaching out to the other. Furthermore, it means recognizing the appeal of social and cultural communities in which everyday needs are shared and time-honoured values are acknowledged, while at the same time looking to the future in order to negotiate a clear ethics with future generations in mind, accepting legacies, and passing them on to others. In Émond's own words:

> Sans une fidélité retrouvée à la signification et à la richesse de *ces* liens, [...] (les liens qui nous attachent les uns aux autres, [...] les liens qui nous attachent au passé, au territoire, il n'est pas de vie qui vaut la peine d'être vécue) la liberté n'a aucun sens." [Without a renewed devotion to the significance and richness of *these* rapports (the rapports that connect us to one another, that connect us to the past, to the land; there is no life

that is worth living), freedom has no meaning.] (Émond "L'usage de la liberté" [unpublished] [italics added])[19]

Occasionally critical comments regarding the auteur's rigid view of the human condition appear upon the release of his films. They miss the point. Life and art are not containable in successful Hollywood feature films. Chekhov's supposedly gloomy plays approach life with more courage and nuance. And once in a while, one has the rare opportunity to spot a Morandi in a corner of the Vatican Museum.

Notes

1 I am grateful to the editors of this volume, André Loiselle and Liz Czach. Unless indicated otherwise, all translations of quoted passages in this article are my own.

2 Translation by Jonathan Griffin. Quoted from Bresson 1977, 17, http://projectlamar.com/media/notes_on_cinematography.pdf (accessed 9 June 2016).

3 Émond often mentions Chekhov in his writings. In one of the crucial passages in his essay "Vitupérer l'époque" [Railing Against Current Times], he delves into the realm of culpability and responsibility, topics that form the centrepiece of his ethics and that have affinities with Chekhov's oeuvre: "C'est Tchekhov, bien entendu, qui a raison lorsqu'il écrit que nous sommes tous coupables. Pour Tchekhov, il faut donc juger, mais en se jugeant soi-même" [Chekhov is indeed right when he says we are all guilty. According to Chekhov, one must be critical, but by being critical of oneself] ("Vitupérer l'époque" [unpublished]). "Vitupérer l'époque" was written in 2010 for a soirée in honour of writer Pierre Vadeboncoeur (1920–2010) and published in 2011. Vadeboncoeur was an important author and public intellectual who wrote on the Quebec labour movement, national sovereignty, and social justice. He was instrumental in articulating the notion of a modern Quebec identity during the Quiet Revolution.

4 In *La Perte et le Lien*, Émond describes his beginnings and formative years in dialogues with Simon Galiero. He points out that literature was his first love: "Alors même si mon amour premier était la littérature, j'ai eu le sentiment que je devais faire quelque chose d'utile, ou en tout cas que je devais comprendre la société dans laquelle je vivais, et c'est ça qui m'a amené vers les sciences humaines" [Even if my first love was literature, I had the feeling that I had to do something useful, or in any case that I should understand the society I lived in. And that is what led me to the human sciences] (*La Perte et le Lien*, 12). Galiero and Émond dedicate another entire section of *La Perte et le Lien* (19–20), "Inspirations Littéraires," to discussing literary preferences and influences,

including French existentialism, Balzac, Zola, Tolstoy, Romain Rolland, and Philip Roth.

5   "[…] après avoir traversé les chambres de Raphaël et la chapelle Sixtine, encore sonné par cette richesse, cette abundance, cette grandeur, dans un recoin de la section d'art moderne du musée du Vatican, je tombe sur quatre petits tableaux de Giorgio Morandi (1890–1964): deux paysages et deux natures mortes. Les natures mortes, en particulier, m'attirent […] Ce n'est presque rien. Pourtant, nous sommes ici devant une sorte de miracle" [(…) after having crossed Rafael's chambers and the Sistine Chapel, still touched by this wealth, this abundance, this magnitude, in a corner of the modern art section of the Vatican Museum, I came across four small paintings by Giorgio Morandi (1890–1964): two landscapes and two still lifes. The still lifes drew my attention in particular (…) It is almost nothing. Nevertheless, we are facing some kind of miracle here] (Émond 2011, 94–95).

6   Poland is one of those resilient "small nations" that fascinate many Quebec nationalists. Legendary author Jacques Ferron, for one, was "enchanted" by Poland (Ferron 1980, 72). Arlette Cousture's bestselling novel *Ces enfants d'ailleurs* (1994), which was made into two successful television series by Claude Fournier (1997–1998), also attests to this Québécois fascination with Poland. Other resilient "small nations" have captured the imagination of Quebec filmmakers—for example, Ireland for André Forcier (*Je me souviens*, 2009), Norway for Denis Villeneuve (*Maelström*, 2000), and Belgium for Philippe Falardeau (*Congorama*, 2006). René Lévesque was well known for his "éloge des petits pays," praising small countries whose ability to govern themselves and thrive in spite of being surrounded by much larger nations was an inspiration for Quebec (Godin 1997, 643–58).

7   "De cette impulsion, il reste tout de même une trace dans le film : la reproduction d'une fresque de Giotto, *La renunciation aux bien paternels*, accrochée au mur derrière la table de travail de Pierre […] J'aime cette fresque : sa palette riche et sa composition tranchée; le personnage retenant le bras du père qui veut frapper son fils" [There remains a trait from this very impulse in the film; the reproduction of a Giotto fresco, *La renunciation aux bien paternels*, hanging on the wall behind Pierre's office desk (…) I like this fresco, its rich palette and its clear-cut composition. The character holding back the father's arm as he tries to strike his son] (Émond, "J'ai dormi parterre dans la maison de nos ancêtres," *Tout ce que tu possèdes. Scénario et regard croisés*, 10).

8   "Pierre est une figure de l'isolement contemporain : il est radicalement seul dans un monde où les liens familiaux ont éclaté et où les rapports sociaux se désagrègent" [Pierre is an example of contemporary isolacionism; he is radically lonely in a world where familial connections have dissolved and where social rapports are disintegrating] (Émond, "J'ai dormi parterre dans la maison de nos ancêtres," 12).

9   http://duszenko.northern.edu/stachura/intro.html. Accessed 5 July 2016.

10   "La petite maison de Saint-Pacôme dans *Tout ce que tu possèdes*, est un peu celle de la maison de mon arrière-grand-père à Verchères" [The little house in Saint-Pacôme in *All That You Possess* is somewhat like the one of my great grandfather in Verchères] (Émond, "Pour vivre ici [les maisons de mes films]").

11   "Ainsi, mes personnages seraient résolument modernes—[*a reference to Saul Bellow and his concept of modernity—which, according to and quoted by Émond, it refers to being nomadic, without attachment, cosmopolitan, indifferent to the fact of being a foreigner in a temporary neighborhood]—, à cette différence près qu'ils ne sont pas indifférents à leur condition d'étrangers mais qu'au contraire, ils en souffrent. Si la culture est le lieu de l'homme, ce qui se pense à travers ces personnages sans lieu, c'est le déracinement contemporain de l'homme Québécois, et sa douleur" [Thereby, my characters would be absolutely modern, except that they are not indifferent to their foreign conditions. To the contrary, they suffer from them. If culture is the place of men, what is thought through these displaced characters is the contemporary rootlessness of Québécois man and his suffering] (Émond "Pour vivre ici. [les maisons de mes films]," 1).

12   This central text refers to all the filmed houses and their meaning. Houses reveal the director's own desire to revisit every time in some way, places that occupy his memory, his own childhood populated by a different Montréal. Émond, "Pour vivre ici (les maisons de mes films)," *Imaginaires de la maison*, ed. Thomas Mainguy. *Contre-Jour. Cahiers Littéraires* 29, Conseil des Arts et des Lettres du Québec (Winter 2012–13): 65–70.

13   Here I refer not only to the filmmaker's well-known trilogy that explores the concepts of faith, hope, and charity, *La Neuvaine* (2005), *Contre toute espérance* (2007), and *La Donation* (2009), but also to his previous films *La Femme qui boit* (2001) and *20h17, rue Darling* (2003). To be considered in this context is also Émond's invaluable work as a documentary filmmaker—see, for example, *Ceux qui ont les pas légers meurent sans laisser des traces* (1992) and *L'Instant et la patience* (1994) (Coulombe, Michel and Marcel Jean 2006, 240–42).

14   Charlton T. Lewis, *An Elementary Latin Dictionary* (New York: Oxford University Press, 1889).

15   Bernard Émond describes Marc Bernard and his wife's moving encounter and the turning point of the writer's life in the following paragraph of his essay "Gratitude": "Elle avait 36 ans, lui 38. Ils auront cette chance inespérée de vivre un grand amour qui ne finit qu'avec la mort d'un de deux amants. C'est Else qui partira la première, fauchée par un cancer en 1968 […] Marc Bernard est inconsolable : sa vie bascule. Lui, qui était un écrivain de la légèreté et du bonheur de vivre va devenir grave […] Et presque toute son oeuvre, pendant les 14 dernières années de sa vie, tournera autour de cette femme aimée et de sa disparition. Il y aura d'abord *La Mort de la bien-aimée* (1972), *Au-delà de*

l'absence (1976), puis *Tout est bien ainsi* (1979), trois livres magnifiques, profonds et simples, sur l'amour et la mort" [She was 36 years old, he was 38. They had this unexpected opportunity to live a great love that ended only with the death of one of the lovers. It is Else who left first, cut down by cancer in 1968. (…) Marc Bernard would remain inconsolable: his life turned upside dowm. A writer of lightness and joy, he would become grave. (…) And almost all his works during the fourteen last years of his life revolved around this beloved woman and her disappearance. There was at first *La mort de la bien-aimée* (1972), *Au-delà de l'absence* (1976), and finally *Tout est bien ainsi* (1979), three magnificent, deep, and simple books on love and death] (Émond, "Gratitude," *Revue Relations* 781, November-December 2015, 10).

16   Similar to Émond's cinematic trilogy, as Émond himself puts it, it addresses "foi" (faith), "espérance" (hope), and "charité" (charity), the three Paulinic virtues (Émond 2011, 19); "La donation" (2009), "Contre toute espérance" (2007), and "La neuvaine" (2005).

17   This is the title of a Morandi exhibit at the Fondazione Ferrero in Alba: "Morandi, l'essenza del paesaggio." See http://www.mambo-bologna.org/museomorandi/moraandinelmondo/2010alba (accessed 15 June 2018).

18   "La *Sehnsucht*, […] n'est pas toujours orientée vers le passé. Elle n'est pas, comme la nostalgie, mal du pays, douleur de l'exil, attente du retour au pays natal, retour sovent accompagné de la déception comme si l'objet perdu devait la plus grande part de sa valeur au fait d'avoir été perdu. La *Sehnsucht* peut aussi bien s'orienter vers le futur, vers quelque terre promise idéalisée, hors d'atteinte immédiate […] là aussi vouées au désenchantement" [*Sehnsucht*, (…) is not always oriented toward the past. It is not, as nostalgia is, longing for the homeland, the return often followed by disappointment as if the lost object owed the main part of its value to the fact that it was lost. *Sehnsucht* can also be oriented toward the future, toward some equally idealized promised land, unattainable in the present (…), also in this case, destined to disenchantment] (Pontalis 2012, 63).

19   Unpublished text.

4

FINGERLESS (ANTI)CHRIST:
A Reminiscence of the Church in 1966 in Denys Arcand's *Les Invasions barbares* and Éric Tessier's *Sur le seuil*

André Loiselle

September 2002 saw the production of two Québécois films that seem to have little in common: Denys Arcand's *Les Invasions barbares* and Éric Tessier's *Sur le seuil*, both released in 2003. The former is a sophisticated male melodrama that won dozens of awards (including an Oscar for best foreign language film) and offers a thoughtful reflection on the centrifugal disintegration of Quebec culture in the early twenty-first century. The latter is a popular horror film that indulges in the gruesome spectacle of sensationalist gore and blasphemous excess. In their drastically different ways, however, the two films present a surprisingly similar commentary on the radical transformation that affected the Catholic Church and all of Quebec society at a precise moment in the history of the province: 1966. In both films, roughly 66 minutes into each narrative,[1] a present-day priest recounts the "very strange phenomenon" that afflicted the Church in 1966. Most astonishingly, both references to 1966 are related to a figure whose fingers have been severed: a damaged statue of Christ with a broken hand in *Les Invasions barbares*, and a horror novelist who cuts off his own fingers in *Sur le seuil*. The two images of a fingerless (Anti)Christ link 1966 to the Church's loss of power and the suffering that ensued. This chapter examines this peculiar connection between the two contemporaneous films to argue that, from the perspective of the early twenty-first century, 1966 represents a painful break from the peaceful, traditional lifestyle of French Canadians towards the futility, meaninglessness, and chaos of fragmented modern existence that seems to have affected primarily Quebec men. The result of this agonizing rupture with the French Canadian heritage has been, at best, the detached, uprooted, nostalgic cynicism of *Les Invasions barbares* and, at worst, the blood-spattered terror of *Sur le seuil*.

Old Priests' Tales

Les Invasions barbares, Arcand's sequel to his first major critical and commercial success, *Le Déclin de l'empire américain* (1986), focuses primarily on the difficult reconciliation between a dying father, Rémy (Rémy Girard), and his estranged son, Sébastien (Stéphane Rousseau). In the original 1986 film, university professor Rémy and his colleagues from the history department where he teaches, Dominique (Dominique Michel), Pierre (Pierre Curzi), Claude (Yves Jacques), and Diane (Louise Portal), were all fun-loving thirty-somethings gathered in a charming country house to enjoy good food, expensive wine, and amusing tales of their numerous sexcapades. Their children exist only as playful noises in the background, or as self-righteous tweens who tediously disapprove of their parents' philandering. By the time of *Les Invasions barbares*, seventeen years later, Rémy is bedridden in a dreary hospital room, he is separated from his wife, Louise (Dorothée Berryman), his friends have moved on, and his now adult children, Sébastien and Sylvaine (Isabelle Blais), have left Quebec; the former is now a hotshot futures trader in London, England, the latter a free spirit who travels the world and the seven seas. In the end, reconciliation is achieved, but only as an elusive precursor to Rémy's death. As I noted in my book-length analysis of *Le Déclin...* and *Les Invasions...* the latter closes on

> deeply nostalgic shots of an empty bench by the forsaken country house as a plane takes off, bringing Sébastien and his girlfriend, Gaëlle (Marina Hands), back to England. An insert of birds flying away suggests that even nature might have given up on Quebec. As the last words of the film are spoken, Gaëlle's "I love you" to Sébastien, Françoise Hardy's bittersweet ballade, *L'Amitié*, enhances the profound sense of loss caused by Rémy's death a few scenes earlier. (Loiselle 2008a, 89)

The ending is undoubtedly the most melancholic moment in the film. But much of the last third of *Les Invasions...*, once Rémy has left the hospital and returned to the beloved country setting of *Le Déclin...*, where he can spend his last few days with his friends before proceeding with a nurse-assisted suicide, wallows in nostalgic reminiscences of a time when people felt a deeper sense of belonging to Quebec. In contrast to the wistful third and final act of Arcand's tragicomedy, where friendship stands out as one of the last enduring values in modern society (Loiselle 2008a, 111), the first act, which shows ailing Rémy confined to a multi-bed hospital room, exposes everything that is wrong with early twenty-first-century Quebec.[2] The ineffectiveness of the Church, the crumbling health care system, the corruption of unions, the callous indifference of bureaucracy, the inability of the police to control drug trafficking, and the fear of foreign infiltration, are all problems that have besieged the province as a whole—and Montreal in particular, according to Arcand. The disease that afflicts the city parallels the illness that eats at Rémy's body.

The second act of *Les Invasions...* performs a gradual shift in tone away from dark cynicism toward nostalgia, as Rémy is moved from his gloomy communal space to a sunny private room acquired by Sébastien, who does not hesitate to bribe the hospital administration and union to provide his father with better living quarters. The second act also sees the return of the band of revelling academics who were at the core of *Le Déclin...* and now come back from the four corners of the country, and beyond, to support their dying comrade. The relief afforded Rémy by the comfortable room and the presence of his beloved colleagues is supplemented by regular doses of heroin, which Sébastien purchases with the help of Nathalie (Marie-Josée Croze). Nathalie, the daughter of Rémy's friend and part-time lover Diane, who makes a brief appearance as an annoying brat in *Le Déclin...*, is now a nihilistic junkie who has a love/hate relationship with her mother. But she is also a deeply intelligent and sensitive woman with whom Rémy develops a close relationship as they chase the dragon together. In a brief scene between the dying man and the self-destructive addict, Rémy describes to his new friend how much he loves life, wine, music, books, and, above all, women. Nathalie reminds him, however, that "it is not your current life you are clinging to. It's your past life. That life is already dead." Nathalie's comment perceptively reframes all of Rémy's elucidation of life and its many sensual pleasures as mere nostalgic musing anchored in a time that is irrevocably gone. Significantly, it is at this point in the film that the narrative breaks and takes a short and seemingly inexplicable detour to explore Quebec history. As such it is difficult not to infer a link between Rémy's nostalgia about his already-dead life and the religious decrepitude that engulfs the subsequent scene.

Following the conversation between Rémy and Nathalie, we see Sébastien's French girlfriend, Gaëlle, receiving a phone call. An art dealer, she is asked to meet with an old priest, Father Raymond Leclerc (Gilles Pelletier), regarding religious artifacts that the Montreal Archdiocese might want to sell. Father Leclerc, who appears in Arcand's 1989 *Jésus de Montréal* as the cleric in charge of the massive Oratoire St. Joseph on Mount Royal, has now been demoted to custodian of a dark basement full of worthless Catholic relics. After surveying the heaps of statues, chalices, and crucifixes, Gaëlle concludes that none of it could be sold on the international market. She does say that surely all of this has great value for the collective memory of the Québécois. But the priest couldn't care less for this condescending opinion from the French art dealer. He closes the discussion by saying: "In other words, this is all ... absolutely worthless. I will show you out." This is an obvious comment on the futility of the Church in early twenty-first-century Quebec. Following this two-minute scene, Father Leclerc is never seen again, and Gaëlle resumes her role as Sébastien's generally silent companion. The exchange could easily be removed from the film and nothing would be lost, except for the commentary on the end of Catholicism in Quebec that the priest offers to the art dealer early in their brief conversation: "At one time, everyone here was Catholic. Like in Spain or Ireland. At a very precise moment—in 1966, in fact—the *churches suddenly emptied out*, in a few months. A very strange phenomenon that has yet to be explained. So now we don't know what to do with this. The authorities would like to find out if it has any value."

The strangeness of the phenomenon is not elaborated upon by the priest, but as eerily understated music starts being heard in the background, the camera lingers momentarily on an old statue of Christ, oddly focusing on its broken fingers. The peculiarity of the historical anecdote related by the priest, the soft creepiness of the music, the eccentricity of the close-up on the damaged hand, and the seeming incongruity of the scene itself, create something of a *punctum* effect, to evoke Barthes (1981, 27), that punctures and disrupts the otherwise straightforward reading of the male melodrama. That this strange little aside in the narrative would refer to a "very strange phenomenon" compels the attentive viewer to further explore the meaning of 1966.

This compulsion becomes even stronger when one grasps the peculiar coincidence between *Les Invasions barbares* and Éric Tessier's horror film *Sur le seuil*, in which there is also a reference to the *emptying out* of the Church in 1966. Based on Patrick Senécal's 1998 novel of the same title, Tessier's film tells the story of psychiatrist Dr. Paul Lacasse (Michel Côté), who must care for a new patient, Thomas Roy (Patrick Huard), a famous horror novelist who has purposefully cut off his fingers before trying to commit suicide. A jaded and cynical middle-aged man who thinks he has seen it all, Dr. Lacasse initially perceives Roy's condition as a relatively banal case of psychosis. As the narrative unfolds, however, he becomes increasingly confused by the succession of strange coincidences surrounding the case. His investigation into the novelist's peculiar history leads him away from Montreal to a remote village, where he meets Father Lemay (Albert Millaire). The old priest relates to Dr. Lacasse the strange circumstances that surrounded the birth of Roy during a black mass on 13 September 1966 (the perfect year for a demonic creature to come to life),[3] and explains how exactly *thirty-six* years later the Evil One has returned to wreak havoc. Nostalgic flashbacks show the peaceful, easy-going life the young Father Lemay (Alexis Bélec) and his two colleagues, the senior priest, Father Boudreault (Jean Pierre Bergeron), and the junior *abbé*, Father Pivot (Nicolas Canuel), enjoyed in their rural parish up until 1965. Father Pivot, in particular, was a friendly and kind young priest. But the violent death of his beloved sister (his niece in the novel) at the end of 1965 transformed the pleasant, ordinary cleric into a bitter, contemptuous man. By July 1966, Pivot's anger had taken on monstrous proportions. He turned his back on Catholicism, took over the village church, and recruited a clan of devil worshippers for a demonic orgy of self-mutilation and blasphemy. In September, Pivot's disciples gathered in the church again for an even more gruesome and bloody ritual, out of which Roy was born—he was forcefully extracted from his dying mother's womb and kissed by a satanic Pivot. At that moment, Roy was granted the supernatural power to write Evil into action. When Fathers Boudreault and Lemay entered the church in the early hours of 13 September 1966, they were faced with the gory spectacle of the deadly black mass. Father Lemay rushed to call the police, but Father Boudreault stopped him in his tracks, warning: "Are you mad? What will happen if the police find out? We'll be labelled Satanists. *The church will empty. It'll be over.*" Fathers Boudreault and Lemay thus decided to bury the bodies and clean up the mess. After putting the child up for adoption, Father Boudreault believed that everything would go back to normal. But the damage was done, and evil was unleashed unto Quebec.

As I have discussed elsewhere (Loiselle 2015, 84), the sequence during which Father Lemay recounts the events leading to 13 September 1966 juxtaposes the quaint kitchen of an old presbytery in the film's present tense, with the ghastly flashbacks in which we witness Father Pivot and his flock of devil worshippers conducting a black mass in an attempt to experience pure evil. The contrast between the appealing simplicity of the presbytery where the old priest reminisces about a pre-Satanist, pastoral time, and the horrors that transpired there thirty-six years earlier, creates an intense sense of fear routed in the uncanny correlation between pleasant, wistful banality and pure, unadulterated evil. This sequence evokes the nostalgic image of a bygone era in French Canadian history, when priests were the benevolent autocrats of small, self-sufficient agrarian communities that had no interest in the petty neoliberal concerns of North American modernity—back then, there was "nothing to disturb our daily routine," says the aging cleric. In her contribution to this book, Miléna Santoro explores at more length the persistent but paradoxical manifestations of this pre-modern rural arcadia in the contemporary Quebec imagination.

Returning to Montreal after having heard the old priest's tale, Dr. Lacasse witnesses a bloodbath as he enters the psychiatric ward at the aptly called Hôpital Ste-Croix (Holy Cross Hospital), where Roy's deadly influence has led the other inmates to rape, ravage, and maim one another. The psychiatrist arrives just in time to see Roy remove the unborn baby from the womb of Lacasse's pregnant colleague, Dr. Jeanne Marcoux (Catherine Florent), and kiss the infant as he, himself, had been kissed thirty-six years before by the then thirty-six-year-old Pivot. As Roy is shot by the police, he *falls against a wall, with his arms spread in a Christ-like position* and his fingerless hands well in view.

The astonishing parallel between *Sur le seuil* and *Les Invasions barbares* in terms of 1966 and the fingerless (Anti)Christ figure suggests that, from the perspective of the early twenty-first century, the "strange phenomenon" that afflicted the Church in mid-1960s had very painful consequences. What is it about 1966 that might have caused such grief in hindsight, and why associate this pain with fingerlessness? In what follows I show that 1966 marks a period of fiercely contested ideologies. While a large segment of the population was eager to adopt a modern Québécois identity, a significant number of French Canadians were deeply afraid that their nation was irrevocably moving away from its heritage toward evil modernity and, most disturbingly, was on the verge of losing its most precious asset: the large Catholic family ruled by a ubiquitous patriarchal mindset. *Thirty-six* years later, at the time of the films' production, the trauma of this loss persisted and nostalgic longing permeated the national ethos. As is discussed elsewhere in this anthology, some filmmakers like Bernard Émond focus on the struggle to regain this core of French Canadian heritage, "le fonds culturel canadien-français" (Émond et Galiero 2009, 110). Arcand and Tessier seem to be suggesting that such recovery is impossible, yet that the longing remains morbidly painful.

1966 and Thirty-Six Years Later

A letter to the editor from an anonymous female teacher, published in the February 1966 issue of the nationalist monthly *L'Action nationale*, was featured in the magazine as an accurate reflection of the state of mind of a large number of Québécois at the time. The letter opens with the following statement: "Je suis inquiète, vraiment inquiète. Tout change ! Le mal est exalté à la radio, à la T.V. et dans les journaux" [I am worried, extremely worried. Everything is changing. Evil is celebrated on radio and TV and in the newspapers] ("Correspondence" 1966, 727). It would be difficult to find a more obvious illustration of how *evil* was on the minds of many French Canadians in 1966. Another offering, this one in the December 1966 issue of *L'Action nationale*, conveys this contemporary fear in the form of a grim fairy tale. Quebec, allegorized through the common metaphor of the suffering orphan, or *enfant martyr* (Loiselle 2003, 46), is oppressed by an evil witch and surrounded by monsters. His revolt is temporally expressed through "les bombes du FLQ", but at the end of the tale he is still stuck in his cage like a wild animal (Lamontagne 1966, 349–50). While it would be a gross exaggeration to claim that there was widespread daemonophobia in Quebec at the time, a brief survey of the contemporary public discourse reveals that the mid-1960s were characterized, at least in some circles, by profound anxiety and dread in the face of an uncertain future.

Strictly speaking, 1966 marks the end of Quebec's Quiet Revolution, with the defeat of Jean Lesage's provincial Liberal Party and the victory of the conservative Union Nationale. Back in 1960, Lesage had defeated the Union Nationale, bringing an end to the ultraconservative Duplessis regime, often referred to as *la grande noirceur* (see Liz Czach's chapter in this book). Upon his first victory, Lesage launched a wave of progressive reforms aimed at modernizing Quebec. As I have demonstrated in other publications, while it is true that the first half of the 1960s was a time of great progress (the secularization of the educational system and social services, the adoption of medicare, the nationalization of hydroelectricity), it is also important to note that this rapid movement forward was accompanied by a strong resistance against the types of changes proposed by Lesage's Liberal government. Many conservatives were appalled by Lesage's discarding of traditional Quebec values; at the same time, many radical nationalists interpreted Lesage's reforms as part of a federalist ploy to bring Quebec closer to the other Canadian provinces. So it is not surprising that by 1966, the isolationist Union Nationale had regained power under the leadership of Daniel Johnson. In fact, the Union Nationale received fewer votes than the Liberals but still won because of the peculiar Canadian electoral system (Linteau et al. 1991, 532). Of course, social progress did not come to an abrupt end after 1966. The transformations undertaken in the early 1960s had acquired momentum and could not be stopped, even with a traditionalist party in power. Indeed, Johnson's government can be credited with implementing some of the most significant innovations initiated by the Liberals earlier in the decade, including the establishment of the Collège d'enseignement général et professionnel (CEGEP) and Université du Québec system in 1967 and 1968, respectively, following the recommendations of the Commission royale d'enquête sur l'enseignement dans la province de Québec (a.k.a. the "Parent Commission"). Thus, what 1966 represents is a moment when fear of irrevocable transformation found expression in a withdrawal toward conservatism that ultimately proved to be powerless to halt change; by 1970 the Union Nationale had fallen from power, never to regain it again. Much of the public discourse in 1966 indicates that the transition toward modernity, while undoubtedly hailed by many, was experienced by a significant portion of the population as painful, even terrifying.

Many federalists saw the return of the Union Nationale in the mid-1960s as the result of rampant trepidation in the province. An article by Jean Pellerin in the July 1966 issue of the federalist journal *Cité Libre*, to which Pierre Trudeau was a regular contributor, argues that Johnson's victory in June 1966 was largely the result of the *fear* that French Canadians, especially outside Montreal, felt in the face of recent social changes. According to Pellerin, rural priests succeeded in rallying their parishioners against the Liberals by evoking "le spectre de la déconfessionnalisation"—that is, the spectre of secularization. The author adds that village doctors found medicare repugnant, that the province's *petite bourgeoisie* dreaded an end to the political graft that flourished under Duplessis, and that the rural lower classes continued to be deeply suspicious of the belated Quebec industrialization embodied by the Quiet Revolution (Pellerin 1966, 6).

Interestingly, the separatist discourse came to the same conclusion: fear was a principal cause of the return of the Union Nationale. Gaëtan Tremblay, in a September 1966 article published in the highly intellectual left-wing journal *Parti Pris*, argues that the fear that afflicted the older generation of French Canadians—the "vieille société," which still dominated much of the Quebec ethos at the time—led them to work against their own best interests, to recoil from progress and vote for regression (Tremblay 1966, 21–22). In his October 1966 article "Histoire sans héros," Nicolas Beaumont of *L'Action nationale* also pointed to the regressive influence of "vieille société," but he placed the blame more squarely on the ruling class, who were afraid of everything, in particular English power: "Ils ont peur. Peur des Anglais" (Beaumont 1966, 132). Throughout history, Beaumont claimed, Quebec's elites had always been terrified, and because of that fear, they had continuously betrayed the people: "notre élite... a trahi le peuple si souvent" (Beaumont 1966, 132). Beaumont warned the elite that the people would rise one day and confront those who had oppressed them. History has shown that the oppressed judge severely those who have maginalized them culturally and socially: "Ceux qui contribuent à prolonger sa souffrance morale, devront tôt ou tard s'expliquer. Et la vraie histoire nous enseigne que les peuples sont très sévères pour ceux qui les ont maintenus dans un état d'infériorité culturel et social dans le but de les mieux gouverner" (133). Unmistakable signs of this rebellious tendency had already started to appear in 1960s Quebec.

The 1966 election was the first one in which sovereignty was discussed as a viable democratic option for Quebec—in this case, by the candidates from the Rassemblement pour l'indépendance nationale (RIN), a precursor to the Parti Québécois (PQ). That the RIN received 10 percent of the popular vote gave hope to some moderate separatists that sovereignty could eventually be achieved through peaceful political means (Angers 1966, 107). But in spite of the RIN's commitment to democracy, many, especially in rural areas, saw its leader, Pierre Bourgault, as a dangerous agitator who was inciting young people to violence ("Pour la révolution violente" 1966, 2). Some young adults were indeed growing more frustrated with the terrified elite and the lack of fundamental change in the province, and they started calling for widespread violence. In January 1966, radical separatist Claude Larivière encouraged his young comrades to oppose the forthcoming 1967 Centennial celebrations and to sacrifice their youth for the cause of dethroning a dominant federalist regime that had become too tyrannical to tolerate (Larivière 1966, 591–92). Since 1963, the Front de libération du Québec (FLQ) had been resorting to terrorism in support of the separatist cause. By 1966, FLQ bombs had killed four innocent people, and in July of that year, a sixteen-year-old FLQ sympathizer, Jean Corbo, blew himself up with a bomb intended for the Dominion Textile factory in St-Henri. In 1966, "vieille société" was clearly terrified by young people's violent urges. Something "evil" was evidently brewing in the province.

But separatist agitators were not seen as the only or even the *main* cause of violence among young people. Rather, the collapse of traditional family values, religious sentiments, and public morality—"la désagrégation de la famille, des sentiments religieux ou de la moralité publique"—was perceived by many as the fundamental reason for the drastic increase in criminality among teenagers ("Pour les jeunes..." 1966, 10). This was viewed as the real evil that was taking over the province in 1966. Widespread anxiety about the breakdown in family values was expressed in small-town newspapers, and in 1966, a large organization of rural women, l'Union catholique des femmes rurales, started lobbying the provincial government for measures that would save the family from ruin. Maintaining the traditional family was the only way to save Quebec from national disintegration, "preserver la nation" ("U.C.F.R..." 1966, 1). Even in the cities, growing violence among young Québécois and the collapse of the traditional family unit were starting to trigger serious apprehension among older generations. An op-ed in the February 1966 issue of *Cité Libre* expressed concern about the dramatic rise in juvenile delinquency, interpreting it as a direct result of the state of crisis ["état de crise"] in which the traditional family unit now found itself (Vennat 1966, 2). From a different perspective, but along the same lines, Patrick Allen wrote in *L'Action nationale* about the devastating impact of divorce in the United States; he saw this social evil, "mal social," as now threatening Quebec (Allen 1966, 148). One article in the regional newspaper *L'Avenir du Nord* even suggested that a group in favour of laicization, Mouvement laïque de langue française, was conspiring with Freemasons and Satanists to undermine the Catholic institution of marriage (Létourneau 1966, 4).

Whether or not Satanists were to blame, marriages were indeed starting to break down at a frightening rate in Quebec in 1966. As Michael Gauvreau reported in *Catholic Origins of Quebec's Quiet Revolution, 1931–1970* (2005):

"Today's married couple," declared Dr. Camille Laurin, a prominent Montreal psychiatrist at the 1966 banquet of the Service de Préparation au Mariage, "is going through a very difficult phase because the foundations, ideals, norms and values upon which it was inspired are undergoing an unprecedented upheaval." As a psychiatrist, Laurin diagnosed the most common symptoms of this upheaval, which, he felt, were typified by a pathology of "incoherence" in the relations between husbands and wives, by which he meant a lack of correspondence between values and behaviour. Family breakdown, he maintained, was increasingly evident in a "conflict of generations" expressed in increasingly violent and abusive language ... What was most significant about Laurin's address was his equation of these symptoms of family breakdown with a wider cultural phenomenon—the "desacralization of Quebec society." (Gauvreau 2005, 149)

The pathology of incoherence resulting from desacralization, which was tearing apart husbands and wives, parents and adolescent children, also seemed to have taken the form of a chaotic culture cluttered with political radicalism and rampant sexual exploitation. The teacher's letter to the editor in *L'Action nationale*, quoted earlier, expressed dread in the face of ideological turpitude and widespread depravity:

Le directeur de la revue *Maintenant* est venu à 'Aujourd'hui' parler en faveur du communisme [...] À la T.V. que de gros seins nus et en gros plans! Que de baisers lascifs et interminables [...] Les danseuses nues, des FRANÇAISES, sont à Montréal [...] Dans les hôtels de villages, des spectacles de nudité ou presque, sont donnés régulièrement. [The editor of the magazine *Maintenant* spoke on the show *Aujourd'hui* about the benefits of communism ... On TV all you see are close-ups of big breasts, and endless lustful kisses ... Strippers from France appear in Montreal ... Even in small-town hotels, nude or semi-nude dancers appear regularly.] ("Correspondence" 1966, 727–29)

The increasing presence of sexuality, for some reason associated with the rise of communism, and the corollary collapse of religious devotion, social decency, and family values, alarmed a large segment of the population.

An especially threatening factor in the minds of conservative French Canadians at the time, one that would exacerbate the "pathology of incoherence in relations between husbands and wives," was the debate around the decriminalization of contraceptives. A 1966 *Maclean's* article explored the emerging reality of a Quebec where women were gaining access to birth control. The article described how René Lévesque, then Minister of Family and Welfare, was speaking publicly in favour of birth-control clinics. It also indicated that a large number of French-speaking physicians were in favour of family planning; even some priests felt free "not only to advise [on] birth control but in some cases to air their opinions on radio and TV programs" (Gray 1966, 2). But while some priests seemed relatively open to the idea of removing the legal prohibition against circulating information about contraceptives, the use of contraception itself remained unacceptable from the perspective of the Church. Indeed, the Congress of Canadian Catholic Bishops stated clearly that contraception was evil and forbidden by God, and those who commit such sin must always answer for their transgression before Him. As reported in the Catholic publication *Relations*, "Les Évêques ont bien dit que 'les actes mauvais' — Et la contraception en est un — sont 'interdits par la loi de Dieu' et que 'celui qui les commet devra toujours répondre de leur transgression devant Dieu'" (Marcotte 1966, 327). Indulging in the "evil act" of contraception—and evil it indisputably was—violated heavenly law.

An opinion piece by a female reader in the regional newspaper *La Vallée de la Petite Nation* in December 1966 expressed fear of this new medical technology, which had not yet been fully tested. But her much more serious apprehension had to do with the impact of the pill on the moral fibre of young women. Because of the pill, young wives might want to continue indulging in the pleasures they had enjoyed as single girls, and they might even hide from their husbands that they were taking contraceptives: "on est marié mais on veut quand même vivre sa vie de célibataire" ("La Pilule..." 1966, 14). Interestingly, a similar response to the potential moral evils of the *pilule* appeared in the erudite and cosmopolitan pages of *Parti Pris*, in which Situationist Patrick Straram seemed appalled at the news that the wives of American soldiers, as of January 1967, would have free access to birth control. Straram sarcastically wrote that women who were cunning enough to get rid of their husbands by sending them to war could then have sex with whomever they wanted: "Une femme qui sait convaincre son homme d'aller au Viêt-nam peut s'envoyer tous ceux qu'elle veut ensuite" (Straram 1966, 129). And the venerable editor of the conservative *Action populaire*, Louis Germain, in his editorial of 9 November 1966, equated the wife who chooses to use the pill to avoid having children to a depraved harlot who sleeps around and does not want a bad surprise: both were morally reprehensible (Germain 1966, 4). Clearly, many men, hipsters and geezers alike, were profoundly concerned about the degree of freedom that women were on the verge of acquiring.

Furthermore, 1966 saw the emergence of the first powerful feminist groups in francophone Quebec: the leftist Fédération des femmes du Québec (FFQ), primarily an urban organization, and Association féminine d'éducation et d'action sociale (AFEAS), which reached out to the more rural areas. Thus, regardless of their geographical location, women in 1966 Quebec were beginning to organize themselves into a force to be reckoned with (Dumont 2008, 104). So the collapse of traditional family values, the destabilizing rise of feminism, and the evil decriminalization of the pill in 1966 might very well have led to voiolence, as well as to the "strange phenomenon" that Father Leclerc argued had emptied out the churches. Or at least, this is what Quebec celebrity Janette Bertrand suggested in a little-known documentary by Thierry Le Brun, *Un certain souvenir / A Licence to Remember* (2002), which, coincidently, appeared at virtually the same time as *Sur le seuil* and *Les Invasions barbares*.

In *Un certain souvenir*, Belgian expatriate Le Brun seeks to understand the meaning of the Quebec motto *Je me souviens* [I remember], which appears on the province's licence plates. Adopting Michael Moore's naive-everyman approach to investigative documentary filmmaking, albeit in a less heavy-handed and uncouth fashion, Le Brun bumbles around the province, interviewing both regular people and celebrities to figure out exactly what it is that Quebec claims to be remembering. Janette Bertrand, who has been a fixture on the Quebec cultural scene since the 1950s as an actress, journalist, screenwriter, and television talk-show host, is something of a French Canadian Oprah Winfrey, firmly entrenched in the radically moderate politics of liberal feminism. Her intervention in *Un certain souvenir* revolves around Le Brun's question of the relationship between the Church and the collective memory as expressed—so it seems—through *Je me souviens*. Bertrand does remember the role of the Church, but not fondly at all:

> It's when you are born a woman in Quebec that you experience Church oppression. The Church wants to know if you've had enough kids. If two years after one child you don't have another, you'd better avoid the parish priest or he'll tell you: come see me because it's time you have another child.

Implicitly referring to 1966, she then describes the stand that women finally took against religious oppression when contraception became available in the province:

So there was a revolution. Women discovered liberty, the choice to have children or not. They no longer obeyed the Church. Then it was women who went to church. Women said … Here it was called family prevention … "I'll prevent a family. And I won't be hypocritical and go to … and I won't confess to it." So women stopped having kids. They found freedom, and that was the end. *The churches emptied out.*

Michael Gauvreau's reading of Catholicism in Quebec during the Quiet Revolution supports Bertrand's suggestion that sexual emancipation at home also meant emancipation from the Church. "In this key respect, Quebec women began to equate rejection of the conventional gender divisions and hierarchies with rejection of the Catholic religion itself" (Gauvreau 2005, 229). This equation between religion and the oppression of women persisted for years and can be perceived to this day. For instance, during the 2013 debate around the xenophobic Charte des valeurs du Québec formulated by the Parti Québécois, which was in power at the time, and which proposed to prohibit the public display of ostentatious religious signs such as the niqāb, a large number of women, including Janette Bertrand, signed a petition supporting the charter in the name of gender equality (Bertrand 2013). The return to power of the provincial Liberals in 2014 put an end to the debate over the charter, though not to xenophobia,[4] which remains part of the political discourse in Quebec, perhaps even more so after the 2018 victory of the right-wing party Coalition Avenir Québec.

Also still resonating in the early twenty-first century, and more relevant to this chapter, is the threat to the family posed by birth control that the conservative group Union Catholique des Femmes Rurales reacted against in 1966 by demanding measures to preserve this sacred cornerstone of French Canadian heritage. Even thirty-six years after the beginning of the end of the traditional Catholic family, there remained a profound fear that the Québécois family was on the verge of disappearing. In October 2003, at the exact same time as *Sur le seuil*'s theatrical release, a conference titled "Les défis pour le Québec à l'aube du choc demographic" focused on the urgent problem presented by the province's extremely low birth rate (one of the lowest in the world, apparently). Rejecting the option of relying on immigration to solve this demographic crisis, the Conseil de la famille et de l'enfance demanded that the government take measures to encourage procreation, "inciter les couples à procréer" (Morisette 2003, A7). Shortly after this conference, in November 2003, Quebec's largest newspaper, *La Presse*, published a special feature on Quebec's birth rate crisis, "Crise des berceaux." Not surprisingly, women continued to be blamed for the problem, thus echoing the dominant attitude of 1966. Women were criticized for being spoiled and for wanting to wait until circumstances were ideal—ideal man, ideal salary, ideal career circumstances—before having children. And the ideal time, of course, never happens: "Il faut aux femmes le gars idéal, le bon budget, le bon *timing* dans la carrière, des conditions idéales qui ne sont jamais réunis, quoi" (Leduc 2003, Plus-4). Conversely, men were largely depicted as innocent bystanders with regard to the demographic crisis (Leduc 2002, A12). Indeed, much of the early twenty-first-century discourse around the effects of the mid-1960s feminist revolution described by Bertrand portrayed men as victims. Having been marginalized at every level of Quebec's current matriarchal society, "les problèmes des hommes au Québec ... sont le résultat du féminisme" (Guy 2002b, F2). Boys could no longer succeed at school because of feminism (Ouimet 2002, A18). Men who were trying to be good fathers experienced a "crise d'identité," having lost the traditional signposts of paternity that had been thrown out the window by "l'idéologie féministe, la pilule, les lois sur le divorce, une libération des structures juridiques" (Landry 2003, A22). A letter to the editor of *La Presse* spoke of the despair of divorced fathers in early twenty-first-century Quebec, who had been reduced to slavery by a type of vengeful feminism, "féminisme revanchard," that had condemned them to forced labour in order to support their ex-wives, who denied them the right to see their children (Rondeau 2002, A12). Men had been made to feel so guilty by women that they had recoiled into impotent silence (Gagnon 2002, 18).

In Le Brun's documentary, as Bertrand speaks the line about churches emptying out in 1966, archival footage shows the tall steeple of a church crumbling to the ground. This brief moment in the film is meaningful, for the image of the disintegrating structure does not merely imply the end of the Church's omnipresence in Quebec, but is an obvious metaphor for phallic ruin. As the mighty steeple loses its erection and collapses to the ground, it clearly suggests the downfall of masculinity.

Le Brun's editorial spin on Bertrand's commentary was no coincidence. Women's emancipation from the tyranny of forced childbearing in 1966 presented a genuine threat to patriarchy and, as shown above, masculine resentment was still alive and well at the time Le Brun, Arcand, and Tessier were making their films in the early 2000s. In fact, in a series of articles published in *Le Devoir* in 2010, on the fiftieth anniversary of the Quiet Revolution, Christian Rioux asked whether the 1960s had witnessed "la fin d'un certain patriarcat" [the end of a certain kind of patriarchy] (Rioux 2010). The crumbling steeple and the severed fingers of the (Anti)Christ illustrate the same phenomenon: the castration of masculine religious power as a result of the evils that were aroused in 1966 and that afflict Quebec masculinity to this day. Amy Ransom in her contribution to this anthology further explores the painful melodrama of the contemporary Québécois man, who longs for the lost home of the patriarchal family. Ironically, it could be argued that the Québécois man actually has nothing to return to, for he had never achieved in the first place what Robert Schwartzwald calls "phallo-national maturity." As Bill Marshall argues in *Quebec National Cinema* (2001), Québécois cinema counts an abundance of films that deal with the French Canadian man's abject failure to achieve phallo-national maturity, that is, a genuine independent masculinity "of concrete achievements, of work and efficiency" (Marshall 2001, 105–6).

Fingerless Nostalgia

The pastoral environment that Father Lemay evokes so vividly in *Sur le seuil*, and that was forever shattered in September 1966, is a world of men, where obedient women play their traditional roles in the background. The scenes in the presbytery, both in the present tense of the film and in the flashbacks, include a few shots of a silent housekeeper, Gervaise (Anne-Marie Labelle), who is dressed the exact same way and appears to be of the exact same age both in 1966 and in 2002. She says nothing, and only obeys the priests' commands. While the men share "a very pleasant life" in the early 1960s, Gervaise, the eternal servant, is seen mutely toiling in the kitchen. Gina Freitag in her chapter discusses the horror that can arise when a domestic space is rendered hostile to female characters because of repression by male power. But unlike the female perspective at the centre of the films that Freitag analyses, especially Maude Michaud's *Dys-* (2014), *Sur le seuil* resolutely assumes a male point of view and, as such, positions the female character as, a best, a peripheral figure and, at worst, the root of all evil. Indeed, the direct cause of Father Pivot's evil turn is a disobedient woman. The film makes clear that the event that radically transformed Pivot's temperament and destroyed this pleasant life was the death of his beloved sister, Audrey (Soleil Guérin). Significantly, in the flashback where Audrey silently passes away at the hospital, Father Pivot *orders her not to die*, in a vain attempt to exert power over her even at the threshold of death. From the moment his authority as a priest fails to control a woman, Pivot loses faith and veers toward evil.

It is typical, from the mindset of Catholic patriarchy, that a woman's disobedience would be the cause of a man losing his faith and turning evil; for ever since the beginning of the Church, woman has been seen as the "reptilian evil" that serves as the "Devil's gateway" to man (Gilmore 2010, 67). As David D. Gilmore writes in *Misogyny: The Male Malady* (2010):

> [The] tendency to link woman with primary evil and to perceive her as a moral threat to mankind finds expression in early Christian theology in the admonitions of Tertullian (c. A.O. 160-220), the theologian who first denounced woman as the Devil's gateway. Accusing women of original sin, as well as all manner of lesser evils, Tertullian addresses them directly: "Do you not know that each of you is Eve? The sentence of God on this sex of yours lives in this age: the guilt must of necessity live too. *You are the Devil's gateway.* You are the unsealer of that forbidden tree. You are the first deserter of the divine Law. You are she who persuaded him whom the Devil was not valiant enough to attack. You destroyed so easily God's image, man. On account of your desert[ion], even the Son of God had to die." (Gilmore 2010, 67–68)

Or to cite Leonard Swidler's pithy summary of what the Bible says about women, "every woman leads the essentially 'good' man down to evil" (Swidler 1979, 151). From this perspective, Pivot appears as just a victim, whose search for pure evil and transmission of dark powers to Thomas Roy is really the woman's fault.

It is also significant that evil is achieved by Pivot and his disciples through the desecration of birth, as the malevolent priest removes the bloody infant from the body of his dead mother lying on the altar, and breathes evil into him. It is no coincidence that the metaphor of loss of control over women would result in the destruction of the family and the defilement of childhood. That a *male character is cursed* with the burden of carrying evil as a result of the events of 1966 seems to reflect the early twenty-first-century discourse on masculine victimization discussed above; for woman's disobedience has condemned men to an impotent existence of pain and agony. It is also meaningful that Gervaise's only momentous gesture occurs *after* old Father Lemay has concluded his tale and Dr. Lacasse has left the presbytery to return to Montreal. In a brief shot, we see that the housekeeper has set up a hangman's noose in the priest's room, where he will proceed to commit suicide. As such, she is the agent of the priest's eternal damnation. She is also the agent of Thomas's continued curse, for she is the one who took care of the baby after the carnage in the church, thus ensuring the survival of evil.

As the man cursed with carrying the burden of evil, Roy chooses to cut off his fingers, not only to eradicate his ability to write, but also to signify his castration and impotence in the face of the horror that surrounds him. No need to rehearse the famous "Hallucination of the Cut Finger" story from Freud's "Wolfman case" to understand that the finger, as "something small that can be removed from the body", easily takes on phallic symbolism, and that its severance amounts to an acknowledgment of impotence and loss of masculinity (Lemaire 2014, 245). What is perhaps most striking in the representation of Roy's digital castration in *Sur le seuil* is the evocation of continuous pain as blood is seen sipping through his hand bandages, especially at the moment when it becomes clear to Dr. Lacasse that the novelist suffers from more than just a typical psychosis. The loss of patriarchal Catholic control that followed the black mass in 1966 and that remains inscribed in Roy's severed, bleeding fingers is experienced as an excruciatingly painful condition on the part of the horror author, who continues to cause suffering around him through doodles that he can't help but draw even from his hospital bed.

It is important to note that Roy did not cut off his thumbs.[5] Similarly, the Christ statue's damaged hand in *Les Invasions barbares* also still has its thumb. This is symbolically meaningful, for while the severed fingers imply castration, the thumb is the digit that most commonly evokes masculine power, and its presence mitigates the impression of impotence (Becker 2000, 301). More specifically, some symbologists argue that "the thumb symbolizes man and the fingers are the four elements which protect him" (Rabanne 1999, 35). As such, Roy's and the Christ statue's severed fingers suggest that the elements (or institutions) that protect man have perhaps been removed, resulting in a loss of some power. But the remaining thumb indicates that man still has a remnant of ascendance that may allow him to regain his position of control. In accordance with the "male under siege" mentality of early twenty-first-century Quebec, it makes sense that only a *man* can try to redeem Roy's lost masculinity and that the only strong female character in the film, Dr. Jeanne Marcoux, must be sacrificed at the altar of science—an operating table—in order to terminate evil. While Lacasse does not manage to fix Roy, he will seek to guard his progeny. The film closes with a domestic scene that includes Dr. Lacasse, Jeanne's widowed husband Marc (Frédéric Gilles), and Antoine, the infant kissed by Roy before he died. Asked by Marc to look after Antoine for a minute, Lacasse responds, "Yes. I'll watch him." He then addresses Antoine directly, promising: "I'll watch you. You can be sure. I won't let you out of my sight. Ever." While expressing Lacasse's apprehension that Antoine has been cursed by Roy's evil kiss, these words could as easily be spoken by a loving father vowing to dedicate himself to the well-being of his male progeny. Freed from the oppressive presence of empowered women (Jeanne is dead, and Lacasse's own wife has left him), the good father may finally be able to reconnect with his son and return to the pastoral tranquility of pre-feminist, pre-1966 patriarchy.

Admittedly, Lacasse is not Antoine's father, and neither is Thomas Roy. As such, the theme of digitally castrated patriarchy trying to re-erect itself upon the ruins of a shattered family unit functions primarily at a metaphorical level in *Sur le seuil*. In *Les Invasions barbares*, however, this theme is at the literal core of the narrative, in which a dying man seeks to reconnect with his son and reconstruct the filial edifice. The flashback to 1966 is much more conspicuous in *Sur le seuil* than the passing reference to 1966 by Father Leclerc and the severed fingers in *Les Invasions*, which might very well go unnoticed. However, the historical event to which Father Leclerc refers—the collapse of the Church and, by extension, the breakdown of the patriarchal family—is far more central to Arcand's male melodrama than it is to Tessier's horror film.

Rémy and his friends belong to what has been called the "génération lyrique" (Ricard 1994)—that is, those Quebec baby boomers who most benefited from the progress made during the Quiet Revolution and who tried the hardest to break with the conservatism of older generations. The nostalgic irony at the core of the film is that in his dying days, Rémy desperately longs to re-create his family, the very institution that his generation aggressively sought to destroy in the mid-1960s. Born in 1950 in Chicoutimi, as he states near the end of the film, he was sixteen in 1966, the same age as Jean Corbo, who blew himself up with a bomb he had intended to plant as a terrorist act. Rémy and his friends were of that generation of delinquents whose wicked ways were related to crumbling family values and the collapse of traditional Catholicism. The clash between parents and adolescents in 1966 revolved primarily around different views on Catholicism. Speaking specifically of the *génération lyrique* and their parents, Michael Gauvreau writes:

> Catholicism had become, by the mid-1960s, the primary element in an increasingly strident cultural conflict between generations, one whose message as articulated by a growing group of personalist critics, fuelled the individualism of young people by ruthlessly exposing the deficiencies of parents in the transmission of religious knowledge. (Gauvreau 2005, 164)

In the mid-1960s, the *génération lyrique* was implicitly influenced by Personalist beliefs, which had emerged from the progressive *jeunesse catholique* movement of the 1950s and espoused the primacy of the human mind over religious faith as well as the individual's capacity to give meaning to social reality through consciousness (Beaudry 2007, 82–94). This philosophy conflicted sharply with the older generation's traditional Catholicism and led young people to vociferously reject their elders. Thirty-six years later, Rémy and his friends are still estranged from their elders. No one refers to the pre-baby-boomer generations in *Les Invasions barbares*, except at the very end of the film, when Claude mentions indifferently that his mother has passed away.[6] Pierre had already made clear in *Le Déclin...* that he has no connection at all to his parents and siblings. Yet a throbbing desire for the kind of close filial connections that characterized the traditional Catholic family is at the aching heart of the film's narrative.

Conclusion: The Age of Nostalgia

I have argued elsewhere that the failure of the second referendum on sovereignty in 1995 reignited in Quebec culture a strong sense of "nostalgia for a time when nationalist dreams were still possible," a time when conservative repression had been, ironically, the necessary condition for fostering independentist aspirations (Loiselle 2007, 153). Coincidently, this national wistfulness emerged at the same time that members of the *génération lyrique* were reaching middle age and, as such, were ripe for nostalgic reminiscences about the good old days of their (pre-modern) innocence. Thus, the nostalgic turn in late twentieth- and early twenty-first-century Quebec is marked by a longing for a heritage that had been radically disowned just a few decades earlier. This point was made in *Le Déclin...*, in which the history professors are shown to be totally indifferent to the history of Quebec (Loiselle 2008a, 59–62). In their later years, however, they have started to long for this past — a past for which they never actually cared much; and indeed, Rémy remains, on the surface, opposed to the Church. But now that he is getting old and his current life is marked by pain and resentment, Rémy is eager to return to an *imaginary* time in his life when the big Catholic family still existed—a pre-1966 arcadia, before the churches emptied out, before parents were violently rejected and before women took control of their own lives. A time characterized by dreadful circumstances that now appear warm and fuzzy trough the contemplative fog of nostalgia.

Rémy now wishes to reconnect with his children, whom he sees as a conduit back to this lyrical past. But of course, this return is impossible. Rémy dies; his friends go their separate ways; and his children resume their lives away from Quebec. Fingers have been cut off forever and cannot be reattached. Ultimately, Dr. Lacasse is more fortunate than Rémy, for at least he has baby Antoine, with whom he may be able to establish some vague filial relationship that holds some promise for the nostalgic future of Quebec. Granted that Antoine is potentially the incarnation of pure evil, and may grow up to wreak bloody havoc on the entire province. But given the sad state of barren masculinity in Quebec in the early twenty-first century, being the surrogate father of pure evil is perhaps better than nothing.

Notes

1   There are two versions of *Les Invasions barbares*: a 112-minute version that circulated primarily within Quebec, and a 98-minute version primarily for the international markets. The scene in which the reference to 1966 occurs begins roughly 66 minutes into the 112-minute version. The same scene begins about 55 minutes into the 98-minute version.

2   It should be noted that Ben-Z Shek, in his review of my book *Denys Arcand's "Le Déclin de l'empire américain" and "Les Invasions barbares,"* criticized me for adopting "too readily and uncritically Arcand's own ultra-pessimistic view of Quebec society and culture." Shek's counter-argument to this pessimism is to claim that in many ways Quebec is enjoying a golden age of artistic expression: "This in a period when Québec cinema is gaining more and more praise internationally, and artists like Robert Lepage, and troupes like Cirque du soleil, thrill thousands around the globe!" (Shek 2010, 475–76). The irony that is apparently lost on Shek is that Arcand himself, as I point out at the end of the book, recognizes that the one thing Quebec still has going for it is its vibrant artistic imagination. Indeed, Arcand always "reaffirms the Québécois' greatest asset: the power of imagination to create compelling art out of the humdrum reality of everyday life" (Loiselle 2008a, 159). Shek does not seem to have read the part of the book where I make this observation.

3   No need to remind the reader that both Rosemary's baby in Polanski's famous horror film (1968) and Damien, the demonic little child of *The Omen* (Richard Donner, 1976), were also born in 1966.

4   *Le Dictionnaire Flammarion de la langue française* defines "xénophobie" as "haine de ce qui est étranger." The hatred of the *stranger* or the *strange* is the issue here. This is why I use "xenophobia" rather than a related but different concept, such as "racism." Indeed, the debate around the *niqāb* seems to me to

have less to do with race per se (although race remains part of the equation) than with the fear, and ensuing hatred, of what is *strange*. Quebeckers have always been pathologically fearful of the "very strange phenomenon" of ostentatious foreign mores that clash with the still very homogeneous culture of the province. See my discussion on the role of the stranger in film adaptations of Quebec horror novels in Loiselle (2008b).

5   This is one of the intriguing differences between Tessier's film and Senécal's novel. In the latter, Roy cuts off all ten fingers.

6   This line of dialogue appears only in the longer version of the film.

SECTION III

Gendered Suffering

5

THE *DYS*-COMFORTS
OF HOME IN QUEBEC
GOTHIC HORROR CINEMA

Gina Freitag

The horror genre is largely concerned with the sense that a troubling past can never remain hidden and cannot be fully resolved when it does come back to light. For as film critic Robin Wood has emphasized, the "return of the repressed" (Wood 1979, 17) is inevitable; no matter how deep one tries to bury the most unseemly of events or the most unsavoury of behaviours, those truths always find a way to resurface. Whether it is through nightmar-ish memories, haunting regrets, or painful nostalgia, the past is unearthed, stirred, dredged up; it returns to disrupt whatever semblance or illusion of peace might exist. Nostalgia has been an especially disruptive metaphor for the return of the repressed in Gothic horror, a subgenre that has most often been "associated with domestic life, private expression, emotion, and the fem-inine realm" (Pierce 2009, 56). As Isabella van Elferen has argued in *Nostalgia or Perversion? Gothic Rewriting from the Eighteenth Century until the Present Day* (2009), "Gothic nostalgia is decisively active, as it transforms the past, turning it upside down, foregrounding its background, corrupting its order. If nostalgia is characterized by the retrospective creation of an idealised home-land, the Gothic renders this very homeland uncanny by perverting its idyllic quality" (van Elferen 2009, 5). When the repressed returns within the walls of a domestically gendered space, Gothic nostalgia functions as the demented stage *par excellence* upon which to re-enact the traumatic drama of the past and rehearse the origins of the shattered female subject. But while Gothic nostalgia allows the female character to recall her authentic self by shedding all the layers of diffidence that have veiled her core identity, the body always painfully incarnates the impossibility of ever being able to return home. As this chapter will discuss, this trope appears in a number of Quebec Gothic horror films focusing on female characters trapped in the womblike confines of private terror from which they seek to experience rebirth.

The Quebec Horror Film

A relatively new genre in the Quebec film industry, the horror film has grown from Jean Beaudin's Satanist film, *Le Diable est parmi nous* (1972), and David Cronenberg's raw early body horror films shot in Montreal, to Robin Aubert's sleek rural zombie movie, *Les Affamés* (2017), and Jeff Barnaby's zombie uprising film, *Blood Quantum* (2019), which was shot primarily at the Kahnawake and Listuguj reserves in Quebec.[1] In Cronenberg's *Shivers* (1975) and *Rabid* (1977), that which is repressed literally oozes or bursts forth from its characters' bodies in the form of viral infections or phallic monstrosities. In these films, Cronenberg set the tone for what would become a notable tendency in Quebec horror cinema, namely, the shocking *extraordinary* erupting from the unremarkable *ordinary*. Moreover, like much of Quebec national cinema more broadly, the Quebec horror film participates in a dialogue on the construction of identity and space—that is, the tension between the terrifying outside and the unbearable inside. It is a reflection of the Canadian "terror of the soul" (Frye 1971, 225), as Northrop Frye called it: the threat posed "when the individual first feels himself becoming an individual, pulling away from the group, losing the sense of driving power that the group gives him, aware of a conflict within himself far subtler than the struggle of morality against evil" (226).

This terror of the soul is discussed at length in a book I co-edited with André Loiselle, *The Canadian Horror Film: Terror of the Soul* (2015), which surveys several aspects of the Canadian imagination as represented through horror cinema. Quebec cinema further illustrates how, as Bill Marshall puts it, the "imagined community of the nation … is spatially organized, projected, and represented on physical and mental maps" (Marshall 2001, 7). In Loiselle's contribution to *The Canadian Horror Film*, "Pure Laine Evil: The Horrifying Normality of Quebec's Ordinary Hell in the Film Adaptations of Patrick Senécal's 'Romans d'épouvante,'" these cinematic mental maps are examined in relation to the ordinary men featured in the film adaptations of popular Quebec author Patrick Senécal's terrifying narratives: Éric Tessier's films *Sur le seuil* (2003) and *5150 rue des ormes* (2009), as well as Daniel Grou-Podz's *Les Sept Jours du talion* (2010). As Loiselle notes, "the one element that recurs in all three novels [by Senécal], and which is foregrounded in the film versions, is the centrality of a male subject who is confronted with a villain whose monstrosity is marked by such banal ordinariness that it calls into question the hero's own sense of his 'normal' self" (68). The analysis below draws a similar connection between banal ordinariness and the monstrous, from within the Gothic-like narratives of the struggling female protagonists in such films as Pascal Laugier's *Martyrs* (2008), Éric Falardeau's *Thanatomorphose* (2012), and Maude Michaud's *Dys-* (2014). Further exploration of these mental maps reveals an underlying trend toward disturbance in domestic spaces. In these films, the imagined community of the nation begins at home, where the solace of the domestic realm is disrupted by conflict and transforms a space of familiar comforts into an uncanny, alienating territory marked by unease, anxiety, and *discomfort*.

Gothic Nostalgia and the Frustrated Feminine

The home space in these films, as in other similarly disturbing narratives, is significant because of the way in which it manifests itself as a place of both rest and unrest, and ultimately of that which is *unheimlich*—unhomely. As psychologist Ernst Jentsch (and Freud after him) pointed out, the term "without doubt … seems to express that somebody who has an uncanny experience is not quite *zu Hause* [at home] in the matter" (qtd. in Vidler 1996, 23). The unsettled home is a recurring image in a number of Quebec films beyond the horror genre, where the relationship between the central female character and the domestic space exemplifies an *unheimlich* quality by focusing on a "space of madness, of the dissolution of identity induced by the inability to sustain the masquerade" (Marshall 2001, 234), a situation that forms an unyielding yearning associated with the past and inevitably leads to breakdown. In this way, the past is a haunting force that invades the presumed safe space of one's home, a space that is "an especially favoured site for uncanny disturbances: its apparent domesticity, its residue of family history and nostalgia, its role as the last and most intimate shelter of private comfort" (Vidler 1996, 17). A Gothic sensibility prevails in this respect, contrasting "home as a place of security and concord [with] home as a place of danger and imprisonment" (Ellis 1989, x). The trope of the Gothic woman tends to "reveal a vision of feminine subjectivity exposed to an anxiety borne out of [a female character's] relation both to the 'external' structures of the patriarchal Symbolic order and to her own 'internal' drives" (Bonikowski 2013, 68).[2] While the concept of the unsettled home is doubtlessly present in many contemporary horror films centred on male characters, there is a longer tradition of this trope as it relates to female characters in literature and cinema, where "the woman is not merely a victim or object of male power; something of her own subjectivity is involved that connects her intimately with the very force that attempts to destroy her" (Bonikowski 2013, 68). The intrinsic connection between female protagonists, the disruption of the self, and their connection to the home (whether in an apartment or house—the two are depicted with almost equal regularity) are visualized in Quebec Gothic horror cinema in a particularly confrontational and visceral manner.

In Falardeau's *Thanatomorphose*, a young artist, Laura (Kayden Rose), struggles with a profound sense of unhappiness: an abusive relationship, a floundering art project, a general sense of aimlessness. Over a matter of days, her depression, her dissatisfaction, and her reclusiveness take a physical toll in the form of gruesome bodily decay, until she literally uses glue, stitches, and duct tape to hold herself together. In Laugier's Canada–France co-production, *Martyrs*, two young women, Anna (Morjana Alaoui) and Lucie (Mylène Jampanoï), are haunted by the trauma of a childhood kidnapping experience. Lucie is driven by a deep-rooted desire for revenge, and her perversely nostalgic urge to return to the site of her tortured youth triggers a chain of horrific actions that leads to her violent death as well as Anna's. Lucie's relentless search for those whom she believes to be her kidnappers leads to an explosive and destructive sequence early in the film. Her sudden appearance at the front door of a house in the wooded countryside disrupts a peaceful morning scene in which a family is gathered around the table, discussing their day over breakfast; she charges into the house amid a spray of bullets, mowing down each of the family members one by one. Through this violent episode, a far greater and more terrible truth about the past is uncovered in the depths of the house. And in Michaud's *Dys-*, in which Gothic nostalgia is the central threat, prolonged reflection on the past inevitably incites violence and horror. As a mysterious epidemic sweeps through Montreal, Eva (Shannon Lark) is confined to her apartment with her estranged husband and forced to confront her inner struggle with self-determination. During this quarantine, the notion of home as a *safe* space is brutally torn from its conceptual framework and converted into the notion of home as a *survival* space—a theme present in Gothic and zombie outbreak narratives alike (Browning 2011, 41). Physical features of the home from which one might typically seek comfort become sites of terror, suggesting that a home built upon regret and resentment can only ever be an unstable one.

In works of Gothic literature and film, "the home as a site of trauma" (Bonikowski 2013, 76)[3] is a thematic truth of the female character's experience. Over time, the architecture of the home has changed: medieval castles, ruins, graveyards, and vast estates have given way to "the old house: as both building and family line, it became the site of where fears and anxieties returned in the present" (Hanson 2007, 35). Significantly, the castle-in-ruins, the Gothic mansion, and the Old Dark House all similarly "look like spectres of ancient times, and permit indulgence in a melancholic nostalgia … where we encounter the mysterious and demoniac beings of romance" (Varma 1957, 17–18, quoted in Wright 2007, 37–38). The image of the house, or as this chapter describes, the unsettled home, is intrinsically connected to female self-consciousness; the Female Gothic. The term, coined by Ellen Moers in her work *Literary Women: The Great Writers* (1977), initially referred to women who authored female-centric Gothic narratives, but Helen Hanson has adopted the term in her book *Hollywood Heroines: Women in Film Noir and the Female Gothic Film* (2007), to refer to films with "a female authorial presence in the gothic" and their "female address" (44). Though Hanson's discussion first focuses on the 1940s cycle with films like Alfred Hitchcock's *Rebecca* (1940) and *Suspicion* (1941), as well as Robert Stevenson's *Jane Eyre* (1943), she then expands the analysis to include a more contemporary body of films, such as *Sleeping with the Enemy* (Ruben 1991), *Deceived* (Harris 1991), and *What Lies Beneath* (Zemeckis 2000).

This analysis departs from the traditional ideology of the Female Gothic in that it views the female protagonist not as necessarily a heroine or solely a victim, to examine a more complex female character. Hanson's discussion allows for this divergence:

> The gothic possesses the ability constantly to renew itself, to assert its relevance in distinct socio-cultural eras, to find new expressions and outlets in evolving cultural forms and productions, while it is simultaneously, and rather paradoxically, a mode that plays on a fraught relationship to the past … Shrouded in secrecy and ambiguity, the past is revealed in horrifying ways, accompanied by violence of an atavistic form. (34–35)

Following Hanson's lead, I will incorporate the term Female Gothic into my discussion to uncover a different kind of interpretation of the female figure and her agency. This figure is marked not by a shifting or oscillation "between the positions of victim and heroine" (60) but rather through an investigation toward the authentic self—a process associated with certain psychological coping mechanisms whereby "nostalgia offers people a means to connect to a past authentic self and doing so may reduce concerns about extrinsic contingencies in the present" (Routledge 2016, 80). Through a reigniting of the past, no matter how mentally unsettling and physically painful, Gothic nostalgia may allow for the re-formation of the authentic self, freed from trappings of gendered alienation and subjugation. Whether the protagonist fully attains a sense of her authentic self through this process is arguable and perhaps beside the point. What matters is that the character moves toward it through a process of self-determination accompanied by what Julia Kristeva refers to as the abject.

As Kristeva describes in *Powers of Horror* (1982), abjection is that which does not "respect borders, positions, rules"; it is "what disturbs identity, system, order" (4). This is precisely what the Female Gothic architype is seen to do to as she struggles to escape the boundaries and restrictions imposed on her by patriarchy. But there is more to the female protagonists of this discussion—the environment in which self-identity is investigated in the Female Gothic narrative plays an important function in visualizing the inner turmoil of the struggling female protagonist. As Julian Fleenor describes in *The Female Gothic* (1983), the spatial element inhabited by the female protagonist utilizes images of enclosed rooms or houses, suggesting a certain repressive force created by society or internalized by the protagonist (12). That "spatial imagery is frequently used intentionally or otherwise to suggest the female body itself" (13). There is an explicit visualization in the films analyzed in this chapter, whereby the protagonist's existence links mind, body, and locale, for "at the centre of the Female Gothic is the conflict of female identity. Sometimes that conflict is expressed as the feminine mystique, sometimes as madness, sometimes as the grotesque" (24). In the process of negotiating her identity through an excavation of the past, the protagonist in the Gothic narrative is trapped amid conservative, patriarchal, objectifying patterns and limitations; she is "always acting in reaction, tension" (24). However, contrary to what Fleenor denotes as something that is "not transcendent" (24), one could argue that the very process of questioning and challenging the systems that create identity is an act toward transcendence. This is most obvious in *Martyrs* but appears in all three films addressed below.

There is much that can be borrowed from works of Gothic literature and their analyses to illuminate the prevailing themes at the core of these three Quebec horror films. Among the most evident elements of these films is the way in which they expose the "inequity and powerlessness of women's lives … transforming domestic spaces into Gothic nightmares" (Bonikowski 2013, 67). Like that of the Gothic woman, the trend of the abject, distressed, isolated female protagonist—what I will call the frustrated-feminine—is frequently visualized within the confines of the home (68). The three films discussed in this chapter all offer, to use Hanson's phrasing, "spaces that powerfully and affectively portray a crisis in women's relation to the home and her agency within it" (Hanson 2007, 185). The frustrated-feminine is further distinguished from other female character types (including the furious-feminine, which I have discussed elsewhere in relation to a female protagonist's monstrousness and the sense of agency assumed therein)[4] through depictions of the female protagonist in provocative, unsexualized, gut-wrenching, grotesque detail. This is especially true of *Thanatomorphose* (whose title, according to the filmmaker's added note on the plot summary on IMDB.com, refers to "an Hellenic word meaning the visible signs of an organism's decomposition caused by death"). In this film, the turmoil endured by the female protagonist is the sole focus; her mental and emotional decay is paralleled by the putrid decay of her physical form, which, as online reviewer Amber Bug puts it, "can be seen as metaphor for the struggle any young woman goes through when trying to find herself and her way in life" (2016). Similar to the abject nature of both *Martyrs* and *Dys-*, the protagonist, Laura, is one of the frustrated-feminine, driven to extremes as she seeks self-definition. As all three of these films convey, this abject process is represented largely through bodily fluids: sweat, tears, blood, pus, and, in some cases, urine and feces. These women are united by the way in which they "lie on the border between life and death with the focus of their strange existence on the physical decomposition of their bodies," as Teresa Lobos observes in her review of *Thanatomorphose* (Lobos 2014). Furthermore, these characters grapple with and confront the idea of their "own inexplicable and insignificant existence … an introspective dance of bodily horror" (Lobos 2014). They are caught in the mire of crises: physical, sexual, and existential. Each of these protagonists is stuck in a transitional space, nostalgically longing for a return to what Elena Liotta calls in another context a "place of origin," a site that "presents itself to the human being in an ambivalent form, as a trustworthy safe space, that furnishes force and propulsion towards the exterior, or as a place that holds in and that threateningly attempts to reabsorb the new creative energies" (Liotta 2009, 48). The place of origin, symbolized by the home environment, affords a point for these characters to confront forces of pressure, regret, and dissonance in their lives. In effect, the home takes on a representation of further significance, reflecting the ultimate place of origin: the womb. As Shoshana Felman relates in *What Does a Woman Want? Reading and Sexual Difference* (1993), there exists "a womb nostalgia, a nostalgia for the woman as a familial and familiar essence, a nostalgia for femininity as snug and canny, *Heimlich*, that is, according to Freud's definition, 'belonging to the *house* or to the *family*'" (63). In the three films examined here, the place of origin is problematized, for the womblike environment where the action unfolds appears as threateningly oppressive and dark even while also strangely comforting and hopeful. The horror framework thus raises questions about the secure nature of the feminine space: "Is this place really as protected as we think when we look at it from the outside? Is it as safe and warm as had always been romantically imagined?" (Liotta 43).

In general, a great deal of horror film theory examines the primacy often given to female physiology: women rarely seem to escape the difference or otherness that is continually anchored in the body. In "Film Bodies: Gender, Genre, and Excess" (1991), Linda Williams argues that "the bodies of women figured on the screen have functioned traditionally as the primary embodiments of pleasure, fear, and pain" (4). Barbara Creed's notion of the monstrous-feminine, a term used to describe certain female character types[5] in the horror genre, emphasizes "the importance of gender in the construction of her monstrosity" and how she "is defined in terms of her sexuality" (Creed 1993, 3) because she is seen as abject, a "partially formed subject" (Creed 1996, 36). The plight of the frustrated-feminine moves significantly beyond the trappings of the physical being to reflect on the inner turmoil: searching the horrific past for a sense of peace in order to reclaim not only the body but also the self. Not surprisingly, this reclamation is frequently situated in the womblike enclosed environment of the home.

Thanatomorphose

The explicit illustration of the frustrated-feminine is central to our understanding of *Thanatomorphose*. The protagonist, Laura, is introduced following a sexual episode with her abusive boyfriend, Antoine (Davyd Tousignant), who steps on an exposed nail in the hallway of her apartment, the isolating setting of the film. As he curses and bleeds, she tends to his wounds but is soon left alone, where she discovers a bruise on her arm. She dismisses it and attempts to work on a sculpture piece in her living room, an artwork with which she has grown frustrated. She soon gives up when she realizes she cannot make any progress and goes to bed. Unable to sleep, she notices water damage on the ceiling that has taken the shape of a vagina-like slit. Over the course of the film, Laura takes to staring at the rotting ceiling as she masturbates, drawing a parallel between the crumbling ceiling and what is to become the progressive decay of her body. In a way reminiscent of Cronenberg's early body-horror imagery, Falardeau's film soon unveils further bruising, her hair begins to fall out, and her nails grotesquely loosen and slide off. As Teresa Lobos observes in her discussion of this film for the online journal *Off/Screen*: "In a decidedly gruesome way, Laura's physical disintegration coincides with a newfound reclaiming of her own body, as loathsome as it has become. She shuns the men ... and takes control of her own sexual pleasure in an, albeit gruesome, scene of self-love" (2014).

Despite this self-love, Laura's body continues to resist enforced servitude as it graphically decays: her body temperature drops (her boyfriend notes how cold her skin is as they later have sex); the few remaining unbruised patches of skin discolour, becoming pale and grey; she finds maggots growing within; and she vomits, urinates, and later defecates, suggesting a disturbed interior state and a rejection of that which contaminates the self. Even as her wounds steadily worsen, she calmly goes about mending herself, cleaning, bandaging, documenting. At one point she sews on a broken finger; later, she duct-tapes one of her arms back together.

As with each of the films and their protagonists mentioned in this chapter, Laura continually returns to specific sites in her home typically associated with comfort and safety. These spaces conjure up an implied past of "normal" femininity that has become untenable under the oppressive gaze of male lovers who lay claim to her body. Laura yearns to reconstitute a body of her own. But this aspiration is unrealizable as her authentic form has been forever obliterated through masculine reification. Therefore, though these domestic sites help facilitate what Liotta refers to in her study of uncanny places as the "journey towards one's own form, which is self-constructed in one's experience with the environment" (Liotta 2009, 55), they are also marked by the horror of her self-destruction as the only escape from objectification. Her decaying body thus becomes a literal incarnation of Gothic nostalgia as it proceeds through perverting its idyllic quality toward an authentic self whose original shape is irretrievable. In other words, the desire for the place of origin to bring about a rebirth or reconstruction of the self necessarily translates into, again borrowing from Liotta, a "return to the uroboric incest and self-dissolution" (47). The kitchen, where she makes bacon, eggs, and coffee for breakfast, and tries to revive her disoriented self, is also a site of violence when she slips and injures her head. The bedroom where she sleeps is also a space where she endures rough sex with her boyfriend. And the bathroom, where she washes and readies herself for the day, is also where she soaks in the tub to soothe her rotting flesh and examine the state of her ever-worsening conditions. Her abjection is harshly visualized in other places in the home as well: the living room where she once held a housewarming party with friends, is also where she performs a graphic fellatio scene, her head wound still fresh with blood. The later brutal bludgeoning of both her boyfriend and another lover (Émile Beaudry) also takes place in the living room. And finally, in one of the concluding scenes, despite her determination to hold herself together and push onward, Laura writhes and crawls down the hallway, her skin melting off her skeleton, her jaw crying out in rage as it dislocates and drops to the floor shortly before she collapses.

In addition to the troubled relationship with her abusive boyfriend (and the apparent threat of eviction), another more significant factor contributes to Laura's despair—that is, the haunting presence of what she longs to achieve through artistic expression: her desire to fashion a body of her own, which takes the form of her frustratingly unfinished sculpture. The raw, coarsely shaped material sits on a pedestal in her apartment, and she returns to it constantly as though it beckons to her. But she grows weary of her lack of progress, and so it sits there while she listlessly waits for a spark of inspiration and motivation. After the one occasion in which she does actually leave her apartment (presumably for work), she returns home, mail in hand, and opens an envelope. In it, she finds a rejection notice from an art program to which she had applied. Later that night, while lying in bed with her boyfriend, she reveals that sculpting no longer gives her pleasure, and emphasizes its pointlessness. Despite this, she continues to fixate on the unfinished work, a reflection of her own unrealized state. And as her body shows increasing signs of putrefaction, she resumes her attempts to sculpt, stopping only in frustration and when her finger breaking off prevents her from continuing. She later goes so far as to even affix to it bits of viscera from the horrific events that are taking place in her apartment. After killing her boyfriend in the living room, she tries to clean up the mess of his dead body by adding pieces of his entrails to the misshapen clay.

Eventually, her sculpture fails to conform to her muddled vision. She returns to put what little remains of her creative energy into the piece, ripping bits of gore into small pieces and working them into the clay. But the sculpture dislodges from its stand under the force of her hands and crashes to the floor. She cries out in exasperation, her voice a rasping banshee shriek. A moment later, she pulls back the sheet cover draped over her mirror and for some time contemplates her body, her other work in progress, before finally reaching up and shoving her fingers into her own eyes. Like the sculpture that sits in her living room, Laura must confront her inevitable destruction. The final mirror scene, in which prolonged self-contemplation culminates in self-blinding, suggests at once the nostalgic longing for the beautiful form Laura once was and often looked at while performing the traditional rituals of femininity such as putting on make-up, and the necessary conclusion of the process of abject self-recovery whereby the ideal image of the feminine must be rejected in search of an original self that is no longer accessible. The alternative is a completely different form: a repulsive pile of shapeless flesh and blood that is unrecognizable as female, or as human for that matter. But at last, it is no longer subjected to the gaze.

Martyrs

The strife associated with a reclamation of the self is also prevalent in *Martyrs*, through a triad identified by Amy M. Green in her article, "The French Horror Film *Martyrs* and the Destruction, Defilement, and Neutering of the Female Form" (2011). She points out that the "triad of the virgin, the matron, and the crone—or the young woman, mother, and elderly woman—still serves as the means by which a woman's life experiences are categorized and understood" (23). Likewise, the film is divided into three main storylines, opening first on footage relating the devastating story of young Lucie, who was held captive, brutalized, and tortured in an abandoned warehouse. Her escape marks the first section in the devastating narrative and sets in motion a haunting force surrounding a troubled woman trying to come to terms with her past the only way she knows how: by destroying those who she believes were her captors.

The imagery of the unsettled home is established in this second storyline, during her vengeful rampage fifteen years later at a peaceful house set in the countryside amid the woods. At first, the film depicts a different young girl (Juliette Gosselin) being chased through the house by her brother (Xavier Dolan) in a moment of sibling horseplay. Their father (Robert Toupin) scolds them and goes about making coffee, drawing attention to an article on the fridge, with its headline proudly proclaiming the daughter's accomplishment: "Marie Belfond regional 100 meter butterfly stroke champion." Outside, the mother (Patricia Tulasne) works on exposed pipes, attempting to fix the low water pressure. Shortly thereafter, the family sits down to breakfast together, discussing an important issue (the son's decision to leave law school for another program). The doorbell rings, marking the final peaceable moments in this house.

When the father answers the door, he is startled to see Lucie on his front stoop. In an instant, she sends him flying backwards with a powerful shotgun blast that splatters blood all over the white walls. Lucie then doggedly pursues each remaining member of the panicked family, with the young daughter's whimpering and crying underpinning the attack. Lucie shoots the mother next, farther down the hallway, then struggles momentarily against her conscience to assault the son in the kitchen at the breakfast table. Finally, she corners the young daughter in a bedroom, where she shoots through the clean white duvet and mattress to injure the girl before shooting her as she tries to flee. At the conclusion of her shooting spree, Lucie doubles over, rocking back and forth, sobbing and contemplating the mother's body in another moment of reflection. She is torn between the fury of her desire for vengeance and an unbearable, heart-wrenching sense of incomprehension at the senseless violence she endured at the hands of this woman. She tenderly kisses the mother's cheek, crying, asking her how she could have done those things to her. But her rage swiftly returns and she swings the gun around, blasting a shot into the ceiling.

Startled by an ominous rasping noise, Lucie soon discovers that the house is host to unexpected sinister elements. She follows the sound and glimpses a filthy, sinewy, naked woman crouched by the kitchen counter. Even her dear friend Anna's arrival in an effort to help cannot subdue the contorting and grotesque woman as she stalks and repeatedly attacks Anna throughout the house. A flashback reveals young Lucie breaking free from her captor in a dark, dank room. She encounters this woman, another victim, tied up in a separate room, lips sewn shut. A realization dawns upon us: Lucie's escape came at the cost of leaving behind a fellow victim, one whose presence still haunts her. Over the years, Lucie has been forced to grapple with a twisted form of survivor's guilt.

In one of Lucie's final scenes, the feral woman embraces her and cuts Lucie's arms from her elbows to her wrists. As Anna witnesses these events, it becomes clear that the naked woman is indeed a hallucinatory manifestation of Lucie's tortured psyche; an abject embodiment of "le démon de la nostalgie," to borrow Linda Lê's term.[6] It is Lucie herself who is inflicting this violence against her body as a form of self-punishment. In a final act of self-mutilation, Lucie slits her own throat and bleeds out in the storm raging outside. Anna scrambles to help her amid thunder crashes and realizes it's too late; her beloved friend is dead.

The third section of the narrative focuses on Anna. Her role is frequently depicted as that of the matron or caring mother: she tends to Lucie, to one of Lucie's surviving victims, and to yet another woman who has secretly been held captive in the house. The bond Anna forges with them contrasts with the disconnection she feels to her own mother (Louise Boisvert), whom she calls the morning after her friend's murderous rampage. As she recovers from the shock of such disturbing violence in a domestic space, Anna reaches out to her mother, hoping to mend the damage in their troubled relationship and to reconnect with a sense of home. However, the call is met by cold, distant conversation, peppered with her mother's disdain for her daughter's friendship and waywardness. Anna is effectively isolated. The conversation is interrupted as Anna uncovers an underground complex hidden in the bowels of the house—the source of all the horror endured and now resurfacing. As Green describes in her article, beneath a hatch in the floor are "labyrinthine, hidden spaces … reminiscent of the womb and the birth canal," images that further "permeate the film with mother imagery, but the womb spaces and watery rites implode inward on themselves leading to death, not to life" (25). This home environment comes to symbolize a disruption, where the underlying nostalgia to return to a place of origin—that illusory space in which these characters attempt to reclaim or reconnect with a previous sense of self and family—proves to only bring about atrocious pain. Just as the womb can be seen as the core of the female body, the basement may be seen as the core of the house. But instead of this womblike space providing comfort and safety, it contains a dark and horrifying truth. The space holds yet another brutalized female captive chained in the dark, her scarred, fragmented, malnourished frame encased by metal contraptions. Previously, Anna had taken pity and tried (against Lucie's wishes) to bring her friend's brutalized captor to safety upon discovering her still conscious after the attack. Here she again guides a victim to safety, but her efforts are rendered futile when an intruding woman armed with a gun and her attendant crew kill the house's captive, and seize Anna as their latest captive.

Another woman arrives, referred to only as Mademoiselle (Catherine Bégin) (what Green identifies as the crone or elderly woman), and educates Anna about this basement and her cult's morbid history of martyr-making, its obsession with "the state between life and death, as the body begins the final process of dying completely" (Green 2011, 26). Somehow, Anna endures the same repeated brutal treatment (force-feedings, beatings, humiliations), which culminates in a gruesome process of being flayed alive, her musculature laid bare, with ecstasy achieved. On this momentous occasion, Mademoiselle rushes to Anna's side to learn the truth of what she has experienced, that which lies beyond death. Only Mademoiselle is privy to the shocking testimony. Ominously, she later puts a gun into her mouth and pulls the trigger, sealing the truth within her. We are left with a final image of Anna's entranced form and some on-screen text. It reads:

Martyr: nom adjectif	martyr: n
Du grec "marturos"	From the Greek "Marturos"
Témoin	witness

As denoted by this text, the audience is called to be witness to Anna, and to the way in which "she loses her agency to the tyranny and despotism of others," both men and women, who "have lost all recognizable humanity" (Green 2011, 23). For both Lucie and Anna, the reclamation of the self is never realized. And, like that of Laura in *Thanatomorphose*, they illustrate the "frustrated-feminine," for all are young women, as Green concludes, "who should be moving forward with their lives, [but] instead regress back physically and emotionally, or both, into grotesque mockeries of the female form" (27). The nostalgic longing to return to the place of origin in search of transcendence leads only to the gothic ruin of the shattered body.

Dys-

The female form is similarly disturbed and distraught within the confines of the home in *Dys-*. Similar to *Martyrs*, this film utilizes on-screen text, thereby encapsulating the essence of the film:

DYS- *(prefix)*

diseased, abnormal, or faulty;

difficult or painful;

unfavourable or bad

Through the provision of this definition during the opening moments of the film, we are prepared for a difficult and painful experience, a depiction of that which is disturbed and unsettled. As noted previously in both *Thantomorphose* and *Martyrs*, this film also presents particular sites of terror within an ordinary home in which extraordinary violence unexpectedly erupts; in *Dys-*, violence is perpetrated on the kitchen table, in the bathroom, and in the bedroom. There is little comfort to be found in the home created by Sam (Alex Goldrich) and Eva, the estranged married couple at the centre of the film. While the threat of a strange and pernicious virus looms around them, it is clear early on that, as Michael Gingold observes in his review of the film, they are not only "surviving against a threat from the outside, but the mental and eventual body horror that results from the two being trapped together inside" (Gingold 2014).

Though far from the typical zombie mythos of George A. Romero's *Night of the Living Dead* (1968), the storyline of *Dys-* does bear some resemblance to the zombie outbreak narrative in its use of a terrifying and mysterious illness that functions as a catalyst for a deeper anxiety. The film also configures its characters in a survival space of their own making. In his article on "modern zombie (cine)myths," John Edgar Browning discusses this particular space where characters "must, together, fortify in order to protect the enclosure from what is 'outside,' coping all the while with the bleak sense of disparity and hopelessness around them" (Browning 2011, 44). Amid all of this, the Gothic-like narrative focuses on Eva's experience, oscillating between her painful recollections and the dreadful present. She recalls uncomfortable conversations with her mother, whose disparaging remarks about her daughter's pregnancy and the end of her career weigh heavily on her mind and ultimately contribute to Eva's anxiety about the direction of her life. The film's visualization of the past as a terrifying presence in various sites within the apartment reproduces conventions of Female Gothic cinema, as Hanson defines it. In such films, "the past is revealed in horrifying ways, accompanied by violence of an atavistic form. In its moves across the present and the past, and its tension between progress and atavism, the gothic forces witness the present as conditioned and adapted by events, knowledge or values pressing on it from the past" (Hanson 2007, 35).

These multiple threats first collide at the kitchen table, a place where family members generally unite to share a meal, news of the day, and details of important matters. However, for Sam and Eva, the kitchen table serves as a space of discomfort and tension. Sam arrives home from his job as a photography instructor and prepares the table for dinner. The typical home-cooked meal is noticeably absent; in its place are white take-away boxes. Sam gently arranges the place settings with chopsticks and folded napkins, laying out the meal with care in an effort to tempt his wife into some sort of interaction. When Eva joins him at the table, she is dejected and withdrawn. They eat silently at first, until Sam tries to bring about conversation and an opportunity to ease the tension between them. He asks: "Do you wanna talk about it?" Something important yet unresolved hangs in the air. A phone call interrupts the moment, bringing the results of a job interview that Eva had earlier in the day. She becomes quite animated, smiling widely, as she learns she has in fact secured the position—she's even delighted—but upon ending the call, her face drops and she falls back into silence. Sam is relieved at her success and the positive change it may bring. He lovingly reaches out to her as he congratulates her, but Eva immediately recoils from his touch. She can no longer contend with the conversation, nor can she match his attempts at a positive outlook; she gets up from the table and goes into another room.

On a night soon after, they are once again seated at the dining table, sharing a meal with a guest: James (Joseph Lazare), a long-time friend of Sam's, with whom he has fallen out of regular contact. James and Eva sit at opposite ends of the table, and a heavy cloud of animosity hovers between them as Sam attempts to engage both in conversation. However, James's snide remarks and continuous provocations toward Eva suggest that an uncomfortable history is threatening to resurface. They are interrupted by a news update emitting from the TV in the living room, telling of the virus symptoms, encouraging viewers to be vigilant and recommending self-quarantines in their homes until further notice. In an attempt to lighten the mood, James muses that it's "like something out of a zombie movie," and imitates the undead ("Brains!"). Exasperated, Eva loses patience with him, and the conversation is soon stripped of any civility as they trade accusations and berate each other. Their exchange abruptly ends when James's comments catch in his throat and he suddenly coughs up blood, spraying the table, the food, and Eva. In a blur of movement, Sam deftly removes his infected friend from the apartment and returns to calm Eva, who is scrambling to clean herself in the kitchen sink. Significantly, this scene confirms Eva's exposure to the virus and marks the inevitable "return of the repressed," a past event that haunts her relationship and threatens to come to light.

The bedroom is another site of trauma for Eva: this soft, warm, restful haven is where we first encounter her repeatedly seeking respite when interaction with her husband becomes too confrontational. It is also a place where Eva experiences recurring and unsettling nightmares of the infected James, coming to her in the night while she is asleep. Because of his diseased body, James might come across as an incarnation of the "man in pain" figure that Amy Ransom interprets in her contribution to this anthology as a central trope of contemporary Quebec cinema. However, his violent hostility toward Eva makes him more of an abhorrent aggressor than a sympathetic victim of an abject ailment. In her first nightmare, James slips into the bedroom shirtless and covered in rashes, and hovers over her as he menacingly reaches for her. She wakes up and rushes to the front door, convinced he has broken in. On a different night, as Eva dreams she lays sleeping cuddled up to the infected James, she cradles a jar containing a lifeless fetus, the remains of her unwanted, self-terminated pregnancy. She stirs when James tries to smother her, waking from the nightmare. With each successive nightmare, it becomes clear that the recurring visions of James are an embodiment of a haunting past that connects her sense of guilt to the secret the two share.

Sam soon uncovers their secret, however, and his actions subsequently turn malicious and irrational. Stricken by a frenzied fear of infection, Sam duct-tapes the cracks in the apartment windows, and rages when he finds that Eva has broken through the safety of the seal to steal away to the balcony for some fresh air. He locks her outside, but retrieves her later when she is unconscious and half-frozen. He brings her to the bedroom and lays her on the bed, where he undresses her and tucks her in under the covers. He undresses as well, down to his boxers, and gets into bed with her, presumably to help warm her with his body heat. At first, he huddles close to her, lovingly trying to revive her, but soon takes advantage of his wife's vulnerable state. She wakes to find that he has already initiated forced intercourse. She writhes in panic, knocking away the pillow she has been using to conceal the jar containing their aborted child, whom she named Jonas. The recurring presence of Jonas brings forth religious undertones in the film, including the evocation of the parable of Jonah and the whale, symbolically enclosed in the womb. The presence of Jonas also reinforces Eva's nostalgia for a place of origin, spurring her increasing withdrawal and even regression as she recalls the nurturing environment of her own womb—what Liotta has called "a symbol of the perfection of the beginnings" (Liotta 2009, 47). However, her fixation becomes a Gothic perversion of nostalgia, transforming the "canniness of the feminine" into a grotesque display of pain, and Sam's enraged reaction when he sees the jar (along with his later pursuit and capture of Eva) emphasizes the extent of its impact.

As in the other films discussed here, the bathroom is yet another significant site of violence and trauma for the female protagonist. Early in the
film, Eva continually seeks refuge and solitude in the bathroom, the smallest
space within the confines of the apartment. This room is the one Eva favours
the most for safety and self-reflection. She turns to this space (as she does to
the bedroom) when she is in need of time away from her husband, and for
gathering the resources to cope with her distress: medicine, a soak in the tub,
an opportunity to cleanse herself and sort through the trouble at hand. But it
is also the most powerful site in its display of the abject nature of her strife.

Prior to learning Eva's secret, during the first news broadcast that confirms the virus as a public health crisis, Sam prepares to leave on a business
trip and Eva prepares for her first day at her new job. A brief argument
ensues when they realize they cannot leave the premises (and thus cannot
escape each other or the tension between them). Sam informs her that he will
give her space and stay in what would have been Jonas's room. The mention
of the name of their deceased child sends her into the throes of an anxiety
attack. She escapes to the bathroom to fend off the worsening symptoms,
which are denoted by a piercing frequency. She tears open her blouse and
quickly slips out of her skirt, trying to free herself of her oppressive clothes
and shed the thoughts weighing on her mind. When the medication she
swallows eventually takes hold, she sinks down to the floor and cries. Eva is
desperate for relief, and she uses this space to shut out all that exists beyond
her. However, she cannot fully escape her reality, and soon the bathroom is
marred by scenes of terror.

Following the previous bloodied outburst from James at the dining table,
Sam runs Eva a bath to calm and cleanse her while he methodically dons
rubber gloves and gathers every contaminated item from the dining room.
Eva rests, soaking in the bathtub until she is confronted by abjection. Like
Laura in *Thanatomorphose*, Eva notices that strands of her hair are coming
loose in her hands. She panics further when she sees that her nails are bleeding and are peeling off her fingertips easily. Strings of blood leak from her
mouth as she coughs. She grabs a towel and rushes out of the tub to examine herself in the mirror, only to realize that all these terrifying things were
imagined. But there is evidence that her body is indeed at risk: she discovers
a small rash on her shoulder, a sign that she is infected and that the imagined
bodily decay will soon be a reality.

One of the most graphic scenes of violence that erupts within the "safe
space" of the home takes place in the bathroom as well: a flashback to the

disturbing scene at the root of her discomfort. Sam is away on a business trip, a photo shoot for a project Eva has been excluded from. In a phone conversation with her mother (Lynn Lowry), she expresses concerns about her modelling career, and about Sam's feelings toward her, as well as doubts about her pregnancy. Her mother's words fall short of comfort and reassurance and only cause Eva further unease. Determined to find relief at any cost, Eva leaves a distraught message for Sam about losing the baby. Upon hanging up, she enters the bathroom and carefully lies down in the shower stall. She removes her panties, and with a moment to consider her sonogram ("I'm so sorry, Jonas"), she performs a brutal self-abortion using blunt force and a bent coat hanger to penetrate her abdomen from within. The violence of this removal from "home" within the secure confines of the bathroom transforms the space and hints at the inevitable failure for it to be restored as a nostalgic place of origin for Eva. It is further tainted by the blood that seeps out and pools around her on the tiles as James arrives to investigate at Sam's request. He calls for an ambulance and, on seeing the coat hanger and all that it implies, he advises Eva that he helped her only for the sake of his friend, who he believes should know the truth. Incensed, Eva threatens James with a vow to lie about the nature of her miscarriage, to tell Sam that James tried to rape her. Through this intense flashback, the truth of their shared secret and the source of their tensions are revealed.

It is this hidden past—the return of the repressed—that brings about another moment of violence at the hands of her husband. Shortly after he learns of her secret, Sam lashes out, capturing Eva in the stairwell and holding her captive, tied to a chair in their dining room. He maniacally spouts religious quotations and engraves the word "liar" on her forehead as punishment for hiding the truth of her abortion. When she later manages to free herself, she stabs Sam with the same condemning coat hanger and bludgeons him to death, only to succumb to her own madness. She hallucinates Jonas's cries as she salvages and cares for the fetus in the bathroom. Only in catching a glimpse of herself in the bathroom mirror, splattered with her husband's blood, and bearing the crudely carved accusation on her forehead, does Eva truly recognize the severity of her state. Something is not right, and the earlier rash on her shoulder, which has blackened with necrosis, confirms it. She climbs into the bathtub armed with a box cutter and digs at the spreading black patches on her arm. Amid the pain of the moment, she passes out. She wakes some time later and wanders out of the bathroom as the infected James enters her apartment. Before he can question the scene before him,

Eva approaches him with a request: "Make me a baby." With this conclusion it is evident that the trauma she has suffered has caused an irreversible break with reality. Like Laura, Lucie, Anna, and many other "women who kill" in horror films, Eva is "emotionally withdrawn, unable to perform normal social engagement and the murders she commits are more an expression of inner torment than an act of violence" (Totaro 2014).

Conclusion

The female protagonists in *Thanatomorphose*, *Martyrs*, and *Dys*- share in the abject representation of an excruciating, unsettled existence visualized within the confines of the home. This symbolic home/womb becomes a paradoxical space: it is both a metaphor for a nostalgic desire to withdraw from the threatening world of men and hide in a female space of comfort, and an abject environment imbued with the disintegrated ego and rendered *unheimlich* through a rejection of the Symbolic realm of social responsibility. In other words, the home is at once the idealized domestic place to which the female character can retreat to find herself, and the Gothic ruin that confronts her with the inevitable breakdown of a body that fails to personify the authentic self. This confrontation is, in effect, necessary so as to "provoke thought in the viewer via our simultaneous loathing and fascination" (Lobos 2014) with the representation of the frustrated-feminine. As Carl Royer and Diana Royer describe in *The Spectacle of Isolation in Horror Films: Dark Parades* (2005), this disconnect is most often visualized through "the isolation of the island apartment tower combined with mass neuroses" (85), the "confinement of the single-room apartment" (89), but arguably, it is true of any setting in which the unsettled home, the *unheimlich*, manifests itself. As noted by Bernice Murphy in *The Suburban Gothic in American Popular Culture* (2009), horror "invariably begins at home," where "even the most ordinary-looking neighbourhood, or house, or family, has something to hide, and ... no matter how calm and settled a place looks, it is only ever a moment away from dramatic (and generally sinister) incident" (2). Indeed, a home haunted by malcontent invariably transforms from comforting sanctum into claustrophobic "survival space."

Notes

1   For further reading on the horror genre in Quebec cinema, please also see Freitag and Loiselle's "Tales of Terror in Quebec Popular Cinema: The Rise of the French Language Horror Film since 2000."

2   This is especially evident in examinations of the works of such Gothic authors as Shirley Jackson, as discussed, among others, by Wyatt Bonikowski (see the essay "Only One Antagonist: The Demon Love and the Feminine Experience in the Work of Shirley Jackson," *Gothic Studies* 15, no. 2); it is also prevalent in many films in the Quebec horror film tradition.

3   This discussion gives reference to Andrew Smith's illumination of this concept in his commentary on Shirley Jackson's work, pointing it out as a "version of the Female Gothic in a way that it implies 'what is really dangerous is a circumscribed life of domestic duties'" (qtd. in Bonikowski 2013, 76).

4   See Gina Freitag, "Unleashing the Furious Feminine: The Violence of Gender Discourse in Canadian Horror Cinema" (MA thesis, Carleton University, 2011).

5   In *The Monstrous-Feminine: Film, Feminism, Psychoanalysis* (London: Routledge, 1993), Barbara Creed outlines an argument "that when woman is represented as monstrous it is almost always in relation to her mothering and reproductive functions ... the archaic mother; the monstrous womb; the witch; the vampire; and the possessed woman" (7). She also looks at the monstrous-feminine in accordance with Freudian theory, that "woman's monstrousness is linked more directly to sexual desire than to the area of reproduction ... woman as the deadly *femme castratice*, the castrating mother and the vagina dentata" (7).

6   To be fair, it must be stated that Lê uses the term to describe an entirely different phenomenon related to nostalgic tendencies in some francophone Vietnamese postcolonial writing. See Lê, *Le Complexe de Caliban* (Paris: Bourgeois, 2005), 86.

MEN IN PAIN:
Home, Nostalgia, and Masculinity in Twenty-First-Century Quebec Film

Amy J. Ransom

The action comedy *Filière 13* (Patrick Huard, 2010) opens with the image of cop protagonist Thomas (Claude Legault) grimacing in pain, in the grip of agonizing migraines that have begun to interfere with his job perform-ance. His soon-to-be partners in crime-fighting, and brothers, Jean-François (Guillaume Lemay-Thivierge) and Benoît (Paul Doucet), also suffer from various job- and home-related maladies. This trio of Quebec's top leading men had already dealt with various forms of physical and mental pain in the earlier hit *Les 3 P'tits Cochons* (*The 3 L'il Pigs*, Patrick Huard, 2007) as they negotiated the pending death of their mother and their relationships with the other women in their lives: wives, daughters, lovers. These emblematic "new men" struggle with what Diane Lamoureux calls "une recomposition imprévue des rôles sociaux de sexe" in Quebec (Lamoureux 2001, 137). Thus, the "men in pain" characters discussed here grapple with changing profes-sional and familial expectations in twenty-first-century Québécois society, in which gender roles and expectations appear to have become unnavigable in the absence of the clear-cut guidelines traced for men and women by the now passé clerico-nationalist patriarchal tradition.

Whereas the above films use comedy to defuse the emotionally charged issues they explore, a number of other recent urban dramas and thrillers—including *20h17, rue Darling (8:17 p.m. Darling Street*, Bernard Émond, 2003), *Nitro* (Alain Desrochers, 2007), *La Ligne brisée* (Louis Choquette, 2008), *Détour* (Sylvain Guy, 2009), *Les 7 Jours du talion* (*7 Days*, Daniel Grou, 2010), *Décharge* (Benoît Pilon, 2011), and *Lac Mystère* (Érik Canuel, 2014), among others—take a more serious look at the theme of men in physical and emotional pain. These films, often reflective of the *film noir* revival in late twentieth- and early twenty-first-century cinemas (Conard 2007; Schwartz 2005), frequently involve a crime or an accident, with the male protagonist as an ambiguous figure, both victim and perpetrator. Frequently featuring the same small group of male leads (most notably, Luc Picard, Claude Legault, Guillaume Lemay-Thivierge, and David Boutin) and directed by some of the province's most popular and/or critically acclaimed directors, the corpus of films examined here, notwithstanding their different genres, all exploit the melodramatic mode in their dual engagement of the family in crisis and male victimhood and aggression. Drawing on scholarship that realigns the melodrama with the "male-oriented" genres of thriller, detective, and action films (Neale 1993; Staiger 2008), and shifting the focus of feminist scholarship on the melodrama from the female protagonist to the male, this chapter explores how these films deploy the spectacle of men in pain as symptomatic of a certain form of nostalgia, conceived as a longing for the lost home of traditional notions of the patriarchal family, with its clear-cut and hierarchical gender roles as the basis of the nation.

Melodrama and Nostalgia as Modes

Originally associated with pre-twentieth-century stage productions, the melodrama combined music with the conventions of the developing form of the drama, which involved the emotional intensity of classical tragedy but was set in contemporary, bourgeois society (Elsaesser [1972]1987; Gledhill 1987). Film studies in the United States appropriated the term in the 1970s and '80s to identify Hollywood "films (largely made in the 1940s and 1950s) which use the family and the social position of women as their narrative focus" and which expose "the tensions and contradictions that lie beneath the surface of post-war suburban American life" (Mercer and Shingler 2004, 2). Viewed as "women's film," the category of the family melodrama resonated particularly with feminist film scholars, including Laura Mulvey ([1977–78]1987), Tania Modleski ([1984]1987), Annette Kuhn ([1984]1987), and Christine Gledhill (1987). In 1993, however, Steve Neale proposed a dramatic revision to melodrama theory by returning to the term's coinage in early trade newspapers, in which it was originally linked to genres featuring and targeting men: "action thrillers with fast-paced narratives, episodic story-lines featuring violence, suspense and death-defying stunts. Dastardly villains, heroines in peril and daring adventurous heroes populated these films, their actions speaking louder than their words" (Mercer and Shingler 2004, 6). Significantly, not only do the twenty-first-century Québécois films analyzed here belong to these male-oriented genres, but the male protagonist reflects many of the same characteristics and dilemmas that feminist scholars attributed as unique to the female protagonists of 1940s and '50s Hollywood melodrama.

Janet Staiger's insightful essay "Film Noir as Male Melodrama: The Politics of Film Genre Labeling" (2008) takes these generic associations one step further and provides the theoretical underpinnings of the arguments I shall make here about twenty-first-century Quebec film. Following Neale's lead, Staiger examines Hollywood *film noir* specifically as melodrama; she argues that in contrast with trends in film studies looking at the "fallen woman" figure in the family melodrama, "some films might well be described as displaying a 'fallen-man' formula and being a male-centered melodrama" (73). This is precisely the trope that we see again and again in the corpus of films analyzed below, which share a number of other features with Staiger's corpus, including "the use of voice-over narration and flashback" (76), "some character flaw [which] propels the protagonist into adventure" (80), "narrative focus ... not on the explication of the crime but resolution of the character's choice-making" (81), and "music creates symbolic commentary" (85). Furthermore, unlike the Hollywood *film noir* made during "the era of the Production Code, [during which] resolutions had to fit conservative norms of moral justice" (82) with the result that "the resolution of the fallen-man story is morally unambiguous" (82), the twenty-first-century films from Quebec analyzed here frequently—although not always—conclude with moral ambiguity.

The thematic link between the melodramatic mode and nostalgia—the organizing theme of this volume—is, of course, the home and family. As Christine Sprengler (2009) explains, nostalgia has evolved over the centuries into its current conceptualization as an aesthetic mode (rather than a "genre," a trait it also shares with melodrama)[1], from its original conceptualization in the seventeenth century as a physical ailment, later diagnosed as a psychological disorder, through the nineteenth century (11–33). In this chapter, I largely invoke these earlier theories of nostalgia as pathology; the corpus examined here regales its audiences with visions of men suffering both physical pain and mental anguish that results largely from a sense of the protagonist's loss of and regret for "home."

Men in Pain

The man in pain has become a dominant trope of twenty-first-century Quebec national cinema,[2] and given the province's well-developed star system, it is not insignificant that the same actors appear repeatedly cast in this role. Indeed, Christine Gledhill (1991) makes compelling arguments linking critical interest in stardom to melodrama. Invoking the work of Richard Dyer and Andrew Britton, Gledhill argues here that "stars function as signs in a rhetorical system which works as melodrama" (207) and that "a major conceptual link between melodrama and stardom is their centrality to both systems of the 'person'" (208). Luc Picard (b. 1961), Claude Legault (b. 1963), David Boutin (b. 1969), and Guillaume Lemay-Thivierge (b. 1976) star in most of the films examined here, so I will introduce my corpus via descriptions of the "men in pain" roles assumed by these actors. Since, as Barry King (1991) asserts, "the theorization of the star [is seen as] as an interplay of representation and identification" (167), these actors' representations of "men in pain" play an important role in audience reception, and they have been chosen by their casting directors in part because they are believed to inspire identification on the part of Québécois men. These actors repeatedly portray characters who are in some way fallen, in a state of rupture with a certain ideal of home, suffering often both mentally and physically in their longing for a paradisial return; furthermore, they frequently struggle to assert their masculinity, often in opposition to stock filmic images of femininity.

In contrast to the classically handsome, Hollywood-style leading man Roy Dupuis (b. 1963), Luc Picard's average looks allow him in particular to portray Everyman characters, so that he easily fosters identification in male audiences. Having established his star image as a "man in pain" through roles in historical dramas by nationalist filmmaker Pierre Falardeau (1946– 2009), *Octobre* (1994) and *Le 15 février 1839* (*February 15, 1839*, 2002), in subsequent films Picard has portrayed an investigator, a cop, or a journalist struggling to unravel a mystery that has deep personal significance for the protagonist as well. This pattern recurs in *Le Dernier Souffle* [The Last Breath] (Richard Ciupka, 1999; see Santoro 2011), *Un dimanche à Kigali* [A Sunday in Kigali] (Robert Favreau, 2006), and *20h17, rue Darling*, in which reporter Gérard Langlois reconstructs the stories of his neighbours, who were killed in a fire that he coincidentally escaped. Langlois's fallen-man status is made immediately clear with an admission of his alcoholism: "Je m'appelle Gérard et j'suis alcoolique. J'suis sobre depuis six mois et deux jours. Normalement je devrais être mort" [My name's Gerard and I'm an alcoholic. I've been sober for six months and two days. I should probably be dead]. The pattern changes only slightly in Picard's directorial début *L'Audition* (2005), in which he plays a petty criminal rather than an investigator, but the film's structure hinges on a surprise ending that reveals that his death occurred at its beginning.

Like Picard, Claude Legault has come to specialize in men-in-pain roles, but his attractive, expressive face coupled with his short but sculpted, muscular frame has resulted in his frequent casting as a charismatic trickster. His portrayal of the charmingly tormented bouncer Marc Forest in *Minuit, le soir* (2005–6), directed by Daniel Grou (a.k.a. Podz) and co-written by Legault and Pierre-Yves Bernard, revealed to television audiences the full dramatic range of this actor. Forest was verbally and physically abused by his father when a child, leaving scars, and his pain manifests itself in bouts of rage, a character pattern that recurs in the recent hit cop show *19-2* (2011–15, also directed by Grou and co-written by Legault and Réal Bossé), and in a number of later big-screen roles. Legault's most serious man in pain is Dr. Bruno Hamel in *Les 7 Jours du talion*, based on a novel by Patrick Senécal (see Freitag and Loiselle 2013). Unable to express the emotional pain of having lost his daughter, Hamel channels it into a cold, methodic rage that allows him to kidnap and torture her rapist and murderer, Anthony Lemaire (Martin Dubreuil—himself a second-tier man-in-pain specialist).

Tall and blonde, David Boutin could portray traditional heroes, as he did in the popular feel-good film *La Grande Séduction* [Seducing Dr. Lewis] (Jean-François Pouliot, 2003). His astonishing range, however, situates him more frequently in quirky men-in-pain roles, such as an ultraviolent biker in *Hochelaga* (Michel Jetté, 2000) and Jacques le Schizo in *Histoires de pen (Inside)* (Michel Jetté, 2002). This pattern continues in *La Ligne brisée* and *Décharge*, which refers in its title both to the literal trash that Pierre Dalpé (Boutin), owner of a successful disposal business, picks up off the streets of Montreal and to the metaphorical treatment of the young runaway, Ève (Sophie Desmarais), whom he tries to help. He risks his wife and family as he attempts to exorcise his own past demons of drug use, shooting Ève's pimp, but the act is seen as self-defence. At the film's conclusion, Pierre has accepted an ultimatum from his wife (Isabelle Richer), and he drives the family van past Ève wandering listless, probably high, out of a bar, suggesting that his attempted intervention has come to naught.

Guillaume Lemay-Thivierge's handsome features, dark hair and eyes, and sculpted (but not imposing) physical form allow him to represent a per-haps accessible ideal of Québécois masculine beauty that appeals to male and female audiences alike. In addition to playing the second male lead in *Détour* (Roch), *Filière 13* (Jean-François), and *Les 3 P'tits Cochons*,[3] he has also por-trayed Sébastien Messier's (Boutin) former best friend turned boxing oppon-ent Danny Demers in *La Ligne brisée*. Although a mediocre, even troubling film in a number of ways, I posit the Lemay-Thivierge vehicle *Nitro* as a case in point for the Québécois male melodrama.

Nitro is best described as an action film, packed with high-speed chase sequences; the protagonist, Julien (Lemay-Thivierge), first appears as a con-struction worker and a (semi-)responsible husband and father. Structurally complex, the film forces viewers to piece together his backstory through its non-linear narrative: formerly a reckless dragster known as Mad Max, seeking only the next adrenaline rush, Julien's current source of pain derives from his wife's precarious health. Hospitalized, she awaits a heart transplant; Julien desperately concocts a ridiculous plan that involves a return to his wild past. With the collusion of a hospital bureaucrat (Réal Bossé), he plans to murder a known criminal, harvest the heart, and deliver it to the hospital to save his dying wife! What could go wrong with such a perfect(ly misguided) plan? Not only does the "criminal" turn out to be an undercover cop (Tony Conte),[4] but Julien is chased around Montreal by the henchmen of L'Avocat (Martin Matté), a nightclub owner and organized crime boss. He recruits his ex-girlfriend, Morgane (Lucie Laurier), a former stripper turned drag racer and now a professional stock car racer, to help him escape his foes (police and criminals alike) and deliver the heart.

The sources of Julien/Max's pain are multiple in this seriously misguided piece of entertainment, written by Benoît Guichard based on director Alain Desrosiers's idea, which opens with a public service announcement to pro-mote organ donation. Flashbacks reveal that he lost his own mother when relatively young and that as a young man, he had fallen in love with Morgane, who betrayed him by sleeping with L'Avocat (The Lawyer). During a street race with Morgane as his opponent, Max has a serious accident that leads him to his true love—he meets his future wife, Alice, in the hospital. Her chronic heart problems trigger the painful crises acted out in the film; but the "happy" ending guarantees her survival, since Morgane's death provides her with a bona fide donor heart. Julien/Max's attempts to preserve his home and family intact, though, ultimately lead him to lose both—the film closes with him in prison.

Home (and Its Violation or Loss)

As already suggested, home and the family are core thematics for the artistic modes of nostalgia and melodrama; they thus play key roles in the plotting of the present corpus. The fallen-man protagonist's suffering is always linked to a problematic relationship with home and the family: either the current home and family situation is a source of dissatisfaction, or they are violated by an external or even internal source. In terms of dissatisfaction, either the home life is unhappy *or* (more rarely) the protagonist is initially alone and longs to establish a home and family. In other cases, the protagonist enjoys an apparently satisfying home and family life until an external force disrupts it. Sometimes the protagonist's own human imperfection leads him to self-destruct his happy home and family life because of vague internal impulses. These films typically follow the equilibrium–disequilibrium–equilibrium narrative thrust that Sprengler (2009, 73) associates with nostalgia films, but in twenty-first-century films the exposition of this narrative rarely follows a straightforward chronology. Indeed, these films tend to commence at a moment of rupture.

Thus, several protagonists are already in pain as the film begins, although this is sometimes an attenuated pain, even numbness, as they live in a generally unhappy state of dissatisfaction with their current home and family life. *Détour's* Léo Huff (Picard) is the henpecked husband of a childless invalid wife and is sexually harassed by his domineering female boss. The mild-mannered male secretary is an easy target for con artists, the sultry Lou (Isabelle Guérard) and redneck Roch (Lemay-Thivierge), whom he picks up when their truck breaks down. Convinced by Lou that she is abused and wants to start over, Léo first violates his marriage vows by sleeping with her and then violates his own home, murdering his wife when she refuses to sign the financial papers that would allow him to leave with Lou. Equilibrium in this neo-*noir* film is restored by death (Lou shoots Léo and will run off alone with his money), as it is in another Picard vehicle, *L'Audition*.

A handful of these male melodramas begin with the protagonist alone and, consciously or not, longing for a home and family; this is the case with

Thomas (Legault) in *Filière 13* and in *La Ligne brisée*, in which aspiring boxer Sébastien (Boutin) has lost everything after fleeing the scene of a hit-and-run and now begins to seek redemption. His physical therapist, with whom he begins an erotic relationship, turns out to have been his victim, Cécile (Fanny Mallette). In *20h17, rue Darling*, as well, Gérard Langlois (Picard) was living alone when his apartment building burned down at the exact hour and on the street referenced in the film's title; his inquiry into uncovering what happened and why, and perhaps finding out why fate spared him from the conflagration, brings him out of his isolation and into contact with others.

In contrast, *L'Audition*'s Louis Tremblay (Picard) is actually becoming increasingly happy in his home life; indeed, his girlfriend Suzie (Suzanne Clément) is pregnant, and he is exploring an acting career—hence the film's title—in order to leave behind his criminal past. The happy home he longs for appears just within his reach when an element from his past intervenes, shooting him dead. *L'Audition* thus reverses the typical trajectory of the man's fall, in that rather than an Everyman figure falling into a crime, for Louis a life of crime is the equilibrium, the prospect of a "normal" family life disequilibrium, and his murder a restoration of equilibrium. A similar external violation of the home and family occurs, of course, in *Les 7 Jours du talion* when Anthony Lemaire murders Bruno Hamel's (Legault) daughter.

The comedies *Filière 13* and *Les 3 P'tits Cochons*, as well as the drama *Décharge*, depict an initial state of equilibrium in which pre-fallen men lead a superficially happy family life. In contrast to Léo in *Détour*, who seems justified in leaving his odious wife (Suzanne Champagne), these protagonists have attractive wives and mostly happy, affectionate children. They do not fall nearly so far as the protagonists of the thrillers and *films noirs*, but some nagging internal itch leads them to violate the happiness of their home and family life. Actor Paul Doucet completes the trio formed with Claude Legault and Guillaume Lemay-Thivierge in the two comedies discussed here; in *Filière 13*, he is Thomas and Jean-François's superior officer, and his wife leaves him because he continually places his job before his family. In the same film, Jean-François's (Lemay-Thivierge) increasing neurosis related to his stage fright destabilizes his marriage (his wife is unhappy and nearly leaves him). In *Les 3 P'tits Cochons*, as the eldest of the three brothers, Paul Doucet's character, Rémy Quintal, is perhaps the most *cochon* since he has both heterosexual and homosexual affairs; although his relationship with his teenage daughter is a source of dissatisfaction, there appears to be no reason for him to be unhappy with his beautiful wife (Sophie Prégent). Given his attraction to a younger woman, the film suggests his bisexuality rather than a closeted homosexuality, although he certainly keeps his ongoing affair with a male neighbour a secret. On the one hand, the film's depiction of a lead character engaged in a homosexual affair can be interpreted as merely another aspect of his overweaning sexual appetite and thus an indication of contemporary Quebec's official ideology of inclusion. On the other, its deployment of stereotyping of the middle-aged male homosexual couple for comedic effect suggests society's lingering ambivalence and the continued prevalence of heteronormative images of masculinity. Following their elder brother's example, both Mathieu (Legault) and Christian (Lemay-Thivierge) also cheat on attractive wives (Isabelle Richer and Julie Perreault, respectively). Whereas Mathieu is able to repair the damage done, Christian's masculinity appears to have been too impaired by his domineering, police-officer wife to allow for reconciliation. Again, the film deploys for comedic effect characters who do not conform to traditional gender roles through the trope of the henpecked husband; the film's sequel provides redemption for Christian and a target for his unanchored libido via a steamy affair with his (older) sister-in-law, Dominique (Prégent).[5]

The dissatisfaction with the current equilibrium in relation to home and family life thus triggers a disruptive event that attenuates the protagonist's "nostalgia," literally, his pain and longing for the lost "home." In many cases, that loss is a literal one, for he has left or been kicked out of the family home; but it is also metaphorical, the "home" also figuring a lost sense of security, a compromised masculinity in a contemporary Quebec in which (the official version of) home life is no longer based on "an agrarian model of manhood which was tied to the land and the family characterized by self-restraint and piety" or even the more modern urban model of "national manhood" developed in the early twentieth century, according to Jeffery Vacante (2017, 3). These films' nostalgia for clearer definitions of masculinity thus participates to a certain extent in the "mouvement masculiniste" that has developed to counter what is perceived as a contemporary crisis in masculinity in Quebec, as discussed by Mélissa Blais and Francis Dupuis-Déri (2008).

Nostalgia (Pain and Longing)

This chapter adopts earlier, medicalized definitions of nostalgia derived from its etymology as pain suffered because of longing for a lost home (Boym 2001, 3; Huffer 1998, 14; Sprengler 2009, 12); before we develop further how the fallen-man protagonists' pain derives from their loss of or longing for home, it is worth briefly noting that some of these films can also be described as "nostalgia films," following contemporary definitions. Critics of Québécois film have identified two types of "nostalgia film" unique to the province: films and television series set in the late nineteenth- and early twentieth-century colonization period like *Séraphin, un homme et son péché* [Séraphin, a Man and His Sin] (Charles Binamé, 2003), *Le Survenant* [The Outlander] (Érik Canuel, 2005), and *Aurore* (Luc Dionne, 2005) (see Bédard 2007–8), some of which Liz Czach discusses in her chapter; and an even larger corpus of films set in the 1960s, including (among others) *Maman est chez le coiffeur* [Mommy's at the Hairdresser's] (Léa Pool, 2008), *C'est pas moi, je le jure!* [It's Not Me, I Swear!] (Philippe Falardeau, 2008), and *Un été sans point ni coup sûr* [A No Hit, No Run Summer] (Francis Leclerc, 2008) (see Charles 2009; Clément 2010; Ransom 2019). Although the male melodramas examined here are all set in contemporary Quebec (or at least the filmmaker's vision of it), the very scenarios of these male melodramas often express either nostalgia for film genres of the past (such as the neo-*noir Détour*) or the perceived simplicity of family structures and gender roles of the past.

As seen in the previous section, again and again, a male protagonist, sometimes through his own doing, but at other times through no fault of his own, suffers a "fall" from an idealized, pre-lapsarian image of home. Léo Huff leaves an unhappy home with every intention of returning, but events take him on a *Détour* and to a point of no return; the situation of Julien (*Nitro*) is somewhat similar, although he has willingly planned the criminal activities that lead to his fall. The lonely protagonists Thomas (*Filière 13*), Christian (*Les 3 P'tits Cochons*),[6] and Sébastien (*La Ligne brisée*) long for a home; indeed, Gérard (*20h17, rue Darling*) has literally lost his home—his apartment building burned down. Most clearly, the married men who lose their families because their wives perceive that they place career first (Louis in *Le Dernier Souffle* and Benoît in *Filière 13*) or who risk their happy family lives because of some internal compulsion to cheat on their wives (Pierre in *Décharge*, Mathieu in *Les 3 P'tits Cochons*) experience a loss of home, often literally as they are kicked out by the angry spouse. In the latter, these fictional men's sexual temptations appear symptomatic of a slightly different form of nostalgia; their yearning here is to recapture the sexual excitement of their youth, the thrill of romance and passion that they believe themselves to have lost in the everyday routine of monogamous family life.

Les 3 P'tits Cochons offers a particularly interesting example of how long-ing for a lost home plays out because of its unique focus on three brothers who jeopardize their home and family lives precisely because of a shared family crisis: their mother lies comatose in the hospital. Nostalgia has been particularly linked with psychological neurosis (Elsaesser [1972]1987, 58–59) and with the longing for the lost home connected to a fantasized desire for reunion with the pre-Oedipal mother (Huffer 1998, 16–19). This film suggests a cause-and-effect connection between the stresses caused by their mother's hospitalization and Rémi, Mathieu, and Christian's "act-ing out," which jeopardizes their own happy homes. The underlying loss of home, then, is the impending threat of the mother's death, perhaps related to the "womb nostalgia" phenomenon explored by Gina Freitag in the previ-ous chapter; home-movie style flashbacks punctuate the film, reinforcing the notion of the Quintal boys' idyllic 1960s to '70s childhood. Indeed, the young-est, least mature brother Christian (Lemay-Thivierge) literally re-enacts this longing —he repeatedly lies down on the hospital bed alongside his moth-er's inert form, seeking comfort and literally dialoguing with her through the magic of postmodern film, which externalizes Christian's interior reality by depicting the comatose matriarch as magically awake and conversing with her son. At the same time, the film comments on the delayed advent of mature adulthood for twenty-first-century Québécois, the baby boomers' offspring, raised in a climate of permissive prosperity instead of the rigorous discipline and self-denial of the pre–Quiet Revolution Catholic past. In its very title, *Les 3 P'tits Cochons* comically alludes to these men's difficulty growing up via a children's tale about adult responsibility, directly referenced in the film as it is read to Mathieu's children at bedtime. The Quintal brothers' childish behaviours represent a way of expressing their longing to return to the home of their childhood triggered by their fear of their mother's loss, a generational turning point that forces them into the unwanted role of responsible adults.

Reaching maturity in a period of evolving gender roles, however, is particularly difficult since these protagonists are denied the simpler task of merely reproducing models of masculinity set by their fathers' genera-tion, a generation frequently accused of being absent, particularly following Guy Corneau's highly publicized *Absent Fathers, Lost Sons* (Corneau 1989). For example, in *Les 3 P'tits Cochons*, we never see or hear mention of the boys' father. Furthermore, a generation of feminist discourse has accused the paternal instinct of oppressing both mothers and children through its critique of the clerico-nationalist model of the patriarchal family (see Baillargeon 2012).

Masculinities

The sense of loss experienced by the protagonists of these male melodramas, the nostalgia for the lost home, is distinctly tied to gender roles and relationships in a number of ways. In the most obvious and basic sense, these films' plotlines are centred on a male protagonist and apply the melodramatic mode to film genres largely associated with a male spectatorship: action comedy (*Filière 13*, *Les 3 P'tits Cochons*), *film noir* (*Détour*, *Lac Mystère*), the thriller (*Les 7 Jours du talion*), and the sport film (car racing in *Nitro*, boxing in *La Ligne brisée*). They interpellate a male spectatorship to identify with a protagonist cast by a sympathetic Québécois actor who easily reads as either an Everyman figure (Picard) *or* an idealized self (Legault, Lemay-Thivierge).

Not only are men the subject of these films in the sense that the films are about an individual man suffering from a problem that affects men "in general," but men are also the object of the cinematic gaze in this corpus. Although women may be featured, as wives and mothers, and also as *femmes fatales*,[7] and although the latter may serve as beautiful objects of the protagonist's desire, the films studied here focus more directly on close-ups of the male actor's visage, frequently revealing images of his anguished face. Particularly for Legault and Lemay-Thivierge, who clearly meet regularly with personal trainers, the actor's body is also frequently featured as both an object of desire for the female spectator, and an object on which pain is inflicted. In a review of *Les 3 P'tits Cochons 2*, for example, one critic underscores the body's significance, noting that Lemay-Thivierge appears frequently "en bedaine" [shirtless], observing that "Oui, mesdames et messieurs, il est *cut, cut, cut*" [Yes, ladies and gentlemen, he is cut, cut, cut] (Meunier 2016). Not insignificantly, the English-language expression for a sculpted abdomen, usually obtained through great physical effort, also refers to painful injury. These filmed images contribute to a certain construction of masculinity, one that allows perhaps for a Latinate or Gallic emotional expressivity, but one that also engages the rhetoric of martyrdom and victimhood long current in the French Canadian/Québécois context.

These men's mental anguish appears written clearly not only in close-ups of their sometimes handsome but now distorted facial features, but also on their bodies. These men in pain suffer beatings, and sometimes shooting and stabbing, resulting in bloodshed and bruises, with further pain incurred during medical treatment. They also mete out suffering on other men, which usually results in moral anguish; for example, during the organ harvesting scene in *Nitro*, Julien/Max's ethical dilemma is writ large on his face, as he must make the fateful decision to take another man's life in order to save his wife. Although he does a better job of masking his own pain, the more superficially stoic Dr. Bruno Hamel (Legault) externalizes the pain of his daughter's loss by physically torturing her sequestered killer during *Les 7 Jours du talion*. The painful loss originally felt by Pierre Dalpé (Boutin) in *Décharge* was that of his sister, who died of a drug overdose as a teenager; the film focuses in medium close-up on the features of both Boutin and his teen-age avatar, played by Charles-Alexandre Dubé (a man in pain in training).

Particularly illustrative of this phenomenon is the boxing film *La Ligne brisée*. Through its depiction of the hypermasculine sport, it necessarily offers viewers the spectacle of its two male leads, Boutin and Lemay-Thivierge, slugging it out, sweating and bleeding, but also emotionally stressed as they contemplate and disagree about how to handle the hit-and-run. It connects its contemporary men-in-pain protagonists with their forebears via its inescapable invocation of the province's film canon and the iconic sport films *La Lutte* (Michel Brault, Marcel Carrière, Claude Fournier, Claude Jutra, 1961) and *Golden Gloves* (Gilles Groulx, 1961). These Quiet Revolution–era films produced by founding fathers of Quebec national cinema working at the National Film Board/Office National du Film similarly connect the national identity crisis to a crisis in manhood and the desire to reassert a hegemonic masculinity on the part of French Canadian men *en passe de devenir des Québécois*. Louis Choquette's more recent film invokes a similar contemporary crisis while at the same time expressing nostalgia for what might be read as Quebec's golden age of self-assertion through the 1960s campaigns for self-determination.[8]

Significantly, through its medical origins, nostalgia proved historically to be a specifically male malady: a longing for home suffered by soldiers serving in foreign lands that manifested itself as both mental and physical symptoms. As seen above, the protagonists of these films have become alienated from their homes and often appear under siege, embattled in their current situations. Julien/Max in *Nitro* is running both from police and from criminals, attempting to complete his mission of delivering the stolen heart for transplant. As law enforcement officers, Thomas and Jean-François serve as the infantrymen of modern urban life, but when removed from their regular duties they are in a sense exiled as questions about their performance in their usual jobs force them into more banal surveillance duties. Dr. Bruno Hamel, exiling himself from the family home, takes his prisoner to a remote cabin for the seven days he intends to use in meting out his own form of justice for his daughter's death. But above all, the protagonists' painful situations derive from and reveal the contradictory roles the transition from traditional Québécois society to a modern and now postmodern society has forced upon both men and women, who are now free to but also burdened with the task of writing new roles for themselves (see Baillargeon 2012; Lamoureux 2001; and Vacante 2006 and 2017 for discussions of gender and national identity in Quebec).

According to Laura Mulvey ([1977–78]1987), "ideological contradiction is the overt mainspring and specific content of melodrama" (75); thus the melodramatic mode reveals the contradictions in a society's dominant ideology, even serving as "a safety valve for ideological contradictions centred on sex and the family" (75). Following Mulvey, I read these Québécois male melodramas as dealing precisely with the contradictions inherent in lingering constructions of masculinity inherited from the past, when men are confronted with late twentieth- and twenty-first-century revisions to the masculine ideal in light of feminism, gay rights, and other anti-patriarchal movements, coupled with ongoing expectations about fatherhood and the monogamous nuclear family. These contradictions place the contemporary Québécois man in a number of double binds, which are underscored in the male melodrama, which concludes in a "no exit" fashion, usually having failed to resolve these issues. Only comedy in the melodramatic mode tends toward a "happy ending."

Except for Léo Huff in *Détour*, the protagonists of these films frequently seem to reflect the once-held and still lingering ideal of hegemonic masculinity. In *Gender and Power* (1987), R.W. Connell defines hegemonic masculinity as "the culturally idealized form of masculine character" that links masculinity with "the subordination of women, the marginalization of gay men, and ... to toughness and competitiveness"(Connell 1990, 94). The term vividly suggests an encroaching aggression that seeks power and control over others, a conception of masculinity that aligns clearly with some of the characters in this corpus. Sébastien in *La Ligne brisée* is a handsome man, a successful boxer who (prior to his fall) demonstrates his sovereignty by defeating other men in physical combat and seducing women; similarly, Julien/Max exhibits his masculinity by winning a series of drag races, thus displaying his nerves of steel and superior cunning (by how he times his nitrous oxide injectors). It goes without saying that policemen—Legault's roles in *Filière 13* and *19-2*, Picard's in *Omertá* and *Le Dernier Souffle*—frequently appear as emblems of Western masculinity, either as heroic ideals or as icons of masculinity gone awry. Investigative journalists, like the ones Picard plays in *20h17, rue Darling* and *Un dimanche à Kigali*, have taken on a similar function: they use their intelligence and courage to uncover the truth, braving war zones and rooting out injustice at home.

From the initial situation of equilibrium, in which the protagonist's masculinity appears to be unquestioned, the dramatic event—the fall, so to speak—frequently involves a *lèse masculinité*, a wound to his manhood. The image of severed fingers discussed by André Loiselle in his contribution to this book immediately comes to mind as a vivid metaphor for this painful emasculation. Although it is not my intention to develop this in detail here, melodrama has been linked to castration (Elsaesser [1972]1987, 10; Nowell-Smith qtd. in Modleski [1984]1987, 327); these films' drama often appears to follow the path of the protagonist attempting to recover a manhood that has been lost. Léo Huff's masculinity appeared non-existent to begin with, his wife and boss having nagged any masculine agency out of him; his adventure with Lou and his attempts to confront Roch represent his desire to "be a man" again. Dr. Bruno Hamel's daughter has been taken from him; as the head of the family, he has failed in his masculine duties by failing to protect her; he feels that only by punishing the man who stole her from him can he regain that sense of mastery. In *Les 3 P'tits Cochons*, Legault's character has also lost control of his situation, although in a less sensational manner: his wife's poor business skills are placing a strain on the family budget, and the tensions in the couple then lead him into the temptation to cheat on her. The film satirizes the hegemonic masculinity he briefly assumes during the crisis period: a debt recovery agent, he aggressively berates his clients. For Julien/Max in *Nitro*, as perhaps for Sébastien in *La Ligne brisée*, the combination of an external tragedy (the former's wife's heart trouble, the latter's hit-and-run) and the overall condition of these men's oppression by the system undermine their manhood, so they take action to recover it.

The melodrama appears to be a particularly apt form, then, for such expressions of male frustration. Thomas Elsaesser ([1972]1987) observes not only that "one of the characteristic features of melodramas in general is that they concentrate on the point of view of the victim" (64), but also that "pathos is the result of a skillfully displaced emotional emphasis ... frequently used in melodramas to explore psychological and sexual repression, usually in conjunction with the theme of inferiority" (67). The Québécois "man in pain" film focalizes the narrative precisely through the point of view of the male victim protagonist: *Les 7 Jours du talion* elides a mother's pain at the loss of her daughter in order to follow the father's grief trajectory; *La Ligne brisée* shifts attention away from the female victim of the hit-and-run accident to focus on the pain of the men in the car that struck her. Furthermore, it engages problems of psychological repression and feelings of inferiority, frequently coupled with issues surrounding the man in pain's sexuality. While some protagonists, such as Léo Huff in *Détour*, clearly suffer from a repressed sexuality (which, in his case, the transgressive situation with Lou unleashes), for others, like the Quintal brothers in *Les 3 P'tits Cochons*, sexual excess is symptomatic of dysfunction.

Of course, the misguided actions taken by the protagonist of the male melodrama in a desperate attempt to recover his lost manhood reveal the contradictions in contemporary Québécois society concerning gender roles and expectations. On the one hand, in many cases the protagonist in the male melodrama can be read as a typical Québécois loser, an archetypal figure in the province's culture that has proven difficult to shake. It seems that even after most of the economic and cultural battles undertaken to reposition the French-speaking majority in Quebec as "maîtres chez nous" have been won, without political sovereignty the myth of the colonized, oppressed French Canadian prevails in certain sectors. Thus, particularly since the 1960s *prise de conscience* and the rise of the sovereigntist movement, the Québécois loser has been an omnipresent character in film and literature.[9] This figure's disempowerment clearly reveals the cultural contradiction of the disenfranchised *man* within a patriarchal society.

The ideological contradictions regarding gender roles in Quebec and North America become quite clear when progressive discourses from the fields of feminist theory, gender studies, and sociology, which frequently critique hegemonic masculinity and the patriarchal family, rejecting traditional feminine roles as too limiting, come face to face with the popular media's often conservative representations of gender. In the North American media market, Québécois viewers continue to receive Hollywood images of hegemonic male heroes, and in spite of a snowballing discourse to the contrary, a large part of North American society associates manhood with physical power, sexual attractiveness, and financial security. The real man defends what is "his" (both people and property), confronting injustice head-on at both the personal and social levels, using his intelligence and his physical prowess. Unfortunately, not only is this ideal of masculine agency an unrealistic, unattainable model for most North American men, but there is also a considerable social discourse contradicting this image. For minority men—be they African American in the United States or francophone in Canada (see, for example, Garfield 2010; Vacante 2017)—a long history of oppression makes this goal even harder to attain. The Québécois male melodrama reveals this contradiction between a centuries-long construction of masculinity as described above, and another few centuries of an ethnic mythology of belonging to an oppressed people, and finally a revised late twentieth-century image of how masculinity "should" be more sensitive, willing to compromise, and accept women as equals in both the public and private domains.

Further exacerbating the problem is the long-standing "double standard" for boys and girls, coupled with men's need to assume a responsible role in what continues to be a patriarchal society despite real and nominal achievements by feminist movements in Quebec. The notion that "boys will be boys" that subtends Western society remains, coupled with the extension of adolescence well into their thirties and forties for many men and women today. Conflicts with notions of responsible male adulthood linger from patriarchy, albeit revised for the twenty-first century. The characters in these films are frequently extended adolescents who continue to apply the "boys will be boys" excuse to their behaviour, a notion reinforced by popular media portrayals of sexy bad-boy characters precisely like those played by Lemay-Thivierge and Legault. Having been raised to believe that their antics are not that serious but rather natural to a healthy young man, as married adult men they find it difficult to change these irresponsible habits to become responsible husbands and fathers. Furthermore, the double standard of sexual desire and behaviour continues to hold sway; the Western norm of the monogamous nuclear family stands in contradiction to received notions that men need an outlet for their sexual desires and that it is impossible for men to be monogamous.

A "Typically" Québécois Genre?

The "male melodrama" thus reveals the double bind faced not just by Québécois but by all North American men in the twenty-first century: continually bombarded with media messages that valorize traditional forms of hegemonic masculinity and that either valorize or trivialize male misbehaviour through the "boys will be boys" axiom or the sexual double standard (it's okay for men to cheat because their sex drive is more active and challenging to control), men are nonetheless expected to "grow up," to assume the role of responsible adult, to adopt a more measured form of masculinity that is not based on female oppression, and to embrace monogamy and fatherhood. Since this situation prevails to one degree or another in all of North America and much of the West, what makes the "male melodramas" examined here a particularly Québécois cinematic form?

Thomas Elsaesser ([1972]1987) asserts in his groundbreaking reassessment of melodrama that "the media and literary forms which have habitually embodied melodramatic situations have changed considerably in the course of history and, further, they differ from country to country" (44). Elsaesser also associates various historical booms in melodramatic forms with times of social crisis, connecting them to evolving "codes of morality and consciousness" (45). In particular, he connects the mid-twentieth-century Hollywood family melodrama to the form's theatrical development in post-Revolutionary France, during a period of "the struggle of a morally and emotionally emancipated bourgeois consciousness against the remnants of feudalism" (45). In the contemporary Québécois context, I read the current male melodrama boom as culturally specific by linking it to gendered discourses surrounding the construction of Quebec nationalism (see Lamoureux 2011; Vacante 2006; 2017) and to the perceived loss of the Catholic Church (chronicled by Loiselle in his chapter), which had once provided the province's inhabitants with a clear moral compass and a distinct set of gender roles for the family as the basis of the nation. Furthermore, Québécois society since the 1980s has increasingly embraced neoliberal capitalism; thus, along with increased secularization, in the late twentieth and early twenty-first centuries, Quebec society has seen a massive bourgeoisification. Formerly viewed as a predominantly traditional and agricultural society (through 1945) and then as an urban proletariat (since 1945), since around 2000 the province has increasingly projected the image of itself as a suburban, white-collar, middle-class nation.

Christine Gledhill's discussion of the link between star systems and melodrama is also useful in its engagement of the ethical concerns addressed in male melodrama: "melodrama sets out to demonstrate within the transactions of everyday life the continuing operation of a Manichean battle between good and evil which infuses human actions with ethical consequences and therefore with significance" (Gledhill 1991, 209). In the almost complete absence of references to the Catholic Church, the corpus of films examined here engages its protagonists precisely in moral dilemmas, in which external battles between good and evil (the protagonist and the "bad guys") are mirrored in internal battles played out within the protagonist's conscience as he makes the questionable choices that lead to his fall, choices sometimes made because he is seeking to serve (what he perceives as) a greater good. Hence the frequency with which the melodramatic mode appears in film genres that thematize crime and punishment, such as the action film, the thriller, the horror film, and the police drama. Twenty-first-century iterations of such battles, however, have become increasingly complex as the black and white of good and evil, God versus Satan, of Catholic ideology become increasingly blurred into fifty shades of grey. Thus the male melodrama frequently portrays its victim protagonist, a generally "good" guy, becoming involved with the forces of evil and making decisions that increasingly soil him, as well: abused husband and employee Léo Huff descends from professional insubordination to sexual infidelity to murder in *Détour*; respected physician and family man Dr. Bruno Hamel becomes a kidnapper, torturer, and nearly a murderer, for example.

Les 3 P'tits Cochons calls attention to the moral ambiguity and reversals inherent in the male melodrama already in its title, which obviously refers to the children's tale of the three little pigs, metaphorically comparing these three brothers to the prey of the Big Bad Wolf. But the term *cochon* in French as in English has numerous colloquial nuances, related in particular to sexuality; whereas in English we might think of someone as a "sexist pig," in French something that is *cochon* is sexually inflected. Of course, the three brothers depicted here are guilty of being both irresponsible and horny—they have succcumbed precisely to the contradictions about male sexual roles inherent in Western society in general and Quebec society in particular, and behave as if they cannot control their sexual appetites. While they do not murder anyone, their behaviours are repeatedly ethically questionable. Mathieu (Claude Legault) begins a sexual affair with a female colleague at work, the single brother Christian (Guillaume Lemay-Thivierge) uses his position as a martial arts instructor to have an affair with a girl barely over legal age, and Rémi (Paul Doucet) not only contemplates cheating on his wife with a younger woman, but also is shown in a long-term homosexual affair with a neighbour. Gledhill observes that "the melodramatic persona is totally committed to living out his or her dominant desires, despite moral and social taboo or inter-personal conflict" (1991, 212). Clearly, the Quintal brothers do precisely that.

Another of Elsaesser's arguments hinges upon melodrama as a channelling of discussions about social injustice on a wider scale into plots concerning the microcosm of the family. Significantly, in an era when the province's institutional film critics are lamenting the decline of a tradition of engaged cinema in favour of increased commercialization (Barrette 2004; Loiselle 1999), we see the rise of the male melodrama in Quebec. As Elsaessar argued in 1972 (1987), "the persistence of the melodrama might indicate the ways in which popular culture has not only taken note of social crises and the fact that the losers are not always those who deserve it most, but has also resolutely refused to understand social change in other than private contexts and emotional terms" ([1972]1987, 47). Elsaesser's analysis here can be fruitfully applied to the films in the present corpus, most of which focus precisely upon private dramas centred on the home and family, but which at times only hint at a larger system of oppression in which the protagonist victim is trapped. *Nitro* provides an example of this: Julien/Max's drama results from his misguided decision to solve his family's problem of the imminent loss of its wife and mother, Alice, by murdering to obtain a heart for her transplant. One reason he feels compelled to do so is linked to the apparent contradiction in Canada's socialized medicine system, which should provide adequate care to all, but which is still constrained by capitalist market concerns regarding the medical professional's labour. As explained to him by the medical administrator (Réal Bossé), there are not enough organs to go around because it costs money to keep potential donors hooked to life support until their organs are needed, and in addition, one has to pay the doctors to perform expensive extraction surgeries.

I conclude by returning to the question of nostalgia. In addition to an often literal expression of longing for a lost home, through their depictions of men in pain the male melodramas of twenty-first-century Quebec also express longing for a return to an earlier time. Québécois men appear in these films to be suffering victims, at a loss in the contemporary world, longing for the earlier ideological system of clerico-nationalist patriarchy that allotted them greater agency and privilege and offered clear gender roles for men and women, which purportedly made negotiating one's own identity and one's relationships with others less complex and conflict-ridden. Furthermore, given the ethical dilemmas found in these films, they also express nostalgia for an idealized simpler time when good and bad were more easily distinguishable (when cops were good and criminals were bad, for example; or when doctors saved lives without concern for compensation) and when the stipulations of the Catholic Church and its teachings gave very clear guidelines for personal action. The men in pain of these films, then, appear sadly symptomatic of "ce passé qui ne passe pas'" [this past that won't pass] discussed by Bédard (2007–8) in relation to successful historical films, that is, the lingering hold of the French Canadian past on the Québécois present. By revealing the contradictions inherent in a contemporary Quebec society in transition, however, the male melodrama offers a glimmer of resistant potential even in its conservative nostalgia.

Notes

1   As it is used here, rather than identifying a specific film genre, "the term [melodrama] is better conceived as a mode which embraces a range of Hollywood genres" (Gledhill 1991, 207).

2   In addition to the comedies, thrillers, and *films noirs* discussed here, a number of realist dramas focus on the pain of boys and young men, and on older men, as well as men in their prime, including *À l'origine d'un cri* (Robin Aubert, 2010), *Amsterdam* (Stefan Miljevic, 2013), *L'Autre Maison* [*Another House*] (Mathieu Roy, 2013), *Camion* (Rafael Ouellette, 2012), *La Cicatrice* [*The Scar*] (Jimmy Larouche, 2012), *Le Démantèlement* [*The Auction*] (Sébastien Pilote, 2013), *Mommy* (Xavier Dolan, 2014), *Le Ring* (Anaïs Barbeau-Lavallette, 2007), and *Le Vendeur* [*The Salesman*] (Sébastien Pilote, 2011), among others.

3   He and Paul Doucet reprise their roles in its sequel, *Les 3 P'tits Cochons 2. Des cochons un peu moins cochons*, released in summer 2016. Legault, however, ceded his role to Patrice Robitaille (Lepage-Boily).

4   The casting of Conte in this role is a delicious wink to his lead in the mafia-themed 1990s TV series *Omertá. La Loi du silence*, in which he plays an aspiring crime boss, with Luc Picard and Michel Côté as the iconic police duo set out to stop him. Conte's baggage as a television mafioso helps blur audience reception of his character in *Nitro* and reinforces audience sympathy with Max/Julien, who justifiably believes the man he shoots to be a criminal.

5   Although space prevents a more complete discussion of the topic, the manner in which this and other contemporary Quebec comedies poke fun at couples who do not meet traditional heterosexual norms demonstrates the continued acceptance of such norms enforced in the past through the practice of the charivari (see Hardy 2015).

6   Although Christian is married, he often appears home alone, as his wife's police duties keep her outside the home—a clear reversal of the former division of labour involving men in the public sphere and women in the private.

7   Space limitations have forced me to cut an extended discussion of these films' recourse to outdated images of female characters and their reliance precisely on the Madonna/whore dichotomy. This appears particularly clearly in *Nitro,*

Décharge, and *Lac Mystère*, which feature female characters who are involved in prostitution; while *Décharge* offers a realistic vision of a young girl lured into drugs and prostitution in Montreal, *Nitro* and *Lac Mystère* offer freakishly outmoded images of their hooker with the heart of gold characters, Morgane (Lucie Laurier) and Kate (Laurence Leboeuf).

8   As an external reviewer for this chapter observes, sport played an important role for Quiet Revolution–era nationalists, seen most clearly in the Hubert Aquin–Roland Barthes collaboration *Le Sport et les hommes* (1959). Elsewhere, I discuss at length the representation of Quebec's most recognized sports hero, Maurice Richard, representations of his body, and the nationalist narrative (Ransom 2014b, 28–38).

9   The persistence of this image appears to be most clearly depicted in twenty-first-century film in Simon Lavoie and Mathieu Denis's *Laurentie* (2011).

SECTION IV

Métropole & Région

7

THE RURAL (RE)TURNS OF YOUNG PROTAGONISTS IN CONTEMPORARY QUEBEC FILMS

Miléna Santoro

From the beginnings of the feature film industry in the province, the association of rural life with either the impasses or promise of young protagonists has produced some of Quebec cinema's most memorable works, including *La Petite Aurore, l'enfant martyr* (Bigras 1952), *Mon oncle Antoine* (Jutra 1971), and *Les Bons Débarras* (Mankiewicz 1980). In what follows, I propose to place the upsurge in rural films of recent years within the context of Quebec film history and to examine the ways in which contemporary films paradoxically evoke both rural nostalgia and the challenging economic and social realities of life in Quebec's more isolated regions. I contend that the contemporary resurgence of interest in rural stories reflects the uncertainties affecting Quebec society today, particularly the absence or loss that haunts both the individual and the collective in the pursuit of a common purpose or identity. The use of adolescent or young adult protagonists in many recent rural films raises the question of what future they will inherit or create, thus transforming a potentially nostalgic cinematic premise into an investigation of the past and future promise of rural spaces. The corpus of films I will draw upon includes Xavier Dolan's *Tom à la ferme* (2013), Pascale Ferland's *Ressac* (2013), François Péloquin's *Le Bruit des arbres* (2015), Catherine Martin's *Une jeune fille* (2013), and Sophie Deraspe's *Les Loups* (2014). While these are not the only recent films set in rural locales, they offer a representative sampling of the contemporary wave of productions that share both an interest in telling stories set in Quebec's hinterland and a focus on adolescent or young adult characters.

A History of Privileging the Rural in Quebec

For the first three hundred years or so after Samuel de Champlain founded the settlement that would become Quebec City in 1608, the French-speaking population of the colony was predominantly rural. Census data show that as late as 1851, 80 percent of the populace was agrarian. By 1901, a little over thirty years after Canadian Confederation, the Province of Quebec was still 62 percent rural, but by 1921 it was 51 percent urban, a trend that subsequently intensified until fully 80 percent of Québécois were living in cities by 1981. In the 130 years between 1851 and 1981, then, Quebec's people transitioned from an overwhelmingly rural way of life to being preponderantly city dwellers (Tétu de Labsade 1990, 69).

Despite the essentially urban reality experienced by most of Quebec's inhabitants since the early twentieth century, however, the mythology of Quebec's rural identity, and a concomitant nostalgia for its rustic past, have persisted both in the province's public policies and in its cultural productions. To cite but two examples from the twentieth century, the Catholic Church applied its social influence to promote conservative pastoral values in Quebec right up until the Quiet Revolution of the 1960s, and the Quebec government, in response to Depression-era urban unemployment, even sponsored a renewed rural colonization of Quebec's remoter regions with its 1935 Vautrin Plan.[1] These are instances of the impulse to resort to a *retour à la terre* or return to the land, often during times of social or economic upheaval, an impulse that retains significant power to this day.

Given Quebec's history, it is not surprising that many of the first feature-length films produced in Quebec were set in rural communities, even if the audience watching them was generally urban. The useful overview offered by Peter Harcourt in his article "Images of the Rural" reminds us that it was during the Great Depression that Albert Tessier and Maurice Proulx, two Catholic clerics, produced a number of documentary films that "extol the virtues of the agricultural life" (Harcourt 2006, 5), and that the feature films produced in the decade that followed — including Fédor Ozep's *Le Père Chopin* (1944), René Delacroix's *Le Gros Bill* (1949), and Paul Gury's

Un homme et son péché (1949), *Le Curé de village* (1949), and *Séraphin* (1950), as well as Jean-Yves Bigras's immortal adaptation of the popular play *La Petite Aurore, l'enfant martyr*, were similarly concerned with rural rather than urban settings. The penchant for creating a *cinéma du terroir* clearly echoed the literary tendency known as the *roman du terroir*, or "rural novel," which dominated literary production through the 1940s. The marked cinematic preference for rural narratives reveals the impetus felt by early filmmakers to exploit audience interest in and nostalgia for Quebec's pastoral roots and traditions by producing films for the domestic market that stressed rural identity.

In her analysis of Albert Tessier's work, Gillian Helfield points out that "both the work and the rural-agrarian way of life that it glorifies form part of a continuing pattern of cyclical returns to the past, which coincide with periods of upheaval and transition" (Helfield 2006, 61) in Quebec, of which the Depression was certainly one. This nostalgic investment in the familiarity and apparent simplicity of Quebec's rural past was thus one kind of cultural response to a society seemingly being destabilized by internal and external forces. In "Reel Images of the Land (Beyond the Forest): Film and the Agrarian Myth," Tom Brass articulates the symbolic stakes this way: "Politico-ideologically [...] 'peasant-ness'—which populism claims is culturally innate and unchanging—comes to symbolize the 'nation' itself, and depeasantization becomes synonymous with deculturation and the erosion (or loss) of national identity" (Brass 2001, 4). Films that celebrate Quebec's rural traditions, like those of Tessier and Proulx, can thus perform the important function of preserving national identity against the feared or actual assaults of progress or change, including urbanization.

Harcourt's survey of the pastoral tendency in Quebec cinema locates a second focal moment in the *cinéma direct* films that emerged in the late 1950s and early 1960s, of which *Les Raquetteurs* (Brault and Groulx 1958) and *Pour la suite du monde* (Perrault and Brault 1963) are prime examples, given their preoccupation with pastimes and practices associated with rurality.[2] Here again, one can cite the massive socio-economic changes of the Quiet Revolution as a backdrop to this cinematic tendency, and to its interest in filming authentic identities and customs that serve as metonymic representations of the province's past *and* projections of its future values, as is artfully underscored by the very title of *Pour la suite du monde*, which can be translated as "for generations to come." In filming real events like an amateur snowshoeing competition with synchronous sound (the hallmark of *cinéma direct*), or even the re-creation of a beluga hunting practice long since abandoned, Brault, Perrault, and their

cohort were creating a national cinema and thus identity for Quebec by legit-
imizing its cultural traditions and language, and by grounding its way of life
in a remembrance of the rural past. Even in key fiction films of the period,
such as 1964's *Le Chat dans le sac* (Groulx), the emerging nationalism and
search for identity of the contemporary generation are reinforced by a strong
connection to the land. In Groulx's award-winning and influential film,
Claude, a francophone *Québécois* and archetypal "angry young man," spends
time in the country in order to "find himself" when his relationship with his
Jewish anglophone girlfriend Barbara is in trouble. Claude's firing of a hunting
rifle across the fields is an overdetermined gesture that associates his quest for
personal and societal change with the virile pursuits of rural life.[3] This association between rustic masculinity and revolutionary nationalism, and the concomitant desire for a *retour à la terre*, would later reach parodic proportions in
films like Gilles Carle's *Les Mâles* (1971), but was contemporaneously appropriated completely without irony by the Front de libération du Québec, which
included a rifle-toting *habitant*, or French settler figure, as its symbol in the
text of its manifesto during the October Crisis of 1970. In this way, we can see
that nostalgia for the rural continues to mark both political and cinematic history in Quebec through crucial periods of upheaval in the twentieth century.

Of course, as many critics have pointed out,[4] even the earliest rural feature films implicitly undercut the nostalgia for the rural with plotlines and
characters that addressed the problems or even the forsaking of rural communities. Yves Lever sums this up neatly in his *Histoire générale du cinéma
au Québec* when he remarks that "dans la confrontation avec la campagne,
c'est toujours [la ville] qui gagne" [in any confrontation with the country, it
is always the city that wins] (Lever 1995, 113).[5] Cinematic critiques of the
moral and economic failures of rural society, which were arguably more latent
than blatant for film audiences in the 1940s and '50s, become much more
explicit in films produced after 1960. The clearest example of this is Claude
Jutra's 1971 masterpiece, *Mon oncle Antoine*, where the adolescent protagonist, Benoît, discovers the pervasive weakness and hypocrisy of his elders,
and expresses his support for rebellion, albeit manifested only in a snowball
thrown by his friend, against the mining boss whose company exploits his
community.[6] Jutra's film is widely considered one of the greatest works of
Canadian cinema, and this is undoubtedly due to its focus on Benoît, who
is memorable precisely because we see the flawed adult world through his
eyes and judge it accordingly. It bears noting that the film, released in 1971,
evokes the mining town of Asbestos in the period prior to the 1949 Asbestos

Strike. From this retrospective position, the film can thus play the nostalgia card (especially clear in the opening acoustic music evocative of the holiday season, and in the community gathering at the general store) even as it implicitly shares with the audience the knowledge of the impending social upheaval of the Quiet Revolution. The changes to come are certainly foreshadowed by Benoît's harsh judgment of the older generation's hypocrisy and weakness, by his lack of respect for the religious rituals and hierarchy of the day (an attitude also modelled by Fernand, notably played by Jutra himself, who irreverently hums during the post-wake undressing of a corpse), and even by Benoît's sexual fantasies, which express a desire to be free of the influence of the Church, symbolized by a dream in which he reaches for Alexandrine's bouncing bosom while still wearing his altar boy outfit.

The decline in the influence of the Catholic Church, examined at more length by André Loiselle in his contribution to this book, and a profound change in attitudes and national self-awareness, were indeed consequences of the Quiet Revolution, which was precipitated by the death of Maurice Duplessis in 1959 and the election of Jean Lesage in 1960. It bears recalling that Lesage's campaign used the slogan "C'est le temps que ça change" [It's time for a change]. Although others have written in greater depth about Jutra's landmark film and the zeitgeist it portrays,[7] I have glossed it here to underscore my point that such portraits of young protagonists in rural settings have marked Quebec cinema in no small measure because they offer a distancing lens through which to comment on Quebec society and, in particular, the identity questions the province has faced during the socio-economic transformations of the past half century.

Nostalgia for rural life in Quebec's feature films did not abate in the wake of the Quiet Revolution. From the bucolic charm of *J.A. Martin, photographe* (Beaudin 1977), to the more recent post-2000 blockbusters discussed by Liz Czach in her chapter, including *Séraphin : Un homme et son péché* (Binamé 2002), *Le Survenant* (Canuel 2005), and *Aurore* (Dionne 2005)[8]—and it bears noting that these three are all remakes of some of Quebec's earliest film successes set in remote villages or on farms—Quebec filmmakers and their audiences have shown an enduring affection for stories that evoke the province's rustic past. However, it is important to recognize that the images proposed by nostalgia films such as these do not depict the facts of Quebec's rural present and thus often perpetuate stereotypes and misconceptions about life in the farming regions and hinterland of the province by continually associating it with days gone by.

The 2014 report *Comprendre le Québec rural* takes great pains to deconstruct the myths that maintain an image of Quebec's economically struggling, demographically declining rural areas, noting a "une renaissance rurale inattendue et observable" [an unexpected and observable rural renaissance] (Jean 2014, 4) among the approximately two million residents of what amounts to 90 per cent of Quebec's habitable land mass (10). As of 2011, citizens of rural regions made up about one-quarter of the province's population (12), but they were often the victims of policies based on representations rather than the realities of their lives. As lead author Bruno Jean puts it:

> ce sont les représentations collectives qui donnent sa signification au monde rural. [...] L'examen de la construction sociale de ces représentations montre [...] que leur contenu est largement défini par les populations urbaines, devenues majoritaires. Il montre aussi que les représentations sont sélectives et souvent en retard sur la réalité. Ainsi en est-il de cette vision du rural qui l'associe à l'agricole alors que l'agriculture n'est plus l'activité principale dans la plupart des milieux ruraux; de même, la présence dominante de la foresterie dans des centaines de collectivités rurales est occultée dans ces perceptions. (21)

> [It's collective representations that give meaning to the rural world ... An examination of the social construction of these representations shows ... that their content is largely defined by urban populations, now in the majority. It also shows that the representations are selective and often lag behind reality. So it is with the vision of the rural as being synonymous with agriculture, even though agriculture is no longer the principle form of endeavour in most rural areas; similarly, the dominant presence of forestry in hundreds of rural communities is overlooked in such conceptions.]

To this one might add the additional points made by Jean, namely, the importance of dairy farming and secondary industry in rural areas, such that less than 2 percent of the province's GDP actually comes from agriculture (40), while fully one-third of the workforce in manufacturing and construction, among other secondary sectors, currently resides in rural areas (60). Finally, in contradiction to the widely held belief that rural populations are in decline and that, in particular, young people have been leaving in droves for the city, Jean offers statistics showing an increase in rural populations since the 1980s (30),[9] as well as a population proportion of youths under fifteen that is approximately the same for urban and rural communities (32).

In other words, "contrairement à une certaine idée assimilant les campagnes à un monde figé, traditionnel, en retard, les indicateurs socioéconomiques témoignent plutôt d'un Québec rural 'en mouvement'" [contrary to the common notion assimilating the country with an inflexible, traditional, and slow-moving culture, the socio-economic indicators bear witness rather to a rural Quebec "on the move"] (29).

Preconceived ideas about the economic and social difficulties of rural life are difficult to counter, however, because those notions are shared largely by those who do not live in the countryside or in remote regions of the province, as Jean has noted. Moreover, and this is where rural films play a key role, many of the representations of rurality that Québécois encounter come from films or other forms of imagery that reinforce stereotypes of the struggling farmer, logger, or fisherman. Indeed, even films set in the contemporary era play very clearly into this narrative, including Jean-François Pouliot's *La Grande Séduction* (2003), Guy Edoin's *Marécages* (2011), and Sébastien Pilote's *Le Démantèlement* (2014), starring Gabriel Arcand in one of his finest performances as a sheep farmer forced to sell the family farm. While it is unsurprising that these adult-centred films deal with the social and economic problems facing rural communities, these issues also crop up in the group of youth-focused films I wish to turn to in the remainder of this essay. This particular strain of rural films depicting protagonists whose promise or destiny appears tied to experiences in the remoter regions of Quebec seems to temper both nostalgic and negative stereotypes and attitudes with respect to Quebec's rural identity.

The Choices of Young Protagonists in Contemporary Rural Cinema: Five Case Studies

Dolan on the Farm

While the award-winning young filmmaking sensation Xavier Dolan is best known as an urban storyteller, the presence of country houses and the propensity of his protagonists to escape to rural retreats is a recurring element in his seven feature films to date, beginning with 2009's *J'ai tué ma mère*.[10] Dolan wrote, directed, and acted in his first film, starring as the volatile gay adolescent, Hubert Minel, who seems both to despise and adore his mother. Hubert initially rebuffs his parents' desire to send him to a rural boarding school, saying "Je ne veux pas aller à la campagne, ok? C'est pas une place pour moi" [I do not want to go to the country, ok? It's no place for me]. The irony of this scene is not just that he ends up attending the school, but that the rural landscape, depicted in a painting over the mantlepiece behind his head but also in the form of the chalet that figures in his childhood memories, is ultimately where Hubert takes refuge and finds a promise of reconciliation with his mother. If Hubert ends up a victim of gay-bashing in the rural setting of the school, he also shows himself to be strongly influenced by the bucolic memories of his childhood, and thus the family vacation cottage on the shore serves as a haven after the violence he experiences.

The attractions and rejection of rural spaces are even more central to *Tom à la ferme* (2013), Dolan's fourth film and the only one to date that is set entirely in the countryside. This was the first film in which Dolan attempted a filmic adaptation, here of an original play by Michel Marc Bouchard. *Tom à la ferme* is also Dolan's first venture into the thriller genre, characterized by dangers often found lurking beneath deceptively calm appearances. Dolan stars as the eponymous young adult protagonist, Tom Podowski, whose lover Guillaume has died in an accident. The film begins with Tom driving from Montreal to the family's dairy farm for the funeral. When he gets there, he quickly realizes that Guillaume's mother, Agathe Longchamps (the surname means long field), does not know about her son's sexual identity, and that her other son, Francis, will stop at nothing to protect his mother from the truth. Because this film is so explicitly framed by its rural backdrop, Dolan seizes the opportunity to develop more fully some of the ambivalent pastoral motifs he hinted at in his prior work, while also pointing to the enduring influence of Quebec's rurality.

In this film, the beauty and vastness of Quebec's countryside contrast with the ways it can incite or exacerbate feelings of loss or entrapment. In this respect, the opening sequence is richly symbolic, with the camera floating over first the river, then the marshes, then the fields, following the paths taken by the settlers of New France who first farmed the fertile valley of the St. Lawrence River. The autumnal beauty of this land is undeniable, depicted here by the cornfields, which by this time of year are golden rather than green. As we see Tom's car from above and then from inside, in subjective shots of the increasingly depressing sight of for sale signs posted on dilapidated trailers and farm buildings, we understand that Tom is a city dweller, out of his element in this rural region, which is seasonally and economically in a season of decline. By the time he reaches Guillaume's childhood home, the sun has disappeared, replaced by fog and the eerie stillness of a dairy farm with no one at home and with no cell signal to permit him to call anyone.

Tom's loss of his bearings after the death of his lover is externally signified by his difficulties finding his way, the enveloping mist, and the unlit, empty house that awaits him.

Tom's grief also clouds his ability to grasp the situation he encounters on the Longchamps farm. Here, young calves unaccountably die, pointing to a bleak future for the farm, and there is clearly too much work for Frank, as he prefers to be called. The rural setting seems largely dreary or dark: many of the scenes take place in dim interiors or at night, contributing to the atmosphere of menace. In one scene, Tom flees into the cornfields to escape Frank's bullying and encounters a surprising hazard—he is slashed by the sharp edges of the dried leaves on the cornstalks. This danger lurking beneath Quebec's pastoral beauty reinforces for urban audiences some of the reasons for the exodus to the city of young people like Guillaume, who seek to escape harsh rural realities. For those who stay, the land can become a kind of prison, where people like the Longchamps try to eke out a living in insular communities characterized by demanding labour, as well as by a lack of opportunity leading to stagnation, desolation, and even violence. This is precisely the kind of stereotyped rural portrait we saw Hubert react against in *J'ai tué ma mère*.

Given that the audience recognizes this dark reality before Tom does, the enigma of this film is how Tom allows himself to be sucked into the web of sinister family secrets. In part this happens because he has convinced himself that somehow both life and his grief are more real in the countryside than in the city. In one of the film's more intense scenes, Tom desperately tries to convince Sarah, a friend of Guillaume's he asks to join him at the farm, of the authenticity of the agricultural way of life:

> *Tom*: T'as pas d'idée ce que ça représente, quarante-huit vaches d'ouvrage. C'est vraiment de la job. [...] [Frank] va se retrouver tout seul sur la ferme. Et pendant ce temps-là je sers à quoi? Je suis inutile. [...] C'est comme la famille, Sarah.
>
> *Sarah*: Il y a trois semaines, tu ne les connaissais pas.
>
> *Tom*: Je sais pas comment te l'expliquer, là. Regarde autour de toi ici. C'est... c'est du vrai, ici. C'est vrai. Il y a un veau qui naît, il y a du sang sur la paille [...].
>
> *Sarah*: Hey! [...] Tu m'as fait venir ici pour faire semblant d'être la blonde d'un mort, et tu me parles du vrai?!

[T: You have no idea the work that forty-eight cows mean. It is really a lot of work … He's going to end up alone on the farm. And meanwhile, what am I good for? I am useless … It's like family, Sarah.

S: Three weeks ago, you did not even know them.

T: I don't know how to explain it to you. Look around you here. It's … it's real, here. It's real. There's a calf being born, there's blood on the straw …

S: Hang on now! You made me come here to pretend to be a dead guy's girlfriend, and you are talking to me about what's real?!]

What this exchange shows, first of all, is the persistence of the idea that rurality is synonymous with authentic experience and identity. Tom is buying into or espousing this tenet as a way to rationalize his masochistic form of grieving and regain a sense of purpose after the death of his lover. Sarah's incredulity counters this discourse by revealing its basis in inauthenticity or deception, given that Tom has enlisted her to preserve Agathe's belief that her son was straight, and given that Tom himself is not telling the truth about his relationships with Guillaume or with Guillaume's ironically named brother, Frank, whose repressed desires and propensity for violence are never openly admitted or spoken of in the family. In Dolan's portrait of rural life, truth and deception coexist, and appearances are a thin veneer masking dark realities.

It is not until Tom ends up in a local bar, tellingly named Les vraies affaires [The Real Deal], that he finally learns the "frank" extent of the brother's violence. He is sufficiently horrified by the revelation that he finds a way to escape from the Longchamps farm. As reviewer Patricia Belzil puts it, "Dans *Tom à la ferme*, c'est résolument un monde hostile, voire barbare […], [un] univers d'esprits étriqués où la différence est condamnée et les apparences doivent être sauves. La campagne est donc un lieu qu'il faut fuir" [In *Tom* … it is definitively a hostile, even barbarous world … a universe of the narrow-minded where difference is condemned and appearances must be maintained. The country is thus a place to be escaped] (Belzil 2014, 5). During the film's closing credits, Tom's nocturnal escape ends with him driving back into the city, with its vaguely reassuring succession of highways, lights, and buildings. However, Dolan also destabilizes the relief of this happy ending. If nostalgia for the traditional rural life is plainly demystified by his portrait of dairy farm families in decline, so too is the superficially familiar cityscape. Any feeling of safety is here undercut by Tom's haunted expression and by the powerful choice of Rufus Wainwright's song, "Going to a Town," in which we hear the words: "I'm going to a town that has already been burnt down / I'm so tired of you, America." With this weary, almost cynical commentary on the urban alienation that plagues most North American cities, Dolan underscores the similarities between rural and urban spaces, since both contain secrets and darkness and neither one preserves its inhabitants from (self-)deception, isolation, and violence. Notwithstanding Lever's valid observation about early Quebec features, this is one film where a return to the city does not signify a clear victory for the urban over the rural.

Of course, as with any genre film, a thriller relies on certain conventions—here an atmosphere of danger and dark disclosures—to affect its audience. So it is hardly a surprise that Dolan offers a stereotypically negative vision of rural life in *Tom à la ferme* that dramatizes the death, decline, and difficulty that Frank and Agathe face, in a family marked by loss and with no healthy progeny, either human or animal.[11] Most interesting to me, however, is that the young protagonist in this film seeks and finds some emotional catharsis in this otherwise dark atmosphere, a process that has him defending his discovery of and nostalgia for the authenticity of rural living. Tom responds to the duties and rhythms of farm life because they make him feel that he is useful and belongs. Tom experiences a *retour à la terre* that is a return to a kind of austere existence visually coded as belonging to an earlier era, and that allows him, literally, to work through his bereavement and loss of direction in a nostalgic rural context. Being "stuck" on the farm is thus the external manifestation of Tom's own emotional blockage and longing for a lost stability and purpose. Dolan's directorial turn in rural Quebec harks back to other such (re)turns, both in films and in Quebec's history, and attests to the continuing power of the land and its "authenticity" to provide a touchstone for personal and national identity during times of trouble.[12]

Escaping the Gaspé: *Ressac* and *Le Bruit des arbres*

Two other recent films offer less exaggerated yet no less telling portraits of life in remote parts of the province. Both Pascale Ferland's *Ressac* and François Péloquin's *Le Bruit des arbres* present stories set in fishing and logging communities in the Lower Saint Lawrence and Gaspé region. Unlike Dolan's Tom, the adolescent protagonists in these two films have grown up in the country, and they are just reaching an age that will allow them to consider leaving for the city. In both films, one focusing on an all-female family, the other on a father–son dyad, the young protagonists are confronted with suicide, feel a desire to escape both responsibility and the boredom of their lives, and reject their parents' choices. By contrast with earlier rural films, however, these features do not magnify the problems of rurality in a way that idealizes the choice to depart.

Ressac (*Riptide*) is documentary filmmaker Pascale Ferland's first fiction feature film. Shot in and near Chandler in Quebec's Gaspé region, whose economic troubles Ferland observed while she was working there on a documentary project, *Ressac* chronicles the impact of a factory shutdown on the townsfolk[13] through the experiences of a family of women: a grandmother, Dorine Bélanger, a middle-aged mother, Gemma, and her adolescent daughter, Chloé. These women are left to fend for themselves after Edouard, Chloé's father, leaves for the city to try to make a living. His death, later discovered to be a suicide, forces the women to confront their meagre options and hits Chloé particularly hard as she prepares to graduate from high school. All three women are swamped by grief, but Chloé is the one most at risk of being pulled under by her feelings, which she cannot seem to express or share with the other women in her life. The title of the film, echoed by the film's slow-building surge to an emotional crest, offers a metaphor for the affective *and* economic losses experienced by these three women, who must struggle to stay afloat.[14] These themes are underscored by the names given to the four chapters of the film in the film's DVD version: "Seules," "Onde de choc," "Ressac," and "Résilience," which can be translated as "women alone," "shock wave," "riptide," and "resilience."

Ressac does not paint a rosy picture of economic life in the Gaspé, with the derelict factory, the demanding fishing or processing jobs, and few other opportunities for the young; nevertheless, it is not univocal in its portrait of a rural community. After Edouard's death, his widow Gemma finds temporary work in the crab-packing plant, and Chloé secures a job at the local Subway franchise after graduation. Chloé's friends Richard and Emilie offer examples of young people who have left for the city or plan to do so; but the fact that her father, Edouard, was unhappy enough there to commit suicide serves as a powerful cautionary counterweight. Chloé herself does not at first commit to going to the city and sharing an apartment with Emilie, but she is momentarily tempted by the idea of leaving with Richard, until she sees him with another girl. Although we see her packing and Dorine offering her money near the end of the film, Chloé's discovery of her mother's commemoration of Edouard in the fish smoker that Gemma builds from Edouard's sketches leads to a moment of reconciliation between mother and daughter that perhaps places Chloé's departure in doubt. Gemma may have found a new way to support the family, inspired by her dead husband's dreams—a sign of her resiliency and resourcefulness that echo her own mother's practice of fishing, harvesting seaweed from the beach, and growing food in the garden. The determination of women like Dorine and Gemma is not necessarily shared by the younger generation, who represent the community's future and who are all at least talking about leaving. As the film's distributor, Louis Dussault, summed it up for *La Presse:* "Que ce soit dans la ville de Chandler, où se trouvait la Gaspésia, ou dans d'autres villes mono-industrielles, c'est toujours la même rengaine. Les gens passent leur temps à se demander s'ils vont rester ou partir. Ce film relate l'histoire du Québec profond à travers trois générations de femmes" [Whether it is in the town of Chandler, where the Gaspésia plant was located, or in other mono-industrial cities, it's always the same old story. People spend their time wondering if they are going to stay or leave. This film tells the story of Quebec's essence through three generations of women] (Duchesne 2013a). Chloé's mother and grandmother are obviously rooted in their community, which remains nameless in order to suggest its universality. Although the film seems to alternate showing the effects of Edouard's death on her and on Gemma, it is Chloé's unresolved choice that provides the main impetus for the story. Even Chloé's name underscores that she represents youth and the future, for it comes from a Greek word meaning "young shoot," and was also an alternative name for Demeter, the Greek goddess of agriculture.[15] Chloé is thus the embodiment of rural promise, and her experiences and attitudes are key to understanding the past, present, and future of such communities.

Bereft after her father's departure and death, and prone to brooding silence around her mother, Chloé is still not a bad seed, even though she smokes, drinks, and occasionally takes the day off from school. Rather, she is portrayed as an ordinary girl, biking around town, wanting to kiss boys and have a dress to wear to the prom, and beneath her superficial boredom, hungering for understanding and truth in her life. Her complex character emerges most clearly in two important scenes. In the first, she is shown alone in the woods after skipping school. The sequence, about thirty-three minutes into the film, is accompanied by birdsong and a rare instance of non-diegetic music, here a meditative melodic line, by contrast with the hip hop, rock, and country music the characters otherwise prefer. Wearing muted warm colours that harmonize with the trees, she looks up through the shifting branches, her faced dappled with sunlight. We know she is grieving, but in this lingering and beautiful moment her face is more serene than sad, until she hears a gunshot and her initial surprise gives way to curiosity. Creeping through the underbrush, she finds poachers eviscerating a moose or large deer, its steaming entrails spilling out onto the forest floor. The revulsion the spectator might feel is not shared by Chloé, who observes the process and later speaks of it quite dispassionately. Clearly, Chloé is not a stranger to the realities of rural life, and her ability to accept its literal viscerality—be it the dressing of the carcass or her grandmother's earlier cleaning of her fish catch—is a sign that she is not afraid to confront hard truths in the world around her.

The second key scene is when Chloé's anger at her mother explodes after she belatedly learns that her father committed suicide. Reproachful that her mother is seeking solace with an old friend, she accuses Gemma of lying to her and of betrayal. Chloé's climactic storm of words, especially striking compared to her earlier reticence, contrasts starkly with the sunny beach where she makes her stand. In the subsequent shot, the beach is shown under a cloudy sky, with larger waves unfurling on the shore that symbolically echo the raw emotions Chloé has finally expressed aloud. We then see the darkened house, hear crickets at twilight, and, in a jump cut to the next day, watch Chloé packing her clothes. This reliance on landscape shots rather than dialogue to translate a character's emotional states is typical of Ferland's film,[16] where conversation is sparse and faces seldom reveal the depths of feeling roiling beneath the surface, like the riptide of the film's title. What this confrontation between Chloé and her mother reveals is that Chloé requires truth and loyalty above all else. She can look death in the eye, as she does the carcass being gutted, but she cannot abide it when others keep secrets or try to protect her from the truth. She is emblematic of any community that has seen promises of economic stability broken by industries that are insolvent, and also of the human ability to deal with adversity, as long as it is named and known. While she may sometimes use sex, drugs, or drinking to escape boredom, Chloé also reveals a strength of character that leads the viewer to believe she will not make the same mistakes as her taciturn, undemonstrative mother. We do not know, ultimately, whether Chloé leaves for the city, but we do come to see her as part of a line of strong women who keep going despite adversity and whose resilience is a source of hope for the future.

In François Peloquin's first feature, 2015's *Le Bruit des arbres* [The Sound of Trees], the focus is on teenager Jérémie Otis from St-Ulric, a small town where logging and farming are both central to the life of the community. As in *Ressac*, the younger generation, represented by Jérémie and his friends, is struggling, both because it rejects the life choices of previous generations and because of the boredom and lack of direction that can result from not wanting to pursue traditional rural occupations. As the film's title suggests, it is by felling and processing the trees on his land that the rugged and laconic Régis Otis—whose name combines the Latin for king or ruler with the surname of a Québécois advocate for resident logging[17]—supports his two sons. Neither of his boys wants to carry on the family business, however. Early in the film the eldest son drives off to the city with his new bride and belongings, leaving seventeen-year-old Jérémie reluctantly responsible for helping his father during summer break. While Jérémie seems to be competent in the family trade, he would clearly rather hang out with his friends, commit petty theft or other mischief, tinker with engines, do donuts in his car, and party all night. His caring but otherwise silent father, for his part, resists modernization, as well as purchase offers from commercial logging conglomerates, and drives away the local drug dealer, seeing him as facilitating the delinquent behaviour and degeneration he sees in Jérémie and his cohort. Much as in *Ressac*, then, *Le Bruit des arbres* explores the generational differences and conflicts that are a factor in the loss of traditional ways of life and labour, a loss hastened if not caused by the departure of the young for urban centres.

Like the unnamed community in Ferland's film, the St-Ulric depicted by Péloquin is characterized by woods and water, whose inherent beauty is largely ignored by the region's youth. Jérémie and his friends Francis and P.O. prefer to raid the junkyard or hit golf balls at the region's omnipresent wind turbines, and even when they do go to the beach, it is to fire potatoes out of their improvised launcher, not to admire the view. The only time someone seems to observe the landscape is when André "Dédé" Veilleux, Francis's father, wistfully stops to look at the river, beautifully framed by the doorway of his dairy barn, just before committing suicide.

If, for rural inhabitants, the landscape is merely the omnipresent yet largely unseen canvas against which teenage boredom and adult despair find expression, its beauty is nonetheless compelling for the audience, which thus feels affected and even shocked by the overhead shots of efficient modern logging machines razing the forest, by the logs stacked high in the lumberyard or hauled away by noisy timber trucks, and by the lines of white wind turbines that seem to usurp the horizon in place of the majestic trees.[18] We instinctively side with Régis when he teases or rejects those who want only the latest equipment or who sell out to corporations. We also absorb the lesson of Dédé's financial ruin, after seeing him buy a new tractor the family

cannot afford, in pursuit of an idea of progress that results in the family having to auction everything off after his suicide.

For the younger generation, there is little to recommend this literally and
figuratively dying rural way of life. In a telling scene in which Jérémie walks
in the woods with his father, impressing the latter with his ability to identify
trees to cull, Régis asks him what he would think if he did sell the land, adding "C'est chez vous icitte aussi" [This is also your home]. Jérémie responds
by rejecting this legacy: "Non, Pa, icitte c'est chez vous" [No, Dad, this is
your home]. While the words exchanged here are few, they speak volumes
about the problems faced by so many rural families in which the younger
generations, like Jérémie, find urban hip hop culture much more compelling
than family traditions and businesses. As one critic puts it, "le thème de la
transmission avortée est [...] omniprésent. [...] Péloquin brosse un portrait
férocement actuel d'une implacable réalité [...] où des régions du Québec se
retrouvent ainsi coupées de leur jeunesse, de leurs forces vives" [the theme of
incomplete transmission is ubiquitous ... Péloquin paints a fiercely pertinent
portrait of a cruel reality ... where some regions of Quebec find themselves
thus cut off from their youth, and their life force] (Lussier 2015). In interviews, Péloquin himself points to the issue of cultural inheritance, suggesting
how his adolescent protagonist echoes the identity issues he sees writ large
in Quebec society:

> Selon mon point de vue, la culture québécoise vit un moment d'adoles-
> cence; elle est mal avec ses origines. Pour moi, la culture, ce n'est pas ce
> qui fait la une [...] ni ce que l'on montre dans les grands médias [...]. Elle
> a de vrais fondements et, ceux-là, on les voit plus facilement en région.
> Les médias devraient prendre soin de nos origines en s'assurant qu'ils
> montrent la mouvance des régions, la culture agricole, les travailleurs, la
> nature et la relation qu'on entretient avec elle. (Dumais 2015)

> [As I see it, Quebec's culture is living through an adolescent period, in
> conflict with its origins. For me, culture is not what makes headlines ...
> nor what major media outlets show ... It has real roots, and that's what
> you see more easily in rural regions. The media should take care of our
> origins by ensuring they show rural trends and mindsets, agrarian culture,
> the workers, nature, and our relationship to it.]

Exactly like Chloé in *Ressac*, Jérémie is a teen whose experience of death
is what propels him into both turmoil and greater maturity. In this film composed of thirty scenes, Jérémie must confront death twice, once at twenty

minutes into the film, when he must put down his own dog after hitting it while driving home from a bender the night before, the second at about twenty minutes from the film's conclusion, when he and Francis discover Dédé's body in the dairy barn. If guilt over his dog's death does little to change Jérémie's delinquent ways at the film's outset, Dédé's suicide seems to be pivotal: from a reaction shot of Jérémie with his distraught face half in shadow, to his doing donuts in the night where the only things visible are the pinpricks of his car's headlights, and finally to his profile, facing the unlit woodstove screen right, as he fruitlessly tries to find warmth, we observe a young man at a loss and in crisis as he looks to what seems to be a cold future. When he asks Régis to tuck him in, which his father does with great gentleness, Jérémie finally voices a plea for help, begging Régis not to let him party anymore because the rift he feels inside will only get bigger. This rift is of course between life and death, past and future, childhood and adulthood, father and son, all rolled into one. That the reticent Régis, played with convincing restraint by Roy Dupuis, answers this plea with only a "Bonne nuit, mon homme" [Goodnight, my man] is strangely affecting, as it articulates both the father's inability to help, and the loving recognition that the pain and longing for a time of unity and wholeness, both his and his son's, is ultimately the price of manhood.

Perhaps recalling his Biblical namesake, who was told that exile in the city could be made fruitful,[19] Jérémie's youthful experience of loss and death is what enables him to choose an uncertain urban future. Indeed, it is in the wake of a man's suicide that he finds the motivation to both help his father and leave him behind. The closing scenes of the film offer proof of Jérémie's newfound maturity and acceptance of the responsibility he initially resented, for he uses most of the money he gets from selling his beloved muscle car to help buy one of Dédé's auctioned tractors for his father, presumably reserving only enough to finance his departure for the city. It is telling that all of this occurs in the last of the film's four sections, labeled "Exode," or Exodus, on the DVD, again underscoring through biblical allusion the cliché of rural youth deserting Quebec's hinterland. However, if Jérémie follows his brother in leaving for the city, the film does not allow us to see this as either entirely positive or negative. His departure comes at a literal high price, but we also see that the resiliency of Régis lives on in his son; as Jérémie himself says in the last line of the film, "Chez nous on est fait tough" [Toughness runs in the family]. Just like Chloé does in *Ressac*, in *Le Bruit des arbres* the adolescent protagonist finds à way through the pain of loss by recognizing the strength inherited from the very family whose influence and lifestyle he leaves behind. Not unlike in the films analyzed by Czach, shared pain is, literally and mythically, the filial bond that nurtures Québécois characters' sense of identity. That this realization passes more through actions than through words is another trait that seems to characterize many recent films about rural Quebec, in which a nostalgia that remains largely unspoken results from a recognition that contemporary economic and social pressures make it nearly impossible to hold on to traditions and family unity.

Returning to Rural Quebec: *Une jeune fille* and *Les Loups*

Two recent films that focus on rural locales seem to counter the trend of showing an exodus of the young to the city. *Une jeune fille* and *Les Loups* both depict young women who leave their urban or suburban lives for places that were once important to their mothers, in the Gaspé and the Îles de la Madeleine respectively. In both films, the protagonists are in search of something they lack, a feeling of solidarity and belonging that eludes them until they reach the remote farm and the island community that are the settings for these two films. Unlike Ferland and Péloquin, Catherine Martin and Sophie Deraspe are no strangers to feature filmmaking, but they opt for a similar strategy of combining compelling images with spare dialogue to tell the stories of vulnerable young protagonists whose experience of loss precipitates change.

Une jeune fille, Martin's fourth full-length feature (English title: *A Journey*), showcases a highly compelling performance by Ariane Legault as the title character, Chantal, whose mother dies after an illness during which the teen was the primary breadwinner and caregiver and the father was mostly absent. Motivated by a photograph of the Gaspé coastline that her mother shows her just before she dies, Chantal takes a bus bound for the northeastern shore of the Saint Lawrence, with nothing more than a backpack with some food and water, both of which quickly run out. Reduced to sleeping under bridges, the grieving Chantal discards her old life and name, preferring to introduce herself as Anne-Marie to the farmer who discovers her in distress by the roadside in Gaspé, takes her in, and offers her both a purpose and a home. Apparently harking back to *Mouchette*, title of both the Bernanos novel and Bresson's 1967 filmic adaptation of it,[20] the film's coming-of-age storyline is simple; its undeniable power is rooted in Chantal/Anne-Marie's response to the landscape and to Serge, the introverted landowner who steadfastly works the family farm despite pressure from his sister to sell. Nostalgia is clearly present here, both for Serge, who listens to his father's old vinyl record collection, and for Anne-Marie, who seems to find solace in the daily rituals, work, and landscapes that likely remind her more of her mother's memories than of any of her own. In the beginning stages of the relationship between the farmer and the teen, it is clear that Serge represents the past, as he is shown facing left, in almost complete stillness, listening to Beethoven's "Clair de lune" from the *Moonlight* Sonata (35 minutes in). Meanwhile, in an alternating shot from behind the bars of the stairs that suggest the defensive walls she erects between herself and others in her grief, we see Anne-Marie looking right, her face illuminated literally and figuratively as she sits in the stairwell to listen covertly to the soothing music. Visually, then, the characters face in opposite directions, even as an appreciation of the music brings them together and foreshadows their ultimate ability to find harmony with each other, translated among other things by later shots that include both of them listening in the same frame, or that show them both facing the same direction, as at the end of the film when they sit side by side on a rock by the river.

The need for beauty, be it natural or artistic, is clearly shared by both characters in the film, which frequently lingers on the sights and sounds of the Gaspé farm and woodlands. Such images help the audience understand Serge's refusal to sell his woodlots to a local bidder. To his sister's financial arguments, he responds: "C'est la terre de notre famille. C'est à nous autres. Il faut que ça reste à nous autres" [It's the land that belongs to our family. It is ours. It must remain ours]. Much like Régis Otis, then, Serge is a loner who is content to live modestly off the land, which inhabits him as much as he inhabits it. By contrast with rural youths like Jérémie and Chloé, however, Anne-Marie responds strongly to the natural beauty around her, and she finds herself being healed by it. Martin represents this visually in Anne-Marie's spontaneous smiles as she looks out over the dried grasses in the autumn fields (49 mins) and feels and smells the pungent sap in the woods (57 mins).

In choosing to stay with Serge, Anne-Marie forsakes her past identity: although she does eventually tell him her real name, she does not go back on her story that both her parents are dead. Significantly, while she truthfully says her mother died from illness, her comment about her "dead" father is that she cares nothing for him. Serge, for his part, reveals that he loved his parents and learned much from them, underscoring his belonging to a bygone era of harmony. His is a heritage of affective and cultural continuity, by contrast with a younger generation that rejects its antecedents. Much of the heart of the film shows Serge gradually introducing Anne-Marie to his knowledge of working the land and hunting, although she is understandably troubled when he shows her the deer he has shot. The beautiful mammal revives Anne-Marie's sense of loss, so much so that she cannot bring herself to eat the venison Serge serves for dinner. While their relationship is not without ambiguity,[21] it seems that Serge's rural lifestyle fulfills Anne-Marie's need for meaningful adult guidance and a sense of stability, as well as for the solace that being close to nature provides.

Several critics have noted Martin's focus on compelling image composition, as well as on the distinctive aesthetic of her films, one that privileges the visual over the verbal[22] in her explorations of the power of rural settings to heal losses, most evident in *Une jeune fille* and in her previous film, *Trois temps après la mort d'Anna* (2010). Of course, *Une jeune fille* does not gloss over the outmoded rural habitus and lifestyle, nor does it sidestep the economic difficulties faced by farmers and by others who work the land. The reality of the loss of traditions and rural lifeways is something that Martin examined closely in her 2006 documentary *L'Esprit des lieux* [The Spirit of Places], in which she returned to the Charlevoix locations photographed in 1970 by Gabor Szilasi and found many inhabitants who expressed nostalgia for their lost farms, declining religious practices, and former pastimes, with the notable exceptions of a baker and carpenter, who continue to pursue their traditional artisanal practices and techniques, for which there still seems to be a demand. However, with her choice to send a fiercely independent young protagonist into a rural setting to find herself in *Une jeune fille*, Martin is pointing to a compensatory reality that rural life may still offer. This contemporary *retour à la terre* is certainly one possible response to the derelictions and afflictions of urban life. In this respect, Anne-Marie embodies the human need for connection and inner peace, and our thirst for beauty, in an era in which urban and suburban uniformity and anonymity often produce feelings of loss of identity. While this may seem retrograde in a society that privileges the cosmopolitan urban modernity that constitutes one of the outcomes of Quebec's Quiet Revolution, Martin's delicate portrait of Anne-Marie's recovery from her loss and isolation makes it arguably the most surprising and moving tribute to the potential benefits of rural simplicity and solidarity among the films that participate in this rural resurgence. In this, it would seem that Martin also echoes her earlier film, *L'Esprit des lieux*, in which a closing quotation from Gaston Miron's poem "L'Héritage et la Descendance," from his landmark collection *L'Homme rapaillé*, reminds us that nostalgia can also hold potential: "Et j'ai hâte à il y a quelques années / l'avenir est aux sources" [I am looking forward to a few years ago / the future is in our origins].[23]

This is the message of the film's final sequence, in which we see Serge and Anne-Marie on the river rocks facing right, or forward-looking, and then her fingers, inching toward his on the rock, their two splayed hands pointing upwards in the frame. The solidity of the rock and the proximity and directionality of their hands suggest that they will build a future together in this setting of water and land that offers a serenity and stability they both desire. In Martin's *Une jeune fille*, then, the lost teen, one among so many in today's world, finds herself in a rural landscape that offers her a place to be and to breathe—literally, in that the film closes, as it opened, with the sounds of her breathing, and figuratively, in that she has freely chosen her new identity and way of life. Anne-Marie left the city in search of the coastline that inspired her mother's nostalgia. Although she never finds the exact location shown in her mother's photo, what she does find in the Gaspé is a new home and a father figure who will both guide and respect her, offering her the chance to reach her potential in the present and presence of the land. Anne-Marie's newfound sense of belonging and purpose is not nourished by rustic stereotypes or nostalgic illusions about farm life, as was the case with Dolan's self-deluding protagonist. Serge is silent, careful, and self-sufficient, but not uncultured or unkind. His farm is not prospering, but his land allows him to make a living and even pay Anne-Marie, who, we sense, will ensure the farm's future. *Une jeune fille* thus offers a rare filmic representation of the potential of rural renewal that is in fact borne out by an analysis of the vibrancy that Bruno Jean underscores in his 2014 report on Quebec's rural regions.

The need for a paternal figure in *Une jeune fille* is also central to Sophie Deraspe's third feature film, *Les Loups*, which was awarded the Best Film prize in Turin by FIPRESCI. Convincingly portrayed by Evelyne Brochu, who also played Sarah in *Tom à la ferme*, Deraspe's protagonist, twenty-six-year-old Elie Marans, leaves Montreal for Quebec's remote Îles de la Madeleine. Like Anne-Marie in *Une jeune fille*, Elie's journey is inspired by an experience of loss, although we do not find out she is recovering from an abortion until eighteen minutes into the film, when she phones her career-oriented mother, who supported Elie's choice not to carry the child. Similar to Chantal, who becomes Anne-Marie when she leaves the city, we will learn that Elie's real name is Elizabeth Droski; she too creates a different identity in a new place, but in her case, it is not because she wishes to reject her family. We eventually discover that Elie's journey, during the off-season month of March, is inspired by her desire to find her unknown father. Although her mother never told her more than his first name and that he had a tattoo, Elie braves the depression caused by her sense of loss and pursues a nostalgic quest for her paternal origins in this fishing and sealing community that clearly does not welcome outsiders.

In this respect, we should note, as others have done (Dunlevy 2015; Houdassine 2015), that the French title *Les Loups* (*The Wolves*) is a double entendre of symbolic importance. Wolves are central not only because this tight-knit community protects its own—an instinct embodied by the matriarch Maria Menquit (played by a fierce Louise Portal), who suspects Elie is an informer for animal rights activists and who nicknames her handicapped grandson Ti-Loup [Wee Wolf]—but also because the seals they hunt for their livelihood are commonly called "loups marins" or "sea wolves." The title sums up in one word both the prey and the predators, and the possibility of both solidarity and predation these two kinds of animals imply. The fact that Elie empathizes with the seals and thus will not eat the meat without vomiting it up afterwards (recalling Anne-Marie's refusal of venison in Martin's film) signals her status as an outsider and possibly a threat to the survival of the community or "pack." The story of the film is thus a double identity quest, for Elie timidly seeks a relationship with her father William, who is Maria's son, even as Maria seeks to discover who Elie really is and what purpose motivates this "fille de la ville" [city girl]. Maria's investigation and the wariness of the Madelinots (the term for the islands' inhabitants) make manifest the tension between the urban and rural populations in Quebec society.

Like Ferland, Péloquin, and Martin, Deraspe wrote the screenplay for her own film and set the story in a community of which she has some knowledge; in interviews, she indicates she spent summers there as a child because her father was a Madelinot (Dunlevy 2015). As in the other three films we have analyzed, the environment directly affects the community's survival: we learn that the weather can sink ships, and we witness the realities of hunting animals that must be killed, dressed, and, in the case of choice morsels, eaten raw, according to tradition. As Deraspe says: "There is a sort of primary idea of ecology—not trendy ecology, but an ecology in which we, human beings, are intrinsically part of nature and live off of nature, are stunned by nature and fed spiritually but also threatened by nature. The link between life and death is immediate, and part of ... daily reality" (Dunlevy 2015). Be it in the opening birth-like sequence in which Elie's car drives off the dark ferry into the light of a new day (noted by Gobert 2015), in the increasingly pregnant motel owner Nadine who gives birth later in the film, in Elie's mourning for her terminated pregnancy, or, finally, in the death of Maria and several others lost at sea in a storm, the implacable and universal rhythm of life and death is inescapable in this film. Deraspe also emphasizes the cycle of the seasons, specifically the transition from late winter to the breakup of the ice in spring that signals the end of the seal hunt. The film's final frames, showing fragmented ice sheets on the ocean's surface, are a visual reminder not only of the spring thaw but also of the thaw in the relationship between Elie and the Menquit clan, specifically her father, who, at the film's conclusion, is encouraged by Elie to bring yet another adrift family member back into the fold.

Like *Une jeune fille*, then, *Les Loups* shows a young woman who has lost her moorings[24] and who travels to Quebec's farthest reaches in order to find a place where she belongs. When confronted by Maria about her identity and her reasons for coming to the community, Elie answers simply: "Je veux juste savoir d'où je viens" [I only want to know where I come from]. This simple desire for a sense of rootedness and for knowledge of one's origins resonates deeply with a nostalgic attachment to Quebec's traditional cultural heritage, born of a recognition that its society has survived largely because of a tenacious desire to preserve a language and a cultural identity at odds with the North American anglophone majority. Deraspe explicitly invokes nostalgia for Quebec's rural traditions by using live fiddle music to accompany the community's dancing and celebrations after the hunt, a sequence that makes a clear intertextual reference to the costumed Eastertide shindig on the Île-aux-Coudres in Brault and Perrault's *Pour la suite du monde*. Speaking admiringly of the cultural endurance of remote communities, the director remarks: "Il y a assez peu d'endroits au Québec où toutes les générations sont capables de chanter une même chanson ensemble. Leur culture est vivante et continue d'exister. C'est aussi dû à l'isolement, mais il y a une richesse et une beauté fascinantes derrière" [There are few places in Quebec where all the generations can sing the same song together. Their culture is alive and persists. It's also due to their isolation, but beneath it all is a richness and a fascinating beauty] (Gendron 2015).

If *Les Loups* encourages appreciation for the rugged beauty of the people and landscape of the Îles de la Madeleine, it also takes pains to reveal the hardships and the price of making a living from the alternating fishing and tourist seasons there. Unlike *Une jeune fille*, this film shows the rural inhabitants to be suspicious of outsiders, largely because seal hunting, a pillar of their economy, has been judged harshly by tourists and environmental activists, putting the community on the defensive. Serge lets Anne-Marie work on his farm and pays her for it; by contrast, Elie's offer to help out on William's boat is rejected, due to what he calls "insurance" complications. Elie's status as an outsider for much of the film allows the audience to follow her discovery of the community's struggles, embodied most clearly by Réal Clark, whose accident has left him unemployed, alcoholic, and unable to sell his house at auction to support his wife and children, because nobody has the money to bid on it or the desire to turn the family out. The fact that every family is one accident or loss away from financial and personal disaster is reinforced by Maria's decision to pilot William's boat on one last, fatal hunting sortie, resulting in William losing his livelihood. Worse still, the family also loses Maria as the primary caregiver and chief authority figure. Just like the animals they hunt, the human inhabitants in remote communities are all potential victims; for them, familial and community solidarity is one of the few ways to ensure long-term survival.

Although perhaps unsatisfying, the film's conclusion, with Elie and William returning to Montreal, where the latter's butchering skills gain him employment in an abattoir, does point to the limited range and availability of rural occupations. It also echoes films like *Ressac* and *Le Bruit des arbres*, in that Elie and her newfound family unit seek a future in the city, a future that would not seem as certain were they to stay in Quebec's remoter regions. Of course, the fact that Sarah Menquit, William's sister, whom they rescue from a seedy bar, is just as much of an alcoholic as some of the islanders, merely underscores the desolation suffered by those who are uprooted and alienated in and by Quebec's contemporary economic and social environment. As Gobert (2015) puts it in a review for *24 images*, in Deraspe's film "[t]out est dit, du vrai et du faux [...], d'un cadre naturel (qui ne ment pas, salutaire) contre une société (qui fabrique, qui emprisonne)" [It is all communicated, the true and the false ... the natural backdrop (which, salutarily, does not lie) against society (that fabricates, that imprisons)]. It is hard to disagree with this summary of the opposition between the rural and the urban in this film, especially given that Elie, the "city girl," does start off by hiding her identity, whereas the Madelinots do not. However, it also bears noting that if rural life is by no means idealized here, neither are the characters stereotyped as backward or violent. Elie is eventually accepted by the Menquits, who place her under their protection. In this way, *Les Loups* contributes to the contemporary wave of films that portray the nuances of rural life, using young protagonists to expose both its problems and its potential benefits.

Conclusion

In the five films I have considered, rural regions offer a formative context for characters who are emotionally inhibited and unmoored by loss. In their search for a place or a purpose in the modern world, Tom, Chloé, Jérémie, Anne-Marie, and Elie are symbolic of young people at odds with an earlier generation that was itself affected by thwarted nationalist aspirations, the unravelling of social and marital cohesiveness, and several periods of economic disruption in Quebec. It is telling that none of the young protagonists in the recent features discussed here have wholly intact or loving families: while Tom's parents are entirely absent, it is clear that Gemma, Régis, Anne-Marie's father, and Elie's mother all have difficulty expressing themselves and showing affection to their children. In this incommunicability that afflicts intergenerational relationships, translated in all of these films by a reliance on facial close-ups and scenery rather than dialogue to convey emotion, we see that both adults and adolescents are yearning for healing, understanding, and connection. A longing for harmony, or a pre-lapsarian time and place, informs the choices these contemporary directors have made to set their stories in remote yet beautiful locales that reveal and sometimes heal the isolation and lack of direction of their young protagonists. Moreover, even in these films that take place in the proximate moment, the province's hinterland is still so closely associated with the idealized rural roots of Quebec's historical identity that it immediately resonates with the audience, evoking a nostalgia for a lost state that facilitates our identification with the characters' distress.

If rural settings offer a fitting backdrop for the existential crises of today's youth, it is in part because they recall the nostalgic possibility of unity and communion with nature, even as the virtual impossibility of recovering these ideals, at least for urban spectators, enhances the poignancy of the struggles and losses these films also explore. Cinematic returns to the rural world seem inescapably bound up with the past, be it a generation, a way of life, or a time of cohesion within the family or community that the audience remembers, even if the protagonists themselves prefer to abandon their origins or deny their past.

This retrospective and affective dimension of rurality is exactly what Fowler and Helfield note in their critical volume *Representing the Rural: Space, Place, and Identity in Films about the Land* when they write that "landscape is not limited to purely physical terrain: another key element of the rural landscape is its emotive, nostalgic power as an idealized space and community—the land imagined or remembered as a dream and that finds its most visceral evocation through the imagery of earth and sand and flesh and bone" (Fowler and Helfield 2006, 6–7). As we have seen, in the gutting of fish, deer, or seal, and in the felling of trees or the deaths of calves, recent rural films expose the profound links between humans and their environment: the natural world is both compelling in its immediacy and a prism for human experience, providing a source of reflection, self-knowledge, and growth. This is no doubt why, in his examination of spirituality in post–Quiet Revolution Quebec cinema, Ian Lockerbie underscores the importance of the "natural wilderness, which in its remoteness and stillness brings greater peace of mind than the harassed world of modern commerce" that characterizes urban living (Lockerbie 2005, 18). Although writing of *Les Loups*, the critic Gobert could be referring to any of the films we analyze here when she similarly observes an underlying "idée d'une authenticité de la nature versus l'artificialité de la civilisation, le rapport de l'homme à son espace (et vice versa), l'inscription du corps humain (périssable, éphémère) dans un cadre naturel souverain, atemporel, amoral" [idea of the authenticity of nature by contrast with the artificiality of civilization, the relationship of beings to their surroundings (and vice versa), the inscription of the (perishable, ephemeral) human body into an amoral, atemporal and sovereign natural framework] (Gobert 2015).

The natural backdrop contributes a certain universality and timeless beauty to these recent films, but the contemporary economic challenges they allude to are equally part of the landscape. Be it because of the plight of farmers who lack the manpower or resources to succeed, the persistent industrial or family pressures to sell land, the lack of job opportunities and guidance for the young, or the environmentalists' challenges to traditional hunting or fishing practices, the rural communities in these five films are obviously not thriving. That said, the only film that paints a uniformly dark portrait of rural life is *Tom à la ferme*, which is not unexpected given that it is a thriller. In *Ressac, Le Bruit des arbres, Une jeune fille*, and *Les Loups*, the Gaspé, Lower Saint Lawrence, and island communities offer portraits of individuals whose destiny is influenced by their experiences in the hinterland at least as much as by the pull of urban centres. If suicide, in particular, is present in two films—both of which suggest that the cause is economic stress—we must note that only one of those occurs on a farm. Several of the protagonists return to or leave for the city, and one is considering it; Anne-Marie is a contrary example—she chooses to leave her urban past behind and work toward a stable future on Serge's farm. In other words, collectively, these films no longer show the supremacy of the city over the country, and the old stereotypes of rural failure are nuanced by more balanced portraits of resilience and persistence despite loss and economic precarity. The very fact that all the young protagonists learn from their time in remote locales, either maturing through hardship or finding a new sense of belonging, points to the rural as a space of becoming and promise, despite its nostalgic connotations—or perhaps, in the case of Anne-Marie, even because of them.

In the wake of much of film criticism since Jameson (1984), nostalgia is more often than not associated with a longing for a time gone by made manifest in films set in the past,[25] among which are many of the coming-of-age or identity quest stories that have reflected Quebec's own political and social development, as the first part of this chapter has shown. For some theorists, "nostalgia is seen as the antithesis of progress, as it proposes a decline narrative in which the past was superior to the present, which continues to erode into the future" (Charles 2009, 40). However, there is another understanding of nostalgia that I think is more applicable to the contemporary rural films I have examined, one in which, as Morgan Charles puts it, nostalgia can become "a creative coping mechanism with which to come to terms with massive societal and technological change" (Charles 2009, 41). This coping mechanism operates both on screen, through specific shared environmental and cultural referents, and in the audience's reaction to those referents, for the viewer must recognize such nostalgia in order for it to become a resource for (self-)reflection. Although the recent films Charles examines are set in the past while the ones I have selected are contemporary stories, I agree that not all nostalgia films produce romanticized or retrograde escapes into superficially reassuring or recuperative memories. The rural films examined here participate in nostalgia implicitly or explicitly through their setting in Quebec's hinterland; but at the same time, their young protagonists inject new life into the equation, in that they are making decisions about their futures, which remain undetermined precisely because their future is as uncertain as our own. I can thus only concur with Charles when she concludes that certain films that display nostalgic aesthetics "do not foreclose an engagement with the future, but contribute to new imaginary landscapes for its foundation" (Charles 2009, 110). It is in this sense, then, that the rural turns or returns of the young protagonists discussed here constitute a recasting of such landscapes as foundations for growth as well as sites of memory, loss, or hardship. In films as in life, even those who leave the rural communities they inhabit or visit are indelibly marked by the experiences they have there. As spectators, we remain haunted by the beauty and the challenges that rural Quebec holds for those who venture into its filmic incarnations, and we are spurred to reflect on what unifies rather than divides the urban and rural possibilities for Quebec's future generations. In a post-9/11, post-recession context, it is little wonder that a number of directors are exploring rural landscapes in an effort to find new ways to frame and imagine the perennial quest for individual and collective identity that has been and continues to be a central theme in Quebec cinema.

Notes

1   In their *Histoire du Québec contemporain,* the authors claim that around fifty thousand people were motivated by the Vautrin plan, as well as federal incentives, to relocate and establish farms in rural areas of Quebec. They note, however, that this "mouvement d'occupation du sol" [the movement to occupy the land] was transitory, as up to two-thirds of those who went would not remain on their farms (Linteau et al. 1989, 40–41).

2   While it is true that *Les Raquetteurs* was filmed in Sherbrooke, a small city two hours from Montreal, the snowshoeing it highlights is a contemporary recreational version of a practice historically associated with French colonial-era hunters and trappers, and with the Indigenous peoples from whom they learned the use of such equipment. As such, the practice connects the Quebec of the late 1950s to its rural roots.

3   Although *Le Chat dans le sac* is arguably more frequently watched and analyzed today, one must also recall a contemporary to Claude's rustic turn, in the rural retreat of a group of would-be revolutionaries in Jean-Pierre Lefebvre's *Le Révolutionnaire* (1965). In this first feature-length film by Lefebvre, a cohort of angry youths drill and plot the government's overthrow until their self-defeating internal conflicts, including their leader's struggle between a woman's love and his revolutionary aspirations, wind up in the group's self-slaughter. As in Groulx's film, it would seem that, in Lefebvre's sardonic take on his generation's ambitions and impasses, amorous relationships attenuate or complicate the nationalist identity formation and resolve of the young male protagonists, who retreat to the country to consolidate their personal and political commitment.

4   Janis Pallister (1995) references Lever, who in turn cites Brûlé, for his affirmation that "contrairement aux idées reçues et aux apparences, le premier cinéma québécois a en définitive systématiquement pris parti pour la ville en montrant à chaque fois l'impossibilité de la vie à la campagne" [contrary to conventional wisdom and appearances, Quebec's early cinema definitively and systematically favored the city by consistently showing the hopelessness of country life] (Lever 1995, citing Brûlé, 514). Harcourt, for his part, names this "Trouble in Paradise" (Harcourt 2006, 6) and notes a similar "painful irony" in films like Brault's 1967 *Entre la mer et l'eau douce*, where "Claude becomes famous as a *chansonnier* through singing songs about a rural life he had to abandon" (Harcourt 2006, 8).

5   All translations are mine unless otherwise indicated.

6   Although Jutra himself grew up in an urban setting, it is interesting to note his interest in stories set in the rural past, of which *Mon oncle Antoine* and *Kamouraska* are the two most famous examples.

7   Recent critics who have focused on *Mon oncle Antoine* include Mary Jean Green (2003) and Jim Leach (2002).

8   *Séraphin* and *Aurore* are ranked numbers 1 and 10, respectively, on the list of highest-grossing, highest-attended Quebec films since 1985, as shown by Quebec's Institut de la Statistique report of 2016 (Fortier et al. 2016). *Le Survenant* is not among the top twenty best-attended Quebec movies, but its relatively high earnings also place it among this elite group of successes.

9   According to Jean, "la population rurale du Québec n'est pas en décroissance. En fait, depuis 1981, elle s'est accrue d'environ 15 %" [Quebec's rural population is not decreasing. In fact since 1981 it has grown by about 15%] (Jean 2014, 30). However, he does distinguish between distinct types of rural regions, adding "il faut distinguer le profil des régions centrales de celui des régions éloignées. Ces dernières régions perdent continuellement de la population au jeu des migrations internes" [You have to distinguish the profile of central regions from that of more remote ones. The latter continually lose population through internal migration] (Jean 2014, 33). In other words, while depopulation does affect some of the more remote regions, overall, rural areas are seeing absolute population increases, although perhaps not at the same rate as urban areas.

10   I first explored this counter-narrative of the rural in Dolan's work for the American Council for Quebec Studies Outreach Seminar held in Minneapolis in September 2015, in a paper titled "Rustic Returns, or Xavier Dolan's Portrayal of 'Roughing It' in Rural Quebec."

11   Frank's past violence and repressed homosexual desires do not lead the viewer to believe he will produce children to perpetuate the Longchamps farming legacy. Indeed, even the calf he helps deliver eventually dies, so he is not even able to ensure the survival of his livestock, let alone nurture any human children. This dead calf motif also appears in *Marécages*.

12   Interestingly, Dolan repeats this narrative of rural return in the celebrated music video he made for Adele's "Hello," where she is shown taking refuge in a country cottage after a breakup. The video was also filmed in Quebec.

13   The pulp and paper plant Gaspésia shut down in 1999, putting more than five hundred people in Chandler out of work. Efforts to restart the industry failed, sending the community into a second wave of psychological distress, given that so many of the men had to leave their families behind to find work elsewhere. Ferland was inspired by her discussion of some of the effects of this double despair with a local psychologist, as several articles on the film point out (see Brisebois 2014; Duchesne 2013a).

14   As Ferland herself states: "Le titre du film est dans la métaphore... Sa structure est faite comme une vague très forte qui arrive pour ensuite se retirer" [the title of the film is metaphorical ... its structure resembles that of a very big wave that arrives and then withdraws] (Duchesne 2013b).

15   See the entry for "xlo/h" in *A Greek–English Lexicon* (Liddell and Scott 1940).

16   Critic Gérard Grugeau calls Ferland's technique an "osmose naturelle entre les paysages et les états d'âme des personnages" [natural osmosis between the landscapes and the mental states of the characters] (Grugeau 2014, 60).

17   This reference is made clear in the press packet for the film: "Ce bas du fleuve, c'est aussi le pays de Léonard Otis, à qui je lève mon chapeau. Promoteur du concept de fermes forestières, il a défendu l'exploitation des forêts par des travailleurs habitant le territoire plutôt que par des corporations" [This lower St. Lawrence region is also the home of Léonard Otis, to whom I tip my hat. Promoter of the idea of forest farms, he defended the exploitation of forests by workers living on the land rather than by corporations] (Péloquin 2015, n.p.).

18   Péloquin himself describes the turbines this way: "les éoliennes, bien que jolies, nourrissent une impression de pillage des ressources régionales au profit des intérêts métropolitains" [the wind turbines, although pretty, fuel the impression of the exploitation of regional resources in favour of metropolitan interests] (Péloquin 2015, n.p.).

19   See Jer. 29:7.

20   Jean-Philippe Desrochers points out this filmic antecedent in his 2014 review of *Une jeune fille*.

21   Serge himself slaps his own sister when she suggests there is more to his relationship with Anne-Marie than a work arrangement. However, near the film's conclusion, Serge admits to Anne-Marie that he needs her and then hugs her, a form of contact she initially tolerates, then flees. Such moments suggest the potential for a physical bond, but we do not see it during the film's diegesis.

22   Desrochers (2013) writes of what he sees as "une volonté de donner à l'image un caractère presque sacré et un désir de concentrer l'attention du spectateur sur les êtres et les choses" [a will to give an almost sacred character to the image and a desire to focus the spectator's attention on things and beings],

while Beaulieu, in his analysis of the cult of the image in Martin's work (2016), also points to the "communion silencieuse des présences" [silent communion of presences], highlighting the scarcity of dialogue in the development of relationships in her films.

23   There is no entirely satisfactory equivalent for the French word "source," which can mean both origin and wellspring or fount, as in the source of a watercourse. Given the importance of water in both films by Martin, it would seem that this quotation from Miron encapsulates her filmic vision that rural origins and ways of life are intimately connected to the water that was and still is a source of much of Quebec's prosperity.

24   Maria's companion, Léon, says of Elie that she is not "anchored. She's adrift."

25   See Smith 2003; Sprengler 2009; Wilson 2005.

8

RETURN TO ABITIBI
IN BERNARD ÉMOND'S
LA DONATION

Katherine Ann Roberts

"[…] dans l'idée de devoir, il y a celle de dette et de transmission"

— Bernard Émond, *La Donation :*
Scénario et regards croisés, 113

Bernard Émond's *La Donation* (*The Legacy*, 2009), the last in a trilogy of films
on the Christian values of faith (*La Neuvaine* [*Novena*, 2005]), hope (*Contre
toute espérance* [*Summit Circle*, 2007]), and charity, ends with a compelling
scene that evokes the rapport between the film's central protagonist and the
landscape. A woman doctor, Jeanne Dion (Élise Guilbault), stands holding
a baby on a lonely road in northwestern Abitibi in the aftermath of a car
accident that has killed the baby's mother. The sequence places Jeanne at
the centre of the vast landscape; she gazes stoically at an immensity of sky,
fields, and trees in a tableau that manages to soften the shock of the adjacent
tragedy. Jeanne has come to the former mining village of Normétal to replace
the aging Dr. Yves Rainville (Jacques Godin), who migrated to the region
when the mine opened in 1963 and remained after its closing in 1976. Over
the course of the film, Dr. Rainville passes away and, unbeknownst to Jeanne,
bequeaths his practice to her in his will. The film's central question is whether

Jeanne will accept this "gift" and remain in the remote village. The story becomes a means for Émond to further explore the themes of loss, debt, and cultural transmission, which dominate his oeuvre (Émond 2011; Émond and Galiero 2009).

If Émond's cinema is about the debt the Québécois owe their ancestors with respect to what he calls "le fonds culturel canadien-français" [the cultural inheritance of French-Canada] (Émond and Galiero 2009), 110), the debt in *La Donation* is also to the Abitibi films that preceded and inspired it such as l'abbé Maurice Proulx's *En pays neufs* (1937) and *Ste-Anne-de-Roquemaure* (1942), Gilles Groulx's unsigned *Normétal* (1960), and Pierre Perrault's "cycle abitibien," notably *Le Retour à la terre* (1976). By setting *La Donation* in Normétal, Émond engages directly with the myth of the North in Quebec culture and the complex legacy of 1930s colonization. The urban migrants of this period were seen by some as heroic trailblazers engaging in an important (symbolic) appropriation of space and by others as charity cases sent up to the "frontier" as a future on-site workforce for the growing mining industry. Émond's film explores the tensions between these competing discourses both in the filmic narrative and in a reinterpretation of images from previous films. Key to Émond's contribution to contemporary Quebec cinema and to the legacy of Quebec regional filmmaking is his ability to bridge the gap between the legendary and the ordinary in his portrait of the people and the landscape. *La Donation* also offers a focus on female subjectivity, which is absent from the previous Abitibi films.

Émond came of age in Quebec at the twilight of traditional religious education and at the dawn of the sweeping changes of the Quiet Revolution. He completed half of what is known as *le cours classique* (a program of Greek, Latin, theology, and literature run by religious orders) before transitioning into the new CÉGEP (secular college) system[1] and turning in earnest to the social sciences, more specifically anthropology, which were at the time heavily influenced by Marxism. His support for Quebec independence in the 1960s and '70s was secondary to his embrace of the socialist cause (Émond et Galiero Galiero 2009, 31). Émond brings to his cinema a deep knowledge of literary classics (Proust, Chekov) and also an appreciation of European cinema (Bergman, Bresson) and particularly what could be called Rossellini's aesthetics of bitterness (30). At a very young age he had what he describes as "un sentiment tragique de l'existence" [a tragic sense of existence], the idea that one's life is "une série de pertes, une série de défaites" [a series of losses, a series of defeats] (Émond and Galiero 2009, 30–31). Émond's foreboding sense of guilt, destiny, and the mysteries of human existence, common to European Catholic cinema, evolved in tandem with his observations of Inuit culture and a renewed interest in Quebec's cultural uniqueness. What might appear at first glance to be nostalgia for traditional French Canadian rural culture is, in Émond's personal philosophy, a complex meditation on the nature of contemporary human interaction in the face of increasing individualism, aggravated by rampant consumer capitalism and neoliberalism. In the Quebec context this atomization and alienation has been exacerbated by a conflict relationship with pre–Quiet Revolution culture, which is now seen as somehow retrograde or shameful. According to Émond, the end result of this historical alienation will be no less than the complete loss of Quebec cultural memory. Commenting on his NFB documentary *Le Temps et le Lieu* (1999), a portrait of rural Quebec, Émond notes how in the parish of St-Denis, for example, both the village and its inhabitants bear witness to Quebec's recent past in ways that are no longer possible in urban Montreal. In what is now a well-known anecdote, Émond recalls how during the shooting of this film he accompanied the wife of Horace Miner (a celebrated American anthropologist) on a visit to the Basilica of Sainte-Anne-de-Beaupré, a church he had not seen since his childhood. The visit brought Émond face to face with what he calls, true to his training in anthropology, "les rituels de ma tribu" [the rituals of my tribe] (Émond et Galiero 2009, 19). He had the sense that he was observing his own people, even though he did not share their religiosity: "J'avais très exactement l'impression de *rentrer chez moi*, tout intellectuel non croyant que j'étais. [...] Qu'on me comprenne bien : le choc que j'ai ressenti alors était plutôt d'ordre culturel que d'ordre religieux. Il s'y glissait pourtant une nostalgie (et j'utilise ici le mot en toute conscience) de la transcendance perdue." [I had the distinct impression of *coming home*, despite being an atheist intellectual ... I don't wish to be misunderstood: the shock that I felt was more cultural than religious. I was nostalgic (and I use the word here consciously) for a lost transcendence] (Émond 2011, 20). The visit to the basilica was the catalyst for his trilogy, which he dedicated to exploring a Quebec cultural heritage increasingly forgotten by a technocratic, postmodern, secular society (Émond and Galiero 2009, 32).

What Émond calls "le fonds culturel canadien-français" is centred on Quebec's rural past, "la culture des rangs, la culture matérielle agricole, le structures familiales, la langue où on sent le XVIIe siècle, le folklore qui nous vient de la vieille France et au centre de ça, il y a bien sûr la culture chrétienne, la culture catholique" [the culture of agricultural plots and materials, family structures, a language that evokes the seventeenth century, a folklore that comes from old France, at the centre of all that, there is of course Christian culture, Catholic culture] (Émond and Galiero 2009, 10). This cultural inheritance was forged by exclusion (from English Canadian capital and positions of power), by adaptation (moving to cities), and by an investment in a two-thousand-year-old Catholic heritage. One does not have to be a believer to recognize the richness of this tradition: "L'héritage chrétien, c'est comme un ensemble de métaphores qui m'aident à penser le monde contemporain et qui recèlent des vérités profondes" [Christian heritage is like an ensemble of metaphors that helps me think about the modern world and that contain profound truths] (Émond and Galiero 2009, 112). Not surprisingly, Émond's defence of French Canadian culture puts him at odds with many contemporary filmmakers and cultural thinkers, who are so confident that Quebec has moved beyond this paradigm toward a dynamic, sophisticated, modern, largely urban, forward-thinking, secular society.[2] Indeed, for those familiar with the representations of faith, family values, and rural life in pre–Quiet Revolution literary classics such as Louis Hémon's *Maria Chapdelaine* (1913), Félix-Antoine Savard's *Menaud maître-draveur* (1937), Ringuet's *Trente arpents* (1938), Germaine Guèvremont's *Le Survenant* (1945), and Claude Henri-Grignon's *Un homme et son péché* (1933), Émond's comments could be misconstrued as an alarming "retour en arrière," evoking a past of poverty, large families, authoritarian priests, and a suffocatingly narrow interpretation of religious doctrine. Surely contemporary Quebec's advances in terms of women's rights, freedom with respect to sexual identity, emphasis on developments in science and technology, modern political sophistication (vs. the paternalism of Duplessis), and the legalization of linguistic rights far outweigh the slow disappearance of what was traditional French Canadian culture? For Émond, this cultural erosion is potentially catastrophic. Yet what he advocates is not retrograde or *passéiste* but pragmatic and idealist. No doubt inspired by his passage through socialism, he measures the loss of Quebec culture on the level of solidarity: loss of "solidarité sociale" [social solidarity] and "solidarité familiale" [family solidarity] and an absence of a "vision du monde partagé" [shared vision of the world] (Émond and Galiero 2009, 117). He calls for us to reflect on the values of common decency—for example, generosity and honour—pre-existent to capitalist society, without which life under neoliberalism would be simply unbearable.

Edmond's trilogy is anchored in these questions of loss. *La Neuvaine* (*Novena*, 2005), discussed by Jim Leach in his chapter, explores the nostalgia for faith in a post-Catholic Quebec through an unlikely encounter between a troubled Montreal doctor, Jeanne Dion (Élise Guilbault), who has lost a child and witnessed an act of savage murder, and a religious youth, François Garon (Patrick Drolet), who is making a novena for his ailing grandmother at the Basilica of Sainte-Anne-de-Beaupré. In the second film, *Contre toute espérance* (*Summit Circle*, 2007), the devoted wife Réjeanne (Guylaine Tremblay) confronts adversity in the form of her husband's illness and suicide and the eventual loss of her job and home. Both films examine the silence of God in the face of human tragedy. While the first film suggests a potential spiritual healing for Jeanne and the second explores a hopeless desperation, the third, *La Donation*, offers a possible secular response to the trilogy: the idea of service to fellow human beings. For Émond, charity is what remains in the absence of both faith and hope (Émond 2011, 39–40; Émond et Galiero 2009, 77). With "le don" [the gift], as he explains, "on entre dans un processus qui implique qu'on va recevoir, mais peut-être pas tout de suite" [we enter a process that implies that we will receive but perhaps not right away] (Émond 2011, 77).

While Émond has provided extended context for the philosophical impetus behind the trilogy, he has commented more summarily on the specific places chosen as the setting for the films. The importance of place is, however, crucial to the analysis of the trilogy, for the first and third films perhaps more than for the second. The communities in the Lower Saint Lawrence and Abitibi regions advance Edmond's ideas about recuperating the positive heritage of so-called traditional French Canadian culture; they are also already *known* to viewers of Quebec cinema through celebrated documentaries dating back to the beginning of Quebec film history. Émond is thus repaying a "debt" both cultural and cinematographic. The idea for *La Neuvaine*, as previously mentioned, came from Edmond's visit to the Basilica in Ste-Anne, repository of French Canadian Christian culture. But the film oscillates not only between Montreal and the basilica but also between the town of Ste-Anne and Petite-Rivière-St-François, one of the oldest settlements in the Charlevoix region, named, as legend has it, by Champlain in 1603. Located just north of Sainte-Anne-de-Beaupré along the north shore of the Saint Lawrence, the town is almost directly across from l'Île-aux-Coudres, the site of Michel Brault and Pierre Perrault's docu-fiction *Pour la suite du monde* (1963). In *La Neuvaine*, Jeanne does not simply escape to a nondescript countryside where she finds peace and solitude; she begins her healing process at a place not far from the most important "lieu de mémoire" in Quebec cinema, where the inhabitants of l'Île-aux-Coudres re-enact fishing practices abandoned for generations as an act of conscious cultural transmission.

Émond decided to set *La Donation* in Abitibi after presenting *La Neuvaine* at the Festival du cinéma international in Abitibi-Témiscamingue; he touring the region's small villages, some now abandoned (Émond and Galiero 2009, 74–75). While he could have made a film about an emergency doctor in, for example, a CLSC (walk-in clinic) in a poor neighbourhood in Montreal, he concluded that there was something profoundly sad, but also symbolically more poignant, about sending Jeanne to what he terms "le bout du monde québécois" [Quebec's end of the world] (Émond and Galiero 2009, 74), where the deserted villages of Abitibi-West could prefigure "notre propre abandon de notre culture et de notre histoire" [the abandoning of our own culture and history] (Émond and Galiero 2009, 74). At the beginning of the twentieth century, the Abitibi region received several waves of migrants that tried their hand at farming; the area then became dominated by mining. These colonization movements speak volumes about Quebec history, politics, identity, and aspirations to autonomy, as well as the creation of legends. The settlement, growth, and decline of the region has been captured in films like *En pays neufs*, *Ste-Anne-de-Roquemaure* and Pierre Perrault's *Le Retour à la terre* (both familiar to Émond).[3] By setting *La Donation* in Abitibi, Émond is engaging directly with the myth of the North in Quebec culture. What he offers the viewer on-screen is decidedly less tragic and moribund than his own remarks suggest. The film presents not the end of Quebec culture but rather the portrait of a small community that despite obvious economic stagnation and geographic isolation continues to survive with dignity and compassion.

The Myth of the North: from Proulx to Perrault

The Abitibi-Témiscamingue region (which covers an area larger than Belgium) was "opened up" for settlement in two waves of immigration. The first occurred at the beginning of the twentieth century after the completion of the Northern Continental Railway; it brought families to the area along with developers, who were drawn to its potential for forestry and mining. The larger second wave occurred in the 1930s and reflected a government-backed plan to encourage unemployed city dwellers from Montreal, Quebec, and the Outaouais—and the sons of settlers already in the region but not yet established on their own land—to come and clear the land for farming. This colonization movement was also meant to discourage French Canadians from following their brethren to manufacturing jobs in New England. The second wave was short-lived; two-thirds of the settlers, ill-prepared for the rude climate, the remoteness of the villages, and the inhospitable soil, returned to the cities or moved on to work in the forestry or mining industries (Linteau 1989, 41). The end result of this precarious settlement was the establishment of 147 parishes between 1930 and 1941, though many were subsequently abandoned. During this period the Province of Quebec reached the maximum of inhabited space. Historians and demographers argue that the history of Abitibi has always been one of conflict between the resource extraction economy (forestry and mining) financed by "foreign capital" (English Canadian or American) and a logic of French Canadian land-occupation and self-sufficiency. Most settlers, or "colons" as they were known, were not subsistence farmers and relied on seasonal forestry work to supplement their meagre incomes from farming. With the growth of mining, the need for a year-round workforce further weakened the incentive to stay on the land (Laplante 1987).

The limited success of the colonization experiment did not in any way diminish its symbolic importance in Quebec history. For the Quebec elites of the 1930s, colonization was a project of territorial aggrandizement and geopolitical expansion, underpinned by an agriculturalist ideology that couched a love for agriculture in an anti-modern philosophy that idealized the past, condemned the present, and denounced the industrial age (Morissonneau and Asselin 1980). At the turn of the nineteenth century, Quebec elites took stock of foreign capital investment in the cities, the English presence in the Eastern Townships, the proximity of the border with Ontario, and the continued migration of French Canadians to the factories of New England, and judged that northern Quebec was the only remaining "free" area awaiting francophone expansion. Described as "new," rich, unknown, and unlimited (which completely ignored the presence of First Nations), northern Quebec became the nodal point around which a new national identity gravitated, an identity inspired by nostalgia for a lost French Canadian continent (a recurrent refrain since 1759) and by the hope of "un pays neuf" that awaited invention/creation. Those who had the strength to settle this region would do so in the tradition of the valiant *coureurs des bois* and the fearless Jesuit missionaries. According to the dominant ideology, critiqued by Morissoneau and Asselin, "la terre du Nord est promise *aux seuls élus*, dont la mission est de l'occuper pour s'y conserver" [the land of the North is promised *only to the chosen* whose mission is to occupy it in order to preserve their culture] (Morissoneau and Asselin 148, emphasis added). Setting aside the lofty rhetoric, these lands were occupied culturally but not economically by the agriculturalists, and in the process, First Nations groups were ignored and then alienated. Churches dot the territory and are visible in the documentary films made in the region. But so are mine headframes, hills of debris, and large saw and pulp and paper mills, all of these reminders of industries financed outside of Quebec that turned the region's farmer-settlers into salaried workers. How different is this, scholars ask, from working in the mills of New Hampshire and Massachusetts? The power of the myth of the North lies in how it succeeded in creating a country ["un pays"] from a territory exploited by others (i.e., foreign capital) (Morissoneau and Asselin 154).[4]

The glorification of the Abitibi colonization is the subject of l'abbé Maurice Proulx's *En pays neufs* (1937), the first feature-length Quebec documentary film. Both *En pays neufs* and its epilogue *Ste-Anne-de-Roquemaure* (1942), shot in colour, are precious testimonials to a particular vision of Quebec society; they use the modern cinematic apparatus to espouse traditional farming methods and the "pure" rural way of life.[5] These films were intended to build public opinion in favour of the colonization of this "grand royaume" [great kingdom], as it was called, hence they elide the history behind the colonizing enterprise and ignore the obvious hardships the colonizers endured. The images in both films have become legendary in part because they are woven into Pierre Perrault's later *Le Retour à la terre*, discussed below. *En pays neufs* opens with a wide shot of two Indigenous canoists on a lake navigating what was up until recently, according to the voice-over, "un territoire sauvage" [a savage/wild territory]. It then chronicles the region's transformation. First there is a portrait of Indigenous inhabitants and their "harmonious" rapport with the missionaries. This is followed by the arrival of the first settlers by train, the building of their rudimentary camps, the collective work of clearing the land by oxen or by hand, shots of the fields of stumps, and later the construction of log cabins and rudimentary log churches. With each visit in 1933, 1935, 1937, the images emphasize progress: new churches, houses that replace logging camps, large chicken coops, small schoolhouses, nursing stations, and so on. The villages themselves are filmed in long shots that emphasize the extraordinary achievement of carving out roads and building houses in neat rectilinear parcels in this remote land. The inhabitants (notably priests, schoolteachers, newlyweds, and children) are featured smiling and laughing in close-ups or are shown in a God-like view that transforms the newcomers into a sort of natural laboratory of human existence.

In *Ste-Anne-de-Roquemaure*, Proulx's camera lingers on plants and flowers (he was an agronomist with a passion for botany) and happy, smiling, frolicking children who symbolize the "land of the future," according to the voice-over commentary. The film's voice-over is all-knowing and reassuring, as was the style at the time; the hopeful aspects of colonization are affirmed in rich, edifying radiophonic voices. The message was clear: Abitibi is a positive place full of energetic pioneers whose work is never done and who extol traditional farming methods and abhor wastefulness and idleness. One commentary especially stands out in this ensemble of soothing pastoral images, which are made all the more languid by the curious use of Erik Satie's *Gymnopédies* as musical accompaniment. The narrator concludes, as the camera lingers on a field of wheat, "nous voyons dans ces champs merveilleux la réalisation des plus belles espérances" [We see in these magnificent fields the realization of our most beautiful hopes]. This phrasing bears an uncanny resemblance to how landscape was used in the dominant discourse of the American West. In this tradition, the white Protestant pioneers "read" the destiny of the American people into the landscape (Comer 1999; Campbell 2008). The end of *En pays neufs* is no less than the beginning of a landscape tradition in Quebec cinema: subsequent filmmakers would have to contend with the "hope trope" suggested by the juxtaposition of image and narration, if only to expose its falsity. Quebec cinematic identity, if we are to take Proulx's film as a possible starting point, was born out of an exaggerated and unrealistic attachment to the land.[6]

The final frames of *Ste-Anne-de-Roquemaure* feature the 1940 visit of Cardinal Villeneuve. The voice-over extolls once again the courage of the settlers, who represent the best of French Canadian society: "Paroissiens de Roquemaure, vivez heureux, vous representez ce que nous avons de meilleur" [Parishioners of Roquemaure, live happily, you represent the best of what we have]. Pierre Perrault's NFB documentary *Le Retour à la terre* (1976), part of a cycle of films about Abitibi farmers, intercuts images of the Proulx films with his own colour footage of abandoned houses and barns and candid interviews with settlers. They are "les gens de paroles," the male speaking subjects typical of Perrault's documentary practice, who remember a far less glorious experience of "opening" the land than the one extolled by Proulx's narrators. However, Perrault does not contradict or erase the heroic masculine discourse that defines the myth of the North in the Proulx films. Hauris Lalancette, farmer-settler and Parti Québécois candidate, the central figure in Perrault's Abitibi cycle, roams from farm to farm denouncing the government's new initiative to help people abandon their farms and relocate to larger cities. With the proper attitude and help from Quebec, he claims, people could remain on their land and even dream of independence (as was typical of the rhetoric of the day). In public meetings, at farmhouse kitchen tables, out in the fields, Lalancette tries to rally his fellow citizens. He engages in lengthy debates with farmers while their wives sit quietly listening (just as they did in the kitchens of l'Île-aux-Coudres in *Pour la suite du monde*). According to Lalancette, Abitibi farms are being abandoned because today's farmers lack the stamina of their ancestors—that is, of people like his own father, who believed in the great colonization enterprise and who worked themselves to the bone for the dream of the "grand royaume." Lalancette even traces his father's strength and courage back to his native village of St-Hyacinthe and to the rebels of the Patriot Rebellion of 1837(!).

In a language both poetic and tragic, Lalancette takes stock of the retreat from the land while Perrault's camera lingers on overgrown green fields. The landscape itself retains its beauty; it becomes ghostly only once Lalancette describes the people and buildings that once were. In an interesting overview of fiction and film inspired by Abitibi and its colonization, Jacques Michaud opposes the discourse(s) of Proulx's film and Perrault's. The former illustrates the "temps de croire" [the time to believe]; the latter, through images and dialogue, shows "le temps de dé-croire" [the time to un-believe] (Michaud 2006, 175). In *Le Retour à la terre*, Perrault suggests that the settlers were the victims of a tragic government-sponsored mistake, symbolized by shots of their abandoned, half-destroyed houses sinking into the earth and the litany of hardships they recount (they were forced to colonize without farming experience by the threat of having their social services withdrawn, they arrived in the remote area too poor to buy the most basic necessities, etc.). But Hauris Lalancette, their de facto leader, continues to believe; he is one of the élu [chosen]. As Michaud concludes, "l'idée que l'Abitibi représentait un royaume à conquérir a rapidement suscité, chez bon nombre de créateurs d'images et de mots, une sorte de fascination" [the idea that Abitibi represented a kingdom to conquer rapidly evoked a sense of fascination for many writers and filmmakers] (182). The notion that Abitibi is a "kingdom of hope" continues to influence literature and cinema set in the region even when, as with Perrault, these cultural texts are dedicated to chronicling its demise.

Émond's *La Donation* references these films, as I will show in the following section. There is, finally, another NFB documentary that informs Émond's version of Abitibi: Gilles Groulx's unsigned short documentary *Normétal* (1960).[7] Once again a portrait of men and men's work, *Normétal* oscillates between an informative documentary on the mining process (showing the men at work underground in darkness) and scenes of the town bathed in natural light, highlighting smiling children's faces in the schoolroom and on the playground. The scenes of the town, in particular a crane shot of the small number of streets laid out in orderly fashion with the mine headframe visible in the background, provide a different "paysage" of the Abitibi region than what we have seen so far. These scenes remind the viewer of different kind of social organization than spaced-out farms. Emphasis is placed on the collective, on life lived as a group, on working, paying mining dues, enjoying evenings out at the cinema on Saturday nights. Like *En pays neufs*, the town scenes show the inhabitants at a distance as if they were ants in a social experiment. What is most striking is the difference in the film's voice-over commentary between the English and French versions, especially in the final frames. The English version is very matter-of-fact, describing the extraction process and closing with a reminder of how copper is essential to modern life. The French version retains the essence of the heroic: the miners came twenty-five years ago to clear the land but now the underground, "riche de promesse," "devrait bientôt les séduire et réclamer leurs efforts" [rich with promise, soon seduced them and claimed their efforts]. In this way, the newcomers' hypermasculine potential is transferred from one "champ" to another. As night descends on the isolated town, the miners become heroes "du fond de la terre" [from down at the bottom of the earth], while the inhabitants of Normétal, drifting into sleep, "veillent à son bonheur" [watch over the town's happiness]. The desire to give agency to the miners in the French version fits with the myth of the North and the lionizing of the French Canadian pioneer/farmer/settler, though the men's status as employees of foreign capital is fittingly captured by the English message "Keep Water Turned Off" scratched into the rock behind a tap deep underground.

Learning to Look at the Land

Émond's *La Donation* differs of course from the social realist documentary style of the 1960s National Film Board. His cinema is highly stylized. *La Donation* features remote landscape shots set to Robert-Marcel Lepage's haunting music, medium shots of characters gazing from windows or alone against the landscape, and extreme close-ups of faces. Jeanne's long drive from Montreal is summarized by a succession of haunting shots looking out from the car window at a highway that weaves through a remote forest against a metallic grey sky. Occasionally, another car or truck passes. She arrives in the village of Normétal, which is captured in a long shot of a series of nondescript white houses, squatting on a grid in a frame that recalls Groulx's "plan d'ensemble" of the town, mentioned above. Jeanne is then welcomed into Dr. Rainville's home, which is also his office. Before his departure for Montreal to visit his disabled son, who is confined to an institution, Dr. Rainville gives Jeanne what amounts to two history lessons: he tells her of how the region came to be settled and of the subsequent importance of mining (now disappeared). These moments embody the two opposing discourses that structure the discussion of the region: the heroic trail-blazing colonizer who was "abandoned" in this inhospitable land, and the mine worker who toiled away in hazardous conditions in an industry whose imprint on the land has been covered up. In the first instance, Dr. Rainville drives with Jeanne through the countryside seemingly devoid of human intervention and evokes the brevity of the colonization experiment. A land that was cleared only one hundred years before by people "left to their own devices" is now returning to the wild.[8] Émond's camera shows fields partly cleared, lush and green against a blue sky. Dr. Rainville's reference here to the first settlers hearkens back to the heroic colonization narrative extolling the virtues of people who, as Dr. Rainville explains, "cleared the land by hand like beasts of burden" only to see their children abandon the fruits of their labour.

In the second "lesson," Dr. Rainville grows more philosophical. He and Jeanne are shown on a ridge under a clear blue sky, overlooking tended fields with the village in the background. What might be a pleasing sight hides an industrial past. This is the mine's former dumpsite; the tailings have only recently been sodded to prevent toxic runoff. Dr. Rainville turns and points to where two headframes once stood, now a hill completely overgrown (though five hundred men once worked there). His movements are slow, his face sober and reflective. Moved by both the landscape and the context provided by the doctor, Jeanne qualifies the scene as "beautiful." Dr. Rainville's response is a warning of sorts. "It's austere," he counters. "Many don't like it." Observing Jeanne looking at the land, he remarks, "I don't know if you will find what you are looking for here." He is in a sense cautioning her to be careful, to avoid easy idealizing of the landscape and its inhabitants, to avoid seeing it and them as the previous Abitibi films have done. One cannot simply read the future into the landscape (as Proulx's narrator suggested) nor can one lament the abandoned past (visible in Perrault). In some instances the land is not what it seems; being "in place," as Émond's film demonstrates, requires a conscious cognitive process of empathy, emotional understanding, and the recovery of ordinary memories.

Michèle Garneau's research on landscape in the Quebec documentary tradition offers an insightful analysis of Émond's rapport with landscape. While Perrault's cinema accords an obvious importance to "la parole," the speaking subject native to the region, the films of Lucie Lambert (e.g., *Avant le jour*, 1999) and others use landscape as "un lieu d'inscription d'affects : consolation, apaisement, baume, palliatif à la douleur" [a place of inscribing affects: consolation, calming, palliative to suffering] (Garneau 2001, 135). In this cinema, the landscape scenes function more personally for the filmmakers as moments of emotive intervention during which an affective register replaces the epic (136). The northwestern Abitibi scenes in *La Donation* are also characterized by an absence of speech; they are infused with a presence that avoids the extremes of the epic and tragic registers. After the departure of Dr. Rainville, Jeanne begins a long process of seeing the region on her own terms. Émond's camera traces her car as she passes through a pleasing landscape toward a quaint covered bridge (blue sky, fall foliage). She is repeatedly shown standing looking out at the lake from the hospital in Macamic. The houses in the villages Jeanne sees are small and nondescript but well maintained. These are, no doubt, following Émond's own argument, places where "le fonds culturel canadien-français" might still exist, having been transported here at the beginning of the century. Instead of the abandoned, half-destroyed farm buildings in Perrault's *Le Retour à la terre*, Émond's camera lingers on barns, closed but intact, devoid of activity but not deserted. These shots occur just before the dramatic crisis in the latter part of the film: two children have run away from home to protest being forced to live with their father, and the film suggests these buildings are potential hiding places. What is important is that these sites are much more than evidence (or traces of settlement)—they have a function within the story for the residents of Normétal, whose lives continue.

A frame from the NFB's *Normétal* is evoked and contextualized in *La Donation* in a similar manner. The NFB documentary features a long nighttime shot of the town bar or music hall, shown at the end of a series of two-storey buildings; the cars are parked at an angle in front, as is common practice in many one-industry Western or frontier towns. Three well-dressed men in black suits linger briefly under the venue's marquee before entering. Where the Groulx film shows the outside of the bar and describes it as place where the miners partake in much needed recreational activities, *La Donation* shows both the space in front on the street and the interior of the bar to be sites of danger, cowardice, drug consumption, and death. Jeanne drives by the bar one evening alone and sees Line (Léalie Ferland-Tanguay), a sixteen-year-old girl, loitering in front with several men; she had just had the girl in her exam room asking for an abortion. Line dies soon after of a crystal meth overdose; she is found out behind the bar. After pronouncing the girl dead at the hospital and breaking the news to the girl's mother (Monique Gosselin), Jeanne marches into the bar demanding that someone speak up. She is met by the stony faces and averted glances of the patrons. Jeanne is gently escorted out onto the street by the town baker, Pierre Grégoire (Eric Hoziel); he warns her that no one will talk about the incident and to leave things to the police. As Jeanne drives away and Pierre walks off into the night, the camera lingers on the same townscape as in the Groulx film—a medium shot of the bar on the bottom left at the end of an empty street. Once again, it seems that Émond's intention is to humanize the region, to tell the story of the people "on the ground," so to speak, of the ones who in the documentary films seem mere pawns in social experiment. In this way, the places in *La Donation*, such as the bar, become real post-industrial sites of struggle; those sites come alive through story even if, as happens here, the story has a tragic end.

The town baker, Pierre, is a key figure in understanding how Jeanne forges her relationship to place and how the film manages to bridge the gap between legend and reality, between the two versions of Abitibi history, one emphasizing heroism, the other victimization. Jeanne first encounters Pierre in her exam room: he has come to her for stitches after a bread-making accident. He explains to her that he left the region for the city to study history but then returned to take over his father's bakery. With his dark hair and eyes, clad in a reddish lumberjack shirt, Pierre exudes a mysterious rugged masculinity. He seems to be unattached and is never shown in conversation with others. He is a sort of solitary, modern-day *coureur des bois* or *survenant* [outlander] figure who has come to the end of his wanderings and has returned to accept the responsibility of cultural transmission (his father's bakery). During their first encounter he asks Jeanne how she likes her surroundings. When she responds that she finds Normétal "far away," he tells her to go into the woods, "that is what's beautiful here." She must take her time and "learn to look at the landscape," as Pierre explains, evoking again the idea of being in place as a cognitive process.

Jeanne later accepts Pierre's offer to spend a day in the woods. This sequence opens with a long shot of two people canoeing on a lake surrounded by forest, an obvious reference to the opening shot of Proulx's *En pays neufs*. The paddlers here are Pierre and Jeanne; once again the Émond film gives voice, story, and context to those who in the earlier films were simply figures in a landscape.[9] In their ensuing conversation, seated side by side on the steps of a rustic shack at lake's edge, Pierre returns to his decision to come home when his father fell ill. At Jeanne's suggestion that he could have "refused," he smiles, telling her by his silence that there are things one cannot refuse (Jeanne has just learned that Dr. Rainville has left his medical practice to her in his will). Pierre explains how, over the course of researching his thesis on the Abitibi pioneers, he foraged through attics to find the written traces of the colonization project. As Marc Chabot writes, Pierre did not find what he thought would be there: "les rêves des habitants, l'utopie foncière du pays, le projet des bâtisseurs, la philosophie de base des défricheurs" [the dreams of the settlers, a land-based utopia, the projects of the builders, the philosophy of the land-clearers] (Chabot 2010, 125). The hundreds of letters he read contained nothing but ordinary life: births, weddings, land-clearings. Though he describes the pioneers in terms that bear the traces of the dominant discourse of epic self-sacrifice—"they were dirt poor" and "worked themselves to the bone and didn't complain"—he nonetheless situates them on the level of regular folk. What might seem like a mundane conversation is in fact crucial for rethinking the Abitibi pioneer settlers in a new cinematic language, one that moves away from Proulx's romanticized pioneers and Perrault's ancestral heroes or what Lalancette calls in *Le Retour à la terre*, "le meilleur de nous autres" [the best of us]. The story of Abitibi is but the story of "le fonds culturel canadien-français" transplanted in the North, the common rituals of Church, family, and work. Pierre admits that he never finished his thesis, which he sometimes regrets. But what counts for him is to have time to read—and to have space. The sequence ends with two long shots of the river, the water gently flowing, bracketed by a greyish fall landscape, evergreens and denuded trees. Émond here suggests that those who have remained in this remote region of Quebec have developed a strong and deeply personal rapport with the land.

I have argued elsewhere that *La Neuvaine*, the first film in this trilogy, can be categorized as women's cinema despite its male director (Roberts

2017, 108). *La Donation* is also a film about female subjectivity, a subjectivity left unexplored in all the celebrated documentary films about Abitibi. As the community doctor, Jeanne is exposed to a broad range of patients who together offer a window onto a community that lost its principal employer many years ago. These women are the ones to suffer, grieve, administer medical care, and provide shelter and comfort. The film thus offers insight into the world of the Abitibi women—women who in the Perrault cycle are shown smiling and smoking (or driving a tractor) but who do not get the chance to speak. From the compassionate secretary Madame Lemay (Danielle Fichaud), to the reckless teenage overdose victim Lise, to Jacynthe (Marie-Josée Laplante) the "deadbeat" mother addicted to painkillers, Émond immerses the viewer in a world of women's experiences, reminiscent of the family of women at the centre of the rural space presented in Pascale Ferland's *Ressac* (2013), discussed by Miléna Santoro in her chapter. In one of the film's most tender scenes, Jeanne visits Madame Cholette, the mother of the deceased teenage girl, and comforts her at her kitchen table. She makes a house call to an elderly woman still bravely running a small gas station and corner store alone despite her advanced age. She watches over Manon (Manon Miclette), a young mother who dies of breast cancer, who is desperate to protect her children, having been abandoned by her husband. She counsels the elderly Madame Laplante (Françoise Graton), who wants to die after she is left alone by her husband's death. All of these characters exhibit a quiet compassion and resolve, far from the heroic discourses of Abitibi settlement and far from the hypermasculine world of the mine (as in Groulx's film). To paraphrase Pierre Grégoire, these women's stories represent "scenes of ordinary life" in which acts of human kindness can still have an impact—hence the importance of charity or "le don." The women are often filmed seated next to Jeanne; glances and gestures are as important as the dialogue. In Perrault's documentary tradition, as Gilles Thérien argues, there is a sense of "un cinéma pour 'homme' avec une sorte de satisfaction virile à *faire le film en même temps que le pays*" [a "man's" cinema with a sort of virile satisfaction of making film at the same time as the country] (quoted in Garneau 163–64, emphasis mine). In Émond's film, as in the documentary films of Lucie Lambert, silence is more important than talk. Émond is no less committed to creating a cinematic world and using that world to reflect on what sort of "pays" Quebec has become—but he substitutes the ordinary for the heroic, women for men, and careful, measured conversation and meaningful silences for epic speech.

The men of this "pays," so it appears, have either stopped working or are absent, having been forced to migrate once again to find work either in the mines of the Arctic or out in Alberta, where the oil boom continuees. Except for Dr. Rainville and the baker Pierre Grégoire, the men in *La Donation* are a frustrated, angry lot, not unlike the "men in pain" examined by Amy Ransom elsewhere in this book. Two men in particular occupy opposite ends of the economic spectrum. Jeanne is threatened in her office by Monsieur Leclerc (Pierre Mailloux), a gruff man in his mid-fifties, who wants to continue receiving workers' compensation, no doubt for a past injury. His anger at her refusal confirms perhaps the man's laziness but also the limited prospects for employment in today's Normétal. Equally angry and potentially violent is the millionaire industrialist Monsieur Roberge (Aubert Pallascio), who reportedly owned half the region before he "sold it to the Americans," according to Madame Lemay (Dr. Rainville's secretary). Jeanne makes two trips by private helicopter to Roberge's isolated lakefront home, supposedly to treat his aches and pains (fibromyalgia); but she finds herself administering to a depressed and lonely man who has become an alcoholic and a danger to himself. The film assigns him an "outsider" status, given the isolated location of his home and the decidedly American way in which he views medical care (he has already consulted specialists at the Mayo Clinic in the United States, and he has the money to buy medical care and thus wants Jeanne to be at his beck and call). Exasperated with his arrogance and reckless behaviour, Jeanne tells him she will no longer come running each time he hurts himself. Roberge, an industrial baron who runs shipping and transport lines and who made a deal with a foreign investor, highlights a particular sore spot for Abitibi scholars, in that so many people settled the region or migrated there for the mines and ended up working for a "foreign" boss—like Roberge.

As previously mentioned, at the heart of Émond's cinema is the question of cultural transmission, of the debt one owes to one's precessors and the need to carry forward cultural heritage for future generations. In *La Donation*, women are the guardians of this process (the exception being Pierre the baker). After the death of Dr. Rainville, his sister Gaétane (Angèle Coutu), who is a nun, comes to Normétal to settle his affairs. The scene of the reading of the will—three women (Jeanne, Madame Lemay, and Gaétane) seated across from the lawyer—underscores yet again the feminization of the transmission process. At Dr. Rainville's funeral, his sister Gaétane describes her brother's life as one dedicated to helping others. "I don't think one can do much better with one's life," she declares, as the camera lingers on the faces of the attendees. She does not pressure Jeanne to accept the "gift," though she shows by her own example that serving others is obviously the preferred path. She reminds Jeanne as she leaves: "My brother's giving you his most prized possession." What is important is that this gift, while it includes the house and exam room, is actually immaterial—it is a gift of human relationships, of trust, of compassion, of a community that has been built up by Dr. Rainville over forty years. As Pierre Grégoire remarks, the deceased doctor delivered more than half the town's population.

While Jeanne hesitates over accepting Dr. Rainville's medical practice—she is not sure she can become as close to her patients as he was to his—the crisis of the missing children arises. Their grandmother, Madame Pelletier (Odette Bouchard-Lampron), is important in this storyline, for she is the one who will ensure a home for the children after their mother's death. Jeanne visits Corinne (Marie-Soleil Corbin-Allyson), the older of the children, in her grandparents' home and encourages her to be brave and set an example for her brother. Nevertheless, the two children run away to escape being taken away by their father after their mother's death. In the end, while the whole town searches for them frantically, the two spend the night in an abandoned school bus. They are found safe and sound, but Corinne, who suffers from a heart defect, falls ill and almost dies in hospital. The narrative concerning the children adds obvious drama to the film's plot. In giving them a certain degree of agency (they choose to stay with their grandparents and avoid their father), Émond evokes and moves beyond the documentaries about the region. In Proulx's and Groulx's films, children are often filmed in the classroom or playing in the distance. They symbolize, obviously, the innocent future of the colonization/mining experiment. Émond gives them, especially the older girl, a certain agency, while still underscoring the importance of responsible adults to their well-being and protection.

La Donation's final scene, evoked at the beginning of this chapter, fittingly involves the passage of life from one woman to another. Jeanne comes across a car accident in the morning light on an isolated road. The driver of the second car, a young mother, is still alive, though she dies in Jeanne's arms soon after uttering a simple "I'm scared." Jeanne removes the infant, who is apparently unharmed, from the car seat and stands on the side of the road looking out over the landscape. As Marie-Claude Loiselle writes, "Jeanne porte dans ses bras la vie tout entière et, les pieds plantés sur cette route déserte au coeur même de l'Abitibi et de ses champs dénudés, elle vient peut-être de trouver la force vitale nécessaire pour occuper la place qui lui revient" [Jeanne holds in her arms life itself. Her feet firmly planted on this deserted road at the heart of Abitibi and its bare fields, she has just found the force needed to take the place that is reserved for her] (Loiselle 2010, 148). Jeanne will not necessarily adopt this child, though viewers familiar with her character in *La Neuvaine* might see it as a likely outcome, given that she had lost a child to illness. In *La Donation,* the baby is "delivered" for a second time, this time into the arms of Jeanne, who will care for it in the interim. This final image brings together the "don" [gift] of serving others, echoed throughout the film, with a decidedly original view of the Abitibi landscape and its inhabitants, who are neither heroes nor victims. Though the film ends without resolving whether Jeanne will take over Dr. Rainville's medical practice, the final frame shows her as having already taken his place. She is a courageous witness to both life and death in an inhospitable landscape.

Notes

1   A CÉGEP (Collège d'enseignement général et professionnel) is a publicly funded pre-university and technical college in Quebec's education system. They are sometimes compared to junior colleges or community colleges; however, they differ differ in that a Diploma of College Studies (or Diplôme d'études collégiales, DEC) is required for university admission in Quebec.

2   See Santoro et al. for an overview of the politics and thematic preoccupations of contemporay Quebec filmmakers, and White on Émond's rapport with debates about the legacy of the Quiet Revolution.

3   After Montreal and Quebec City, Abitibi was the most filmed region by the NFB between 1950 and 1966. See Véronneau 2006, 20.

4   See Dupuis for an opposing view that assigns more agency to the colonizers.

5   An agronomist by training, Proulx was a skilled 16mm filmmaker who travelled extensively in the region. The Quebec government had in fact commissioned the film to be shown at the Colonisation Pavilion at the Provincial Exhibition in September 1937. Proulx thus had the funds to record and produce the film's narrative commentary and soundtrack in studios in New York (Véronneau 2006, 16).

6   Harcourt makes a similar argument about how the pastoral tradition in Quebec cinema is more aspiration than reality.

7   According to Scott Mackenzie, the film was commissioned by the Quebec branch of the United Steelworkers' Union. Because of NFB intervention, the union was mentioned only once in passing, which prompted Groulx to withdraw his name from the film (134).

8   Quoted dialogue is taken from the film's English subtitles.

9   The canoers in the Proulx film were Native people; Émond does not evoke the Native presence in the region.

9

QUEBEC-MONTREAL:
Time, Space, and Memory in
Robert Lepage's *Le Confessionnal* and
Bernard Émond's *La Neuvaine*

Jim Leach

Un lien important avec le passé a disparu. De plus en plus, nous vivons, au Québec, sans mémoire. [An important link with the past has disappeared. More and more, we are living, in Quebec, without memory.]
— Bernard Émond (qtd. in Haïm 2005a, 43)

On a poignardé notre père, car c'est l'Église catholique qui a gardé la culture québécoise pendant une couple de siècles. [...] Alors, tout en subissant le joug de la religion, nous lui devons notre survie culturelle. [We have stabbed our father, because it was the Catholic church that protected Quebec culture for a couple of centuries ... Thus, in submitting to the yoke of religion, we owe our cultural survival to it.]
— Robert Lepage (qtd. in Caron 1995, 28)

My title is borrowed from Ricardo Trogi's darkly comic road movie *Québec-Montréal* (2002), a film that depicts three groups of young people travelling between the two cities. It makes no reference to Quebec's past or to the differences between the cities in the ways they have figured in present-day debates about the significance of that past. In particular, while all the characters seem to feel a sense of emptiness in their lives from their failure to live up to the ideal represented by the Barbie and Ken couple who periodically pass them in a shiny sports car, there is no suggestion that they would find spiritual sustenance in Quebec's cultural or religious heritage. A case could be made that the film expresses the consequences of living without memory, but this is never overtly addressed, and the film's slick visual style declares it to be a postmodern text even as it portrays the superficiality of the characters' lifestyles.

Quebec's Catholic past was a major point of contention in the debates over the Charter of Quebec Values proposed by the Parti Québécois government in 2013 and again over the policies of the Coalition Avenir Québec, which unexpectedly came to power in the 2018 provincial election. Placing restrictions on the public display of religious insignia, the ostensible aim of these measures is to affirm that Quebec has now become a modern secular society, but their impact mainly affects members of the non-Christian diasporic communities whose presence is viewed by many as a threat to traditional values. Crosses such as the ones in the provincial legislature and on Mount Royal are exempted on the grounds that they are cultural rather than religious symbols, but this distinction points to the ambiguity of a secular cultural identity signified by a symbol derived from a religious heritage that was decisively rejected fifty years ago.

In this chapter I focus on how the past is represented in two films whose titles evoke the Catholic religious practices associated with Quebec's traditional cultural identity that was supposedly swept away in the Quiet Revolution, which caused a seismic upheaval in Quebec culture in the 1960s and whose impact is still being assessed by historians. *Le Confessionnal* (Robert Lepage, 1995) and *La Neuvaine* (Bernard Émond, 2005) are very different films, but, unlike *Québec-Montréal*, they clearly address the psychological and ideological implications of this rejection of the past. I compare these films, and the contexts in which their directors framed them, in order to examine their contributions to contemporary debates about Quebec's heritage and its relevance to the present.

A Not-So-Quiet Revolution

La révolution tranquille was quiet in the sense that it was accomplished without violence, but although historians have traced its roots back at least to the end of the Second World War, it was experienced in the 1960s as a sudden and radical break with the past. In Denys Arcand's *Les Invasions barbares* (2003), which André Loiselle discusses at length elsewhere in this collection, a priest laments the abrupt decline in Church attendance in Quebec, which he says happened in 1966. He is standing in a room full of objects of religious art that once reinforced the spiritual values of Catholicism but which now, an appraiser assures him, have no material value. If the priest exaggerates slightly by attributing the decline to a specific year, historians are generally agreed that "in the space of little more than fifty years, between the end of the Second World War and the close of the twentieth century [...] Quebec went from being one of the most socially traditional, politically conservative, and religiously devout regions of the developed world to one of the least" (Christiano 2007, 21).

However, unlike the priest in his film, Arcand, who studied history at university, has argued that the Quiet Revolution actually changed very little, because "mentalities change much more slowly than governments and social structures" (qtd. in La Rochelle 2005, 274). If this is so, "the extremely rapid disintegration of Catholicism as an institutional presence and as a system of public and personal values during the 1960s" (Gauvreau 2005, 3) must have generated a potent brew in which the emergent modern society clashed with powerful but often repressed residual values. Although the new Québécois identity that replaced the hybrid "French Canadian" one was seen as more dynamic and self-assured, the sudden changes could also be experienced as "une crise identitaire" [an identity crisis] (Beauchemin 2002, 132). This sense of uncertainty was already apparent in "direct cinema" fiction films such as *À tout prendre* (Claude Jutra, 1963) and *Le Chat dans le sac* (Gilles Groulx, 1964), whose production coincided with these social and cultural developments, and which focus on adolescents who feel uncomfortable in the new social order. An iconic moment occurs at the beginning of Groulx's film when the young protagonist declares, "Je suis Canadien français, donc je me cherche" [I am French Canadian, therefore I am searching for myself].

Nevertheless, for many years, the dominant story about the Quiet Revolution depicted it through the metaphor of a movement from darkness into light. According to this account, it swept away *la grande noirceur*, the great darkness of a past in which Quebec's development was held back by the dominance of the Catholic Church and the conservative Union Nationale government led by Maurice Duplessis, which held power almost continuously from 1936 to 1960. Accompanying this metaphor was another in which the Quiet Revolution was a movement from childhood into adulthood, "the veritable coming-of-age of a people in its belated encounter with modernity" (Christiano 2007, 22). However, as with the euphoria associated with the emergence of youth culture and the various liberation movements of the 1960s, the changes in Quebec could be seen as the triumph of individualism over collective values. In Quebec, as elsewhere, this trend led to denunciations of the materialism of the new consumer society, as promoted by the mass media, which disseminated or imitated American popular culture. From this perspective, the metaphors were replaced by another story in which the break with the past did not lead to greater enlightenment or the desired maturity.

Originating with the influential sociologist and theologian Fernand Dumont, this story challenged intellectuals to think of Quebec "in terms of the metaphor of a child carried in one's arms: as a being that is fragile and incomplete and needs protection" (Létourneau 2004a, 116–17). Dumont initially saw the Quiet Revolution as "une révolution culturelle" [a cultural revolution] that needed to be followed by "transformations économiques et politiques" [economic and political transformations] (1971, 92); then, when these changes failed to appear, his later writings developed a vision of a Quebec that had lost touch with the collective project that in the past had provided a sense of purpose and identity. While critical of the Church and lamenting the lost opportunities that followed the Quiet Revolution, he remained a committed Catholic and argued that Quebec could not progress without renewing its ties with its "héritage," insisting that the fundamental issue was "le problème de la mémoire" [the problem of memory] (1995, 18).

By 1995, the year of the second referendum on independence, it seemed that many people were, like Dumont, nostalgic for a past "où l'on priait ensemble, où l'individualisme ne semblait pas menacer l'intérêt collectif" [when people prayed together, when individualism did not seem to threaten the collective interest] (De Koninck 1995, 6). Serge Cantin, in an essay originally published in 1988, could write that, "près de trente ans après le déclenchement de notre Révolution tranquille, il semble que nous sachions moins que jamais qui nous sommes et que nous voulons" [nearly thirty years after the start of our Quiet Revolution, it seems that we know less than ever who we are and what we want] (1997, 27–28). He argued that "en voulant rompre à tout prix avec un passé dit de 'grande noirceur' pour entrer de plain-pied dans la modernité, le Québec s'est sans doute exposé à un danger... dont l'avait préservé jusque-là son conservatisme culturel et religieux" [in wanting to break at all costs with a past known as the "great darkness" to enter straight into modernity, Quebec certainly exposed itself to a danger ... from which its cultural and religious conservatism up to then had protected it] (1997, 29). As this suggests, those who rejected the old story of the Quiet Revolution but did not want to reject all aspects of modernity, had to distinguish their position from a simple nostalgia for a past in which the Church held sway over Quebec's cultural life.

More recently, thinkers like Jocelyn Létourneau have attacked "this pessimistic view of the community" for failing to address "the Québécois reality in its diversity and its nuances." For Létourneau, "Quebec is not incomplete and not like a child that is slow to grow up and refuses its responsibilities," and "the Québécois place of historical being is precisely one of ambivalence" (2004a, 105, 124). This ambivalence has also been described as a marked schizophrenia in that "most Québécois secularists who have abandoned their Catholicism nevertheless embrace that Catholicism as an important part of their cultural heritage" (Adelman 2011, 109). Of course, the diversity of the Quebec population has become even more evident in recent years with the arrival of many immigrants from different ethnic backgrounds, but, as in the two films to be discussed here, the debate on the impact of the Quiet Revolution has been framed almost entirely in terms of Quebec's Catholic heritage.

The renewed interest in heritage has been very apparent in Quebec cinema during the last several decades. While critics have tended to value films in the tradition of the direct cinema films, with their documentary roots, set almost by definition in the present, Quebec also has a tradition of popular cinema that can be traced back to a group of melodramas produced in Quebec during the postwar period, with the moral support of the Church. A remake of one of these films, *Séraphin : Un Homme et son péché* (Charles Binamé), was a huge commercial success in 2002, inspiring a succession of films set in the past. As Éric Bédard suggests, however, while the appeal of these films is often defined as nostalgic, their viewers are more likely "se réjouir d'être sorti de cette époque d'intolérance, de rigorisme, de fermeture d'esprit, de sacrifice et de misère" [to rejoice at having left behind this period of intolerance, strictness, closed minds, sacrifice, and misery] (2007–8, 81). These so-called heritage films clearly respond to a felt need to recover the cultural memory supposedly lost after the Quiet Revolution, but the result is a far from nostalgic gaze; rather, they represent the past as "un vaste musée des horreurs" [a vast museum of horrors] (2007–8, 93).

Catholicism thus seems to function in the present as a marker of identity rather than as a meaningful belief system. However, Heinz Weinmann has suggested that "depuis quelque temps, on a assisté à ce qui a été appelé un 'retour du religieux'" [for some time, we have witnessed what has been called a "return of the religious"], which is "un phénomène global qui dépasse le seul Québec" [a global phenomenon that goes beyond Quebec alone] but takes on specific forms there in relation to the memory of the Catholic past (1990, 24). He argues that the first major cinematic manifestation of this phenomenon was Arcand's *Jésus de Montréal* (1989), a film that subjects the Church as an institution, and the media networks that have replaced it, to the mordant satirical gaze that has earned the director a reputation for cynicism.

Yet the film's plot, in which Daniel (Lothaire Bluteau), a young actor, responds to the request of a priest for a new version of the Passion Play that will be more relevant to modern audiences, affirms the continued relevance of Jesus's teachings. The innovative play created by Daniel and his fellow actors attracts large audiences and becomes a media sensation both locally and internationally, but it proves to be too much for the Church authorities, who try to ban it, which leads to a disturbance during the depiction of the crucifixion in which Daniel is seriously injured. He dies because of the overcrowded Montreal hospital system, and in the final sequence his organs bring new life and hope to the sick. As Arcand's title suggests, the film places the story of Jesus against the backdrop of the modern city, above which the Oratory, where the play is performed, looks down on high-rise buildings and busy streets. The spiritual drama enacted on the mountain contrasts with the materialistic and fashionable activities down in the metropolis.

The spatial structure of the film sets up a tension between religious values, which have been consigned to the past, and the materialism of modern-day Montreal. Yet the diversity and nuances of Quebec culture that Létourneau emphasizes mean that the history of post–Quiet Revolution Quebec has another important spatial dimension. As he points out, "depuis quelque temps, le territoire québécois est marqué de manière exacerbée par des dynamismes de développement concentrés et inégaux" [for some time, the Québécois territory has been marked in an exacerbated manner by concentrated and unequal dynamisms of development], with the result that "certains n'hésitent plus à opposer le Grand Montréal au 'Reste du Québec'" [some people have not hesitated to oppose Greater Montreal to the "Rest of Quebec"]. If Montreal "se différencie des autres cités... par le volume et la diversité culturelle et linguistique de sa population" [is differentiated from the other cities by the size and the cultural and linguistic diversity of its population], the old cultural traditions remain much more influential in Quebec outside Montreal (Létourneau 2004b, 102).

These cultural differences are evident, but in a complicated way, in the work of Robert Lepage and Bernard Émond. Lepage was born in 1957, Émond in 1951, which means that they both grew up during the sudden changes that accompanied Quebec's supposed attainment of adulthood. While Lepage was born in Quebec City, which remains his home and the base for his theatre company Ex Machina, with which he has gained an international reputation as a theatrical innovator, his work reveals a cosmopolitan sensibility more usually associated with Montreal. Conversely, Émond was born in Montreal, the city in which he still lives and which figures in most of his films, but he has said that he has "l'impression que le coeur français du Québec bat à l'extérieur de Montréal" [the impression that Quebec's French heart beats outside Montreal] and that he no longer recognizes himself in that city (qtd. in Coulombe 2012, 13). These geographical coordinates point to the complexity of Quebec's cultural identity after the Quiet Revolution, and, as we will see in exploring *Le Confessionnal* and *La Neuvaine*, issues of time and memory are as intricate as those of space.

In the Name of the Father: *Le Confessionnal*

Robert Lepage, who played one of the actors in the Passion Play in *Jésus de Montréal*, cast Lothaire Bluteau, that film's Daniel/Jesus, as Pierre Lamontagne, the protagonist in his own first feature film, drawing on the spiritual aspects of the actor's persona to depict a character who embodies the spirit of the Gospels, mediating between past and present with no apparent desires of his own. In *Le Confessionnal*, Lepage creates cinematic equivalents to his theatre work, which has "souvent été qualifié de cinématographique" [often been described as cinematic] in its fluid transitions in space and time (Perron 1994, 48), as the action moves back and forth between the near present (1989) and the past (1952). The film draws on the duality in Lepage's own relations to space and time, to the new and old Quebec: on the one hand, he has earned a reputation as "the consummate Québec internationalist" (Fricker 2005, 170), but, on the other, his work constantly depicts the influence of the past, "remembering and engaging with the political trauma of lost territory and integrity" (Dundjerovic 2003, 20).

At the beginning of *Le Confessionnal*, Pierre returns to Quebec in 1989 from a three-year stay in China, where he has been studying art. He has come home for his father's funeral, and his return leads him to investigate a mystery that involved his family in 1952, the year of his birth. His opening voice-over refers to three events that marked that year: the coming of television, the re-election of Maurice Duplessis, and the presence of Alfred Hitchcock and his film crew during the production of *I Confess*, a thriller about a priest accused of murder. Of these three, the first was a key factor that led to the Quiet Revolution, while the second demonstrated the persistence of the forces opposed to change. In Lepage's film, the third event becomes a catalyst that brings out "l'indélébilité du passé et son impact irrémédiable sur l'avenir" [the indelibility of the past and its irremediable impact on the future] (Larue 1995, 29). Yet the film's temporal structure elides the key events in the period between 1952 and 1989 that shaped the culture of contemporary Quebec: the Quiet Revolution, of course, but also the October Crisis of 1970 and the 1980 referendum.

At the Catholic funeral service, the church is deserted except for Pierre and his cousin André (Richard Fréchette). Pierre is especially disturbed by the absence of his adoptive brother Marc (Patrick Goyette), who seems to have disappeared. When he finally tracks Marc down, Pierre finds that he is currently in a relationship with Massicotte (Jean-Louis Millette), a government official, and that he has a child by his former partner Manon (Marie Gignac). Marc is troubled that he does not know who his real father was, and Pierre agrees to try to solve the mystery. His efforts are intercut with events in 1952 that coincide with the filming of *I Confess*, in which Montgomery Clift plays a Catholic priest accused of murder who cannot expose the real killer who has spoken to him in the confessional. At the same time, a priest in the church where Hitchcock's film is being shot is suspected of being Marc's father but cannot clear his name because he learned the identity of the real father in the confessional. Rachel (Suzanne Clément), Marc's mother, commits suicide apparently because she cannot face the shame of being an unwed mother, but the film will reveal that there were other factors that intensified her distress.

The funeral sequence establishes the principle of fluid transitions between time periods that will characterize the film's narration. As the camera tracks away from the two mourners, it passes pews full of people, including Hitchcock (Ron Burrage) and his assistant (Kristin Scott Thomas), finally coming to rest in front of the closed door of the confessional, evoking an uneasy sense of the dark secrets inside, whose threat is reinforced when the film's title appears over this image with a cutthroat razor entwined with the letter C. Without a cut, the camera movement has brought out the difference between present and past, but here the contrast is complicated not only by the presence of the Hollywood filmmakers (Hitchcock was Catholic) but also by the transition on the soundtrack from the priest's voice intoning the funeral rites to Sarah Vaughan's recording of "A Blues Serenade," which becomes diegetic in the next sequence when it is heard on a radio in the Lamontagne home in 1952. The past is thus signified not only by the dominance of the Church but also by the pleasures of (American) popular music.

Such seamless transitions recur throughout the film, but there are also several abrupt cuts from the film's action to black-and-white sequences from *I Confess*, filmed on location in Quebec City. Ironically, Hitchcock's Hollywood fiction offers a more accurate visual representation of the city's past, albeit filtered through the lighting codes of *film noir*, than Lepage's re-creation can possibly provide. According to Lepage, Hitchcock's thriller effectively captured the *grande noirceur* that lay "derrière cette belle ville historique en sucre pour les touristes" [behind this beautiful historical city of sugar for tourists] (qtd. in Caron 1995, 28). In juxtaposing present and the past, film and film-within-the-film, *Le Confessionnal* sets up a tension between fluidity and what Claudie Massicotte calls "le motif de la scission" [the motif of scission] (2012, 100). The film itself foregrounds this tension when Rachel takes a cutthroat razor from a bathroom cabinet in 1952, apparently intending to commit suicide, and there is a cut to red liquid running down a sink, which turns out to be paint washed by Pierre from the paintbrush he is using to cover the marks left by old photos on the wall of the family home in 1989.

The tension between continuity and cutting is also apparent in Pierre's attitude toward the past. On the one hand, he investigates it to solve the mystery of Marc's birth; on the other, he tries to cut himself off from it by taking down the photographs of his family and painting over the marks left by the picture frames. However, the marks of the past remain persistently present and will not disappear whatever colour paint Pierre uses. The implication is that, while the attempt to erase the past has led to a loss of meaning in the present, the present is nevertheless still shaped by the deeply embedded values of that past.

In the film's depiction of the past, the close-knit community of Quebec City is disturbed by outside influences in the form of the production of a Hollywood film that uses authentic locations but with only a token acknowledgment of the French-speaking population; in the present, Quebec is part of a new global culture, with references to the 1989 Tiananmen Square massacre in China, sequences set in Japan, and English-language rock music on the soundtrack. The intercutting between past and present, coupled with the omission of the period in between, creates a play of similarity and difference and raises the question of the film's attitude toward the modernization of Quebec. If the "smooth temporal transitions ... establish a narrative continuity on the level of the image track" (Lajoie 2001, 52), there is often a strong sense of contrast between the periods.

For some critics, the overall effect is to stress the difference between traditional and modern Quebec; for others, the film ultimately shows "à quel point le Québec a peu changé" [how little Quebec has changed] (Larue 1995, 30). Lepage himself seems to support the former viewpoint, pointing out that "le drame de la fille-mère de 1952 serait une bien petite chose aujourd'hui, mais dans ces années-là, c'était terrible" [the drama of the unwed mother in 1952 would be a small thing today, but in those years, it was terrible] (qtd. in De Blois 1995–96, 17), a difference that he illustrates in the movie by contrasting Rachel's fate with that of Manon, who lives as a single mother in a disreputable motel where she performs in a sex show. However, while Manon may not feel shame, she lives in poverty with her son in a motel attached to the bar where she performs.

Rachel's story bleeds into the apparently more open society of 1989, in which the Catholic confessionals of the past have been replaced by the "sexual spaces" (Marshall 2001, 308) of the cubicles in the gay sauna where Pierre searches for Marc and in the sex club where Manon is called to a "confessional" to dance for a customer. As Claudie Massicotte suggests, however, the difference may not be as great as it seems since in both eras the confessionals "s'offriront comme refuges des désirs inavoués" [offer themselves as refuges from unacknowledged desires] (2012, 105). The present mirrors the past when Marc replicates his mother's despair by committing suicide on a visit to Japan with Massicotte, a similarity the film underscores by intercutting between the two events. If Rachel committed suicide because of the shame of being a single mother, Marc does so after apparently learning the identity of his father (although we do not hear what Massicotte says when he reveals the secret to Marc). His motives are not entirely clear, but Martin Lefebvre suggests that he is "unable to strike a balance between continuity and discontinuity" and thus "has no real identity and cannot survive" (1998, 95–96).

The final sequences resolve the mystery of the identity of Marc's father and strive to give it allegorical significance. After Pierre discovers that Massicotte, now a diplomat, was the priest to whom Rachel confessed and that he was forced to leave the Church because he was suspected of being the father of her child, he demands his help to save Marc's son from the conditions in which he is living. The fact that the boy has diabetes, which, as Massicotte points out, is almost always an inherited disease, suggests a link with Pierre's father, Paul-Émile (François Papineau), who went blind from the disease. Since both Marc and Pierre also have symptoms, the clear deduction is that Paul-Émile is also Marc's father. However, while some critics complained that the solution was too obvious, others thought that, since the truth was never explicitly stated, there was room for doubt.

If there is some ambiguity regarding the literal resolution of the plot, the drive toward an allegorical reading in the two final sequences also does not produce the straightforward interpretation that it seems to be reaching for. Intercut with Pierre's confrontation with Massicotte in 1989, we see Hitchcock leaving the premiere of *I Confess*, complaining that the censors have "cut my film," and insisting on returning to his hotel in Paul-Émile's taxi. On their journey, Paul-Émile tells Hitchcock he has a "suspense story" for him and proceeds to outline a plot based on his own affair with his wife's sister. When Hitchcock asks how it ends, Paul-Émile replies that, because the man cannot live with his guilt, he plucks out his eyes. As the cab pulls up outside the hotel, Hitchcock comments that it is not a suspense story but a "Greek tragedy," an allusion that resonates with Lepage's sense that his story "se passe dans une petite cellule familiale dans une petite ville dans un petite province, chez un petit peuple" [takes place in a small family unit in a small city in a small province with a small population], which "évoquait l'inceste, l'oedipe" [evoked incest, Oedipus] (qtd. in Coulombe 1995, 22). As Monique Tschofen points out, it also evokes the motif of blindness and not seeing that emerges from Pierre's investigation (2006, 205).

The Oedipal metaphor suggests both the ritual and psychoanalytical implications of the events depicted in the film, but the final sequence adds another dimension to the possible allegory. In the last, rather improbable, image, Pierre carries his young nephew precariously along the railing of the Quebec Bridge across the Saint Lawrence River. This bridge is first seen at the beginning of the film and again when Rachel throws herself from it. It is also reflected in the windows of a limousine as Massicotte reveals the secret of his birth to Marc. According to Peter Clandfield, the actual bridge is "a symbol of a progressive, outward-looking Québécois consciousness—one akin to that which Lepage himself espouses" (2003, 9), implying that Pierre is carrying his nephew into a new and better future. Yet as the credits begin to roll, we hear Pierre's voice repeating the words from his opening voice-over: "Dans la ville où je suis né le passé porte le present comme un enfant sur ses épaules" [In the city where I was born the past carries the future like a child on its shoulders], a fairly overt allusion to the "pessimistic" story of Quebec's cultural history according to which, as described by Jocelyn Maclure, "ontologically fragile and insecure, Quebec must be carried like a child to the threshold of maturity" (2003, 47).

In interviews, Lepage has encouraged readings of the ending that are more specifically related to the visual evidence, framing it as "a metaphor for vertigo, an image evoking the danger of living," and acknowledging that some audiences saw it as suicidal, assuming that Pierre and the child must fall from the railing, especially since Pierre suffers from bouts of dizziness that we finally realize are a symptom of his diabetic condition (qtd. in Clandfield 2003, 6). Ultimately, Lepage accepts the ambiguity and insists, "il ne faut pas décider de ce que les gens font avec le film, leur conclusion leur appartient" [there is no need to decide what people do with the film, their ending belongs to them] (qtd. in Caron 1995, 27). In the film's press kit, Lepage suggested that *Le Confessionnal* deals with "the transition to modernity, with all the re-questioning ... that involves" (qtd. in Tschofen 2006, 205). Its juxtaposition of past and present depicts the contrast between a culture in which the making of a movie was a special event and the "time-space compression" (Harvey 1990, 284-308) of postmodern culture.

Lepage's film has frequently been seen as belonging to this postmodern culture, as in Christopher Gittings's description of it as "a hybrid amalgam of the old and the new, of cliché and originality, in the manner of a postmodern collage" (2002, 132). Unlike many of his fellow filmmakers (including Bernard Émond), Lepage is quite open to such readings, and the treatment of time in *Le Confessionnal*, and the unstable relations of past and present, cause and effect, explore postmodernism's emphasis on "the perpetual present" and "the loss of historical grand narratives" (Marshall 2001, 305). The buried secret from the past that comes back to haunt the characters in *Le Confessionnal* parallels the repression of Quebec's past after the Quiet Revolution, but the film's structure and style construct a temporality that suggests an alternative to the paralysis that destroys Marc. When Pierre takes responsibility for Marc's son, he differentiates himself from his own father and accepts the instability and ambivalence of the cultural identity he must assume. Although he speaks of the present carrying the past, the experience of the film's representation of time makes past and present equally present, creating a "une temporalité spectrale plutôt que linéaire" [a spectral rather than linear temporality] (Massicotte 2012, 111) in which the past haunts the present because of the secrecy and shame associated with the confessional.

Living without Memory: *La Neuvaine*

Lepage established his reputation in the theatre, whereas Émond, like many Quebec filmmakers, was well known as a documentary filmmaker before turning to feature films, beginning in 2001. With a background in anthropology, he is more aligned with the realist tradition in Quebec cinema than Lepage, whose formalism and theatricality have alienated some critics. Émond's films have been accompanied by a succession of writings and interviews in which he has developed a devastating critique of contemporary culture and, in particular, of the impact of postmodernism and neoliberalism on Quebec. The titles of the two books that most fully express his thinking encapsulate its key themes. *Le Perte et le Lien* (2009), literally "The Loss and the Bond," is a book-length interview with a younger filmmaker, Simon Galiero, and its title could well serve for any of Émond's feature films. *Il y a trop d'images* (2011) [There are too many images] is a collection of essays and other writings, whose title points to the imperative behind the filmmaker's austere style. According to Émond, the proliferation of images in contemporary society serves to mask the loss of meaningful cultural values, and he argues that, in the case of Quebec, this situation can be remedied only by re-establishing the bond with the distinctive identity that was swept away by the Quiet Revolution.

La Neuvaine was Émond's third fiction film and the first in a trilogy on the theological virtues of faith, hope, and charity. It tackles issues of faith through the experiences of Jeanne Dion (Élise Guilbaut), a Montreal doctor who witnesses the brutal killings of a battered woman and her child whom she has tried to help. She has lost her own child to an incurable disease and is now haunted by the idea that her actions, the malpractice" of getting involved with a patient, contributed to this act of violence. Refusing psychological help, she leaves the city and drives, apparently aimlessly, to the village of Sainte-Anne-de-Beaupré, the site of a Catholic basilica where the faithful come to obtain miracles from the saint. However, Jeanne's recovery is made possible not by the saint but by a chance meeting with François (Patrick

Drolet), a young man from a small village who is saying a novena, which requires him to visit the Basilica over a nine-day period, in the hope of saving his dying grandmother. Like Pierre in *Le Confessionnal*, François seems to have no desires of his own, but his intervention saves Jeanne, who, in turn, is able to help him cope with his grief when his grandmother finally dies.

As Émond himself points out, the narrative is based on a clear-cut structure of "les symétries et les oppositions (ville/campagne, foi/incroyance, ésperance/désespoir, simplicité/complexité)" [symmetries and oppositions (city/country, faith/unbelief, hope/despair, simplicity/complexity)] (2007b, 14). Yet even though this structure is more straightforward than that of *Le Confessionnal*, time is distorted, in that the present action is punctuated by flashbacks representing Jeanne's repressed memories, with the result that we do not discover the full reason for her traumatic state until about three-quarters of the way through the film. Her journey from the city to the country is like time travel into the past, and the movement from the darkness of the city (filmed mainly at night) to the light and open spaces of the natural world beside the river reverses the direction of the metaphor of the Quiet Revolution as an escape from the "great darkness" of the past.

Jeanne lives in what the screenplay describes as "une maison cossue d'Outrement" [an opulent house in Outremont], where "tout est discret et de bon goût" [everything is discreet and in good taste] (Émond 2007a, 30). This house is contrasted with the cottage to which François takes her to examine his grandmother, where "le temps semble s'être arrêté en 1950" [time seems to have stopped in 1950] (2007a, 93). In between, he proudly shows Jeanne round the basilica, an ornate building filled with religious art, evoking the Catholic past but now very much a tourist site. Although the worshippers are few in number and mainly old people, an adjoining building houses the "Cyclorama de Jérusalem," which François proudly claims to be "le plus grand panorama du monde" [the biggest panorama in the world], and this is bustling with visitors. When François takes her to see this spectacle, Jeanne is clearly not impressed with the naive realism of its depiction of the crucifixion or with the commercial exploitation that goes on around it. The basilica represents the past, and it does provide spiritual sustenance for François and others in its small congregation, but it cannot escape the materialist trappings of the consumer society. The boulevard Sainte-Anne that runs between Jeanne's motel and the river is a modern highway that, according to the screenplay, could be "n'importe où en Amérique du Nord" [anywhere in North America], with "les mêmes fast-food, les mêmes libre-serves" [the same fast food joints, the same self-serves] (Émond 2007a, 50).

Although François clearly expects Jeanne to be impressed by the basilica, it is his simple morality that offers the most positive representation of the past. They first meet when Jeanne is standing beside the river, apparently on the verge of jumping in. He drives up behind her and stops to eat his lunch. When she sits down on a bollard, he patiently waits through the rest of the day and then takes her back to her motel, brings food to her room, and returns the following morning with warmer clothes. As the screenplay puts it, "il a le temps, il est comme hors du temps" [he has time, it is as if he is outside time] (Émond 2007a, 55). François's unassuming faith encompasses the other theological virtues of hope and charity. Thus, as Monica Haïm suggests, "ce n'est pas religion qui est en jeu dans cette histoire; c'est la morale, une morale sociale simple—faites pour les autres ce que voudrez que l'on fasse pour vous—une morale qui n'exige pas la croyance en Dieu" [it is not religion that is at stake in this story; it is morality, a simple social morality—do unto others what you would want them to do unto you—a morality that does not require a belief in God] (2005b, 42). From this perspective, Émond argues, "L'héritage chrétien, c'est comme un ensemble de métaphores qui m'aident à penser le monde contemporain et qui recèlent des vérités profondes" [The Christian heritage is like a collection of metaphors that help me to think about the contemporary world and that conceal profound truths] (Galiero and Émond 2009, 112).

If this is the case, Émond's position is not very different from that expressed by Arcand, a director with a very different sensibility, in *Jésus de Montréal*. Yet things are not so simple. In describing his own first encounter with the basilica at Ste-Anne, Émond explains, "le choc que j'ai ressenti alors était plutôt d'ordre culturel que d'ordre religieux" [the shock that I felt then was of a cultural rather than a religious order], but he also admits, "il s'y glissait pourtant une nostalgie [...] de la transcendance perdue" [nevertheless a nostalgia (...) for a lost transcendence slipped in there] (2007b, 13). Although Émond insists that he is a left-wing thinker and a non-believer, he attributes the problems of contemporary Quebec to the break with traditions that fostered a collective identity grounded in the teachings of the Church, an analysis that has much in common with that of Dumont, who remained a convinced Catholic. Thus Émond's opposition to globalized and neoliberal culture, which he shares with many radical thinkers in the Western world, leads to an appeal to lost traditions more usually associated with conservative thinkers.

Although he admits that "dans ce processus récent, on a gagné la liberté, and [...] les femmes ont gagné l'autonomie" [in this recent process, we have won freedom, and [...] women have won autonomy], Émond feels that these gains have come at a significant cost: "il y a tout un réseau de liens sociaux, de solidarités—que sont des liens de dépendance sur lesquels se fonde la société—qui se sont défaits et maintenant, c'est comme s'il n'y avait pratiquement plus de société" [a whole network of social bonds and solidarities—which are the bonds of dependence on which society is founded—have been demolished, so that there is practically no society any more] (qtd. in Loiselle 2005, 35). The idea that society has disappeared seems to be an allusion to Margaret Thatcher's notorious claim that "there is no such thing as society," and clearly Émond's argument is a response to social changes instituted by right-wing governments in the Western world since the 1980s that have "prioritized the values of individualism, 'efficiency' and profit" (Holland and Eglezou 2010, 50). Although he accepts that "le phénomène est universel" [the phenomenon is universal], he argues that the consequences are even more serious in Quebec "parce que notre identité est incertaine" [because our identity is uncertain] (qtd. in Haïm 2005a, 45).

Émond rejects what he calls "la logique postmoderne" [postmodern logic], which, he claims, is "une logique de minoritaires [...] où tout se vaut, où on ne juge pas" [a logic of minorities ... where anything goes, where one doesn't make judgments] (Galiero and Émond 2009, 139), thus working against the idea of a collectivity whose values are rooted in a common heritage. However, there is no need to accept the totality of Émond's negative view of contemporary culture and the postmodern condition to appreciate his films. A more productive way of viewing *La Neuvaine* and his other films might start from his observation that "dans un monde soumis à un véritable déluge médiathique et publicitaire [...] tout se passe comme si nous ne croyions plus au réel, comme si nous avions abandonné d'avance l'idée que nous pouvions y vivre" [in a world subjected to a veritable flood of media and publicity [...] everything happens as if we no longer believe in the real, as if we have given up in advance the idea that we can live there] (Émond 2011, 9, 11). As Robert Daudelin says of *La Donation* (2009), the last film in the trilogy discussed by Katherine Ann Roberts in the previous chapter, the austere film style in *La Neuvaine* stresses "matérialité (poids des corps, épaisseur de la lumière) qui lui permet d'échapper à tout interprétation métaphysique" [materiality (the weight of the bodies, the density of the light) which allows it to elude any metaphysical interpretation] and offers "une approche matérialiste de la dimension spirituelle de l'homme" [a materialist approach to man's spiritual dimension] (2009, 49).

This approach is reinforced in *La Neuvaine* by one crucial change that Émond made to the ending. Throughout the film, Jeanne's voice is heard speaking to an unseen male. Initially, it seems she may be speaking to a psychiatrist (even though she has refused to see one), but his responses are more like those of a priest in the confessional. It could be her inner voice speaking to God (who replies), but the screenplay makes clear her voice-over is addressed to the priest in the Benedictus boutique outside the basilica, which seems to be part of the touristic paraphernalia, where François had gone earlier to seek consolation. However, the film ends with Jeanne standing outside as the priest looks through the window at her, leaving open the question whether they will ever make contact.

Conclusion: Time, Space, and Memory

According to Yves Lever, the city, "décriée par l'idéologie agriculturiste de Duplessis" [decried by the agricultural ideology of Duplessis] became a "symbole de modernité" [symbol of modernity] in the direct cinema films of the Quiet Revolution (1991, 23). This is especially true of Montreal, and, as Bill Marshall reminds us, Quebec City is "not Montreal" (Marshall 2001, 307). Yet Lepage's modern Quebec City is not much more attractive than Émond's Montreal, and the negative depiction of the cities in both films would thus seem to point to the failure of modernity. Lepage refers to "l'absence de moralité" [the absence of morality] in Quebec City in 1989, as depicted in the film (qtd. in Caron 1995, 29), but despite the dominance of the Church, morality does not seem much more present in 1952. The difference is that the immoral acts remain hidden: the priests turn their backs when the janitor caresses Rachel, and fire Massicotte because of rumours, and nobody suspects Paul-Émile. The past is depicted in *La Neuvaine* only in the traces it has left in the present, and it is thus much more open to idealization, enabling Émond to contrast what he sees as the spiritual wasteland of modern urban life with a rural culture that still embodies the traditional values the Quiet Revolution rejected.

The different visions of the two films can be seen in architectural terms. Each film depicts a monumental building, the Chateau Frontenac in *Le Confessionnal* and the basilica in *La Neuvaine*. The luxury hotel in Quebec City is a secular edifice that figures as a looming presence in Hitchcock's film and exists apparently unchanged in 1989, when Pierre gets a job as a waiter there. It is contrasted in 1989 with the cheap motel in Charny, on the other side of the river, where Manon lives with her son. Although a church appears in the plots of both *I Confess* and *Le Confessionnal*, it is never seen from the outside, and the main focus is on the social rather than religious dimensions of the contrast between past and present. In *La Neuvaine*, the basilica offers a link to the Catholic heritage, one that is debased by the way it is exploited to take advantage of those who suffer from the spiritual vacuum of modern culture. It is contrasted with the simplicity of the rural home of François's grandmother, situated close to the banks of the Saint Lawrence River, which is a dominant presence in both films, a reminder of the natural environment within which the cultural changes take place. As often in Quebec cinema, bridges (two of which Jeanne passes on her journey from Montreal) act as visual metaphors for the need to construct links between past and present.

Both films explore the relations between personal and cultural memory through the idea of filiation, a term that usually applies to family relationships but can also signify the transmission of culture from generation to generation. It is frequently used by Émond to describe what has been lost in a culture that has cut itself off from its past. He insists that, "s'il n'y a pas de lien avec le passé à travers une filiation et l'acceptation d'un héritage [...] nous sommes isolés et condamnés au présent" [if there is no bond with the past through filiation and an acceptance of a heritage (...) we are isolated and condemned to the present] (Galiero and Émond 2009, 70). Lepage is less concerned with heritage, but the centrality of the family in *Le Confessionnal* means that "the myth of filiation is upheld even in 1989, characterized by Marc's desire to find his father and Manon's frustration with her son's lack of a father" (Manning 1998, 53). Here, the Catholic heritage is problematic since the secrecy of the confessional and the shame attached to single motherhood lead to a blockage in the relations between past and present.

In solving the mystery of his family's past, Pierre exposes the differences and continuities between his cultural past and present. In *La Neuvaine*, Jeanne's memory of the killing for which she feels responsible emerges in fragments as she recovers from its effects by engaging with cultural traditions whose loss has created the present social breakdown. Both films thus invite audiences to reassess the past and the difficulty of defining a distinctive Québécois identity without drawing on a heritage with its roots in Catholicism. The key question thus becomes how to define a culturally Catholic identity as distinct from the religious doctrines that imposed what Lepage calls the "yoke of religion" in the past. Neither film offers a simply nostalgic view of the past; rather, they suggest, in very different ways, that the modern Quebec that emerged from the Quiet Revolution depended on an unhealthy and ultimately impossible desire to deny the past. In these films, the return of the repressed incites not nostalgia but rather a sense that the present is haunted by the failure to create a secular alternative to the spiritual values of the Catholic past (Émond) or to deal with the long-term effects of that past (Lepage).

WORKS CITED

Adelman, Howard. 2011. "Conclusion: Religion, Culture, and the State." In *Religion, Culture, and the State: Reflections on the Bouchard–Taylor Report*, edited by Howard Adelman and Pierre Anctil, 100–16. Toronto: University of Toronto Press.

Allen, Patrick. 1966. "Le divorce en marche aux Etats-Unis et au Canada." *L'Action nationale*, 2 October, 144–48.

Allen, Paula Gunn. 1986. *The Sacred Hoop: Recovering the Feminine in American Indian Traditions.* Boston: Beacon Press.

Angers, François-Albert. 1966. "Editorial : La marche vers l'indépendance." *L'Action nationale*, 2 October, 105–13.

[Anon.]. 2005. "En Bref—Aurore récolte plus de 3.5 millions." *Le Devoir*, 28 July. http://www.ledevoir.com/culture/cinema/87103/en-bref-aurore-recolte-plus-de-3-5-millions

Austin, David. 2013. *Fear of a Black Nation: Race, Sex, and Security in Sixties Montreal.* Toronto: Between the Lines.

Bacqué, Marie-Frédérique, and Michel Hanus. 2010. *Le Deuil*, 4th ed. Paris: P.U.F.

Baillargeon, Denyse. 2012. *Brève histoire des femmes au Québec.* Montréal: Boréal.

Barnaby, Jeff. 2012. Online video interview with André Dudemaine. "Jeff Barnaby, cinéaste Mi'gmaq filmmaker." 3:44, posted 19 September. https://www.youtube.com/watch?v=dSVQk5s40_g. Last accessed 1 September 2018.

———. 2013. "'Big year' for First Nations films at TIFF." *CBC News Online.* http://www.cbc.ca/news/entertainment/big-year-for-first-nations-films-at-tiff-1.1344791. Accessed 1 September 2018.

Barrette, Pierre. 2004. "Le genre sans la différence : Le cinéma québécois à l'heure de la séduction." *24 images* 116–17: 8–11.

Barthes, Roland. 1959. *Le Sport et les hommes. Texte du film d'Hubert Aquin.* Montréal: Les Presses de l'Université de Montréal, 2004.

———. 1981. *Camera Obscura: Reflections on* Photography, translated by Richard Howard. New York: Hill and Wang.

Basso, Keith. 2000. *Schooling the Symbolic Animal: Social and Cultural Dimensions of Education*, edited by Bradley A.U. Levinson et al. Lanham: Rowman and Littlefield.

Beauchemin, Jacques. 2002. *L'Histoire en trop. La mauvaise conscience des souverainistes québécois.* Montréal: VLB éditeur.

Beaudry, Lucille. 2007. "Emmanuel Mounier, le personnalisme au Québec, variations d'un apport critique." In *Une pensée libérale, critique ou conservatrice?*, edited by Lucille Beaudry and Marc Chevrier, 81–94. Québec: Presses de l'Université Laval.

Beaulieu, Etienne. 2016. "L'image inquiète : Le manque d'être chez Catherine Martin." *Nouvelles vues* 17 (Winter–Spring): N.p. http://www.nouvellesvues.ulaval.ca/no-17 -hiver-2016-cinema-et-philosophie-par-s-santini-et-p-a-fradet/articles/limage -inquiete-le-manque-detre-chez-catherine-martin-par-etienne-beaulieu. Accessed 5 May 2016.

Beaumont, Nicolas. 1966. "Histoire sans héros." *L'Action nationale*, 2 October, 129–33.

Becker, Udo. 2000. *The Continuum Encyclopedia of Symbols*. London: A and C Black.

Bédard, Éric. 2007–8. "Ce passé qui ne passe pas. La grande noirceur catholique dans les film *Séraphin. Un homme et son péché, Le Survenant* et *Aurore*." *Revue Internationale d'Études Québécoises* (10.2 and 11.1): 75–94.

Bellemare, Denis. 1992. "La mélancolie et le banal. Essai sur le cinéma québécois." PhD diss., Université de Paris III—Sorbonne Nouvelle.

Belzil, Patricia. 2014. "Tom… au cinéma." *Jeu. Revue de théâtre* 151.2: 5.

Benjamin, Walter. 2003. "On the Concept of History" [1940]. In *Selected Writings*, vol. 4, edited by Howard Elland and Michael Jennings, translated by Edmund Jephcott et al., 389–400. Cambridge, MA: Belknap Press of Harvard University Press.

Bertho-Lavenir, Catherine. 2008. "Le Québec. Une identité en péril." *Médium* 14: 42–63.

Bertrand, Janette. 2013. "Le manifeste des 'Janette'—Aux femmes du Québec." *Le Devoir online*, 15 October. http://www.ledevoir.com/politique/quebec/389956/aux-femmes -du-quebec.

Bhabha, Homi K. 1994. "DissemiNation." In *The Location of Culture*, 199–244. London and New York: Routledge.

Blais, Mélissa, and Francis Dupuis-Déri. 2008. *Le mouvement masculiniste au Québec. L'antiféminisme démasqué*. Montréal: Remue-ménage.

Bock-Côté, Mathieu. 2015a. "Finkielkraut, Le Goff, Delsol. Qu'est-ce que le conservatisme?" *Le Figaro*, 28 April. Accessed 9 September 2018. http://www.lefigaro.fr/vox/ politique/2015/04/28/31001-20150428ARTFIG00287-finkielkraut-le-goff-delsol -qu-est-ce-que-le-conservatisme.php

———. 2015b. "Les ruraux sont-ils des attardés?" *La Vie agricole* 15.24 (April): 34.

———. 2016. "Brèves réflexions sur notre passé pour ceux qui m'imaginent en nostalgique du duplessisme." *Le Journal de Montréal*. 13 August. https://www.journaldemontreal .com/2016/08/13/breves-reflexions-sur-notre-passe-pour-ceux-qui-mimaginent-en -nostalgique-du-duplessisme. Accessed 17 September 2018.

———. 2018. "La lâcheté du Festival de Jazz." *Le Journal de Montréal*. https://www .journaldemontreal.com/2018/07/05/la-lachete-du-festival-de-jazz.

Bonikowski, Wyatt. 2013. "Only One Antagonist: The Demon Love and the Feminine Experience in the Work of Shirley Jackson." *Gothic Studies* 15, no. 2 (November): 66–88.

Bouchard, Gérard. 2015. *Interculturalism: A View from Quebec*. Toronto: University of Toronto Press.

Bouchard, Gérard, and Charles Taylor. 2008. *Building the Future: A Time for Reconciliation*. Québec: Gouvernement du Québec.

Bourdieu, Pierre. 1987. *Distinction: A Social Critique of the Judgement of Taste*, translated by Richard Nice. Cambridge, MA: Harvard University Press.

Boym, Svetlana. 2001. *The Future of Nostalgia*. New York: Basic Books.

Brass, Tom. 2001. "Reel Images of the Land (Beyond the Forest): Film and the Agrarian Myth." *Journal of Peasant Studies* 28, no. 4: 1–56.

Bresson, Robert. 1977. *Notes on Cinematography*, translated by Jonathan Griffin. New York: Urizen.

Brisebois, Isabelle. 2014. "*Ressac*, là où le temps s'arrête." *Le Droit*. 15 March, A2.

Browning, J.E. 2011. "Survival Horrors, Survival Spaces: Tracing the Modern Zombie Cine(myth)." *Horror Studies* 2, no. 1: 41–59.

Bug, Amber. 2016. Review: "Thanatomorphose (2012)." *Ain't It Cool.com*. http://www.aintitcool.com/node/65209#11. Accessed 26 July 2016.

Campbell, Neil. 2008. *The Rhizomatic West. Representing the American West in a Transnational, Global, Media Age*. Lincoln: University of Nebraska Press.

Cantin, Serge. 1997. *Ce pays comme un enfant. Essais sur le Québec (1988–1996)*. Montréal: L'Hexagone.

Caron, André. 1995. "La Première Confession de Robert Lepage." *Séquences* 180 (September–October): 24–29.

Chabot, Marc. 2010. "La fin de l'histoire." In *La Donation. Un film de Bernard Émond. Scénario et regards croisés*, edited by Renaud Plante, 123–33. Montréal: Les Éditions Les 400 coups.

Charles, Julia Morgan. 2009. "La maison où j'ai grandi. The Changing Landscape of Nostalgia in Quebec's Contemporary Coming-of-age Films." MA thesis, McGill University. http://digitool.library.mcgill.ca/webclient/StreamGate?folder_id=0&dvs=1475020768321~306&usePid1=true&usePid2=true. Accessed 13 July 2016.

Charles, Morgan. 2011. "Coming of Age in Quebec: Reviving the Nation's 'Cinéma orphelin.'" *Nouvelles vues sur le cinéma québécois* 12 (Spring–Summer): 76–95. http://www.nouvellesvues.ulaval.ca/en/no-12-le-renouveau-dirige-par-jean-pierre-sirois-trahan/articles/coming-of-age-in-quebec-reviving-the-nations-cinema-orphelin-par-morgan-julia-charles/. Accessed 21 July 2016.

Cheng, Anne Anlin. 2000. *The Melancholy of Race*. Oxford: Oxford University Press.

Chevrier, Marc. *La République québécoise. Hommages à une idée suspecte*. Montréal: Boréal, 2012.

Christiano, Kevin J. 2007. "The Trajectory of Catholicism in Twentieth-Century Quebec." *The Church Confronts Modernity: Catholicism since 1950 in the United States, Ireland, and Quebec*, edited by Leslie Woodcock Tentler, 21–62. Washington, DC: Catholic University of America Press.

Clandfield, Peter. 2003. "Bridgespotting: Lepage, Hitchcock, and Landmarks in Canadian Film." *Canadian Journal of Film Studies* 12, no. 1: 2–15.

Clément, Frédéric. 2010. "Voix de femmes, voies de femmes. La fin des années 60 dans le cinéma récent." In *Perspectives étudiantes féministes. Actes électroniques du colloque étudiant le*

12–13 mars, 2010, edited by Valérie Soly, 158–76. www.academia.edu/1214638/Voix_de
_femmes_voies_de_femmes_la_fin_des_années_60_dans_le_cinéma_québécois_récent.

Comer, Krista. 1999. *Landscapes of the New West: Gender and Genre in Contemporary Women's Writing.* Chapel Hill: University of North Carolina Press.

Conard, Mark T., ed. 2007. *The Philosophy of Neo-Noir.* Lexington: University of Kentucky Press.

Connell, R.W. 1987. *Gender and Power: Society, the Person, and Sexual Politics.* Stanford: Stanford University Press.

———. 1990. "An Iron Man: The Body and Some Contradictions of Hegemonic Masculinity." In *Sport, Men, and the Gender Order,* edited by Michael A. Messner and Donald F. Sabo, 83–96. Champaign: Human Kinetics.

Corneau, Guy. 1989. *Absent Fathers, Lost Sons,* translated by Larry Shouldice. Boston: Shambhala.

"Correspondance : le désarroi du Québec fidèle!" 1966. *L'Action nationale,* 6 February, 727–29.

Coulombe, Michel. 1995. "Entretien avec Robert Lepage." *Ciné-Bulles* 14, no. 4: 20–24.

———. 2012. "Bernard Émond." *Ciné-Bulles* 30, no. 4: 10–16.

Coulombe, Michel, and Marcel Jean. 2006. *Le Dictionnaire du cinéma Québécois.* Montréal: Boréal.

Creed, Barbara. 1993. *The Monstrous-Feminine: Film, Feminism, Psychoanalysis.* London: Routledge.

———. 1996. "Horror and the Monstrous-Feminine: An Imaginary Abjection." In *The Dread of Difference: Gender and the Horror Film,* edited by Barry Keith Grant, 33–65. Austin: University of Texas Press.

Daudelin, Robert. 2099. "Visages-paysages." *24 Images* 144: 49.

De Blois, Marco. 1995–96. "L'Iconoclaste de Québec." *24 Images* 80: 14–17.

De Koninck, Marie-Charlotte. 1995. "Introduction." In *Jamais plus comme! Le Québec de 1945 à 1960,* edited by Marie-Charlotte de Koninck. 5–13. Montréal: Fides.

Desrochers, Jean-Philippe. 2013. "*Une jeune fille.* Simplicité du récit, richesse et profondeur du propos." *Séquences* 287 (November–December): 56.

Duchesne, André. 2013a. "Gaspésia, après la fin." *La Presse,* 18 May.

Duchesne, André. 2013b. "Pascale Ferland/*Ressac* : après la lame de fond." *La Presse,* 15 December. Web. news.20131215.CY.4721042.

Dumais, Eric. 2015. "Entrevue avec François Péloquin pour *Le bruit des arbres.*" *La Bible urbaine,* 29 June. http://www.labibleurbaine.com/cinema/entrevue-avec-francois -peloquin-pour-le-bruit-des-arbres. Accessed 19 September 2016.

Dumont, Fernand. 1971. *La Vigile du Québec. Essai.* Montréal: HMH.

———. 1993. *Genèse de la société québécoise.* Montréal: Boréal.

———. 1995. *L'Avenir de la mémoire.* Québec: Nuit Blanche.

———. 1996. *La genèse de la société québécoise.* Montréal: Boréal.

Dumont, Micheline. 2008. "La culture politique durant la Revolution tranquille. L'invisibilite des femmes dans Cite libre et l'Action nationale." *Recherches Féministes,* 21, no. 2: 103–25.

Dundjerovic, Aleksandar. 2003. *The Cinema of Robert Lepage: The Poetics of Memory.* London: Wallflower Press.

Dunlevy, T'Cha. 2015. *"Les Loups* leads Évelyne Brochu to her place at 'the end of the world.'" *Gazette* (Montreal), 26 February. http://montrealgazette.com/entertainment/arts/les-loups-leads-evelyne-brochu-to-her-place-at-the-end-of-the-world. Accessed 23 September 2016.

Dupuis, Jean-Pierre. 1993. "Le développement mineur en Abitibi. Les projets des colons." *Recherches sociographiques* 34: 233–60.

Duran, Eduardo, and Bonnie Duran. 1995. *Native American Postcolonial Psychology.* Albany: SUNY Press.

Dyer, Kester. 2017. "Indigenous Cinema, *Hamlet,* and Québécois Melancholia." In *In the Balance: Indigeneity, Performance, Globalization,* edited by Helen Gilbert, J. D. Phillipson, and Michelle H. Raheja. Liverpool: Liverpool University Press, 105-122. https://www.oapen.org/viewer/web/viewer.html?file=https://www.oapen.org/document/636305.

Ellis, Kate Ferguson. *The Contested Castle: Gothic Novels and the Subversion of Domestic Ideology.* Champaign: University of Illinois Press, 1989.

Elsaesser, Thomas. [1972]1987. "Tales of Sound and Fury: Observations on the Family Melodrama." In *Home Is Where the Heart Is: Studies in Melodrama and the Woman's Film,* edited by Christine Gledhill, 43–69. London: British Film Institute. Originally published in *Monogram* 4: 2–15.

Émond, Bernard. 2007a. "Le Silence." *La Neuvaine. Scénario et regards croisés,* 13–17. Montréal: Les 400 Coups.

———. 2007b. *La Neuvaine. Scénario et regards croisés.* Montréal: Les 400 Coups.

———. 2010. *La Donation. Scénario et Regards Croisés.* Montréal: Les 400 Coups.

———. 2011. *Il y a trop d'images. Textes épars 1993–2010.* Montréal: Lux.

———. 2012. "J'ai dormi parterre dans la maison de nos ancêtres." *Tout ce que tu possèdes. Scénario et regards croisés. Suivi de contributions de Gilles McMillan, Jean-François Nadeau, Lucien Pelletier et Melissa Thériault.* 9–17. Montréal: Lux.

———. 2012. *Tout ce que tu possèdes. Scénario et regards croisés. Suivi de contributions de de Gilles McMillan, Jean-François Nadeau, Lucien Pelletier et Melissa Thériault.* Montréal: Lux.

———. 2012–13. "Pour vivre ici (les maisons de mes films)." *Imaginaires de la maison,* edited by Thomas Mainguy. *Contre-Jour.* Conseil des Arts et des Lettres du Québec. *Cahiers Littéraires* 29 (Winter): 65–70.

———. 2015. "Gratitude." *Revue Relations* 781 (November–December): 10.

———. 2016a. "De la nostalgie," *Revue Relations* 785 (July–August): 50.

———. 2016b. "Elle pleure." *Revue Relations* 782 (February): 50.

———. 2018. "Vitupérer l'epoque." http://cjf.qc.ca/revue-relations/publication/article/vituperer-lepoque. Accessed 12 June.

———. (unpublished). "Entrer dans une église." *Texte pour le Forum sur le patrimoine religieux du Québec.*

———. (unpublished). "L'usage de la liberté." Texte lu le 7 avril 2012 au Monument National dans le cadre de l'événement *NOUS.*

Émond, Bernard, and Simon Galiero. 2009. *La perte et le lien. Entretiens sur le cinéma, la culture et la société.* Montréal: Médiaspaul.

Falardeau, Éric. 2016. "Thanatomorphose." *Internet Movie Database.* https://www.imdb .com/title/tt2385074/plotsummary. Accessed 18 September 2016.

Fanon, Frantz. 2002. "Sur la culture nationale." *Les damnés de la terre* (1961), 195–223. Paris: La Découverte.

Felman, Shoshana. 1993. *What Does a Woman Want? Reading and Sexual Difference.* Baltimore: Johns Hopkins University Press.

Ferron, Jacques. 1980. *Une Amitié bien particulière. Lettres de Jacques Ferron à John Grube.* Montréal: Les Éditions du Boréal.

Fleenor, Juliann E. 1993. *The Female Gothic.* Montreal: Eden Press.

Fortier, Claude, et al. 2016. *Statistiques sur l'industrie du film et de la production télévisuelle indépendante.* Québec: Gouvernement du Québec, Institut de la statistique du Québec.

Fowler, Catherine, and Gillian Helfield, eds. 2006. *Representing the Rural: Space, Place, and Identity in Films about the Land.* Detroit: Wayne State University Press.

Freitag, Gina. 2011. "Unleashing the Furious Feminine: The Violence of Gender Discourse in Canadian Horror Cinema." MA thesis, Carleton University.

Freitag, Gina, and André Loiselle. 2013. "Tales of Terror in Quebec Popular Cinema: The Rise of the French Language Horror Film since 2000." *American Review of Canadian Studies.* Special Issue: *Québec Cinema in the 21st Century.* 43, no. 2: 190–203.

Freitag, Gina, and André Loiselle. 2015. *The Canadian Horror Film: Terror of the Soul.* Toronto: University of Toronto Press.

Fricker, Karen. 2005. "Robert Lepage: Product of Quebec?" In *Staging Nationalism: Essays on the Theatre and National Identity,* edited by Kim Gounaridou, 167–85. Jefferson: McFarland.

Frye, Northrop. 1971. *The Bush Garden; Essays on the Canadian Imagination.* Toronto: House of Anansi Press.

Gagnon, Jean-Pierre. 2002. "Réplique à Maryse Vinet du centre des femmes l'Essentielle." *L'Oeil régionale,* 23 March, 18.

Garfield, Gail. 2010. *Through Our Eyes: African American Men's Experiences of Race, Gender, Violence.* New Brunswick: Rutgers University Press.

Garneau, Michèle. 2001. "Le paysage dans la tradition documentaire québécoise. Un regard off sur la parole." *Cinémas. Revue d'études cinématographiques / Cinémas: Journal of Film Studies* 12, no. 1: 127–43.

Gaudreault, André, Germain Lacasse et Isabelle Raynauld eds 1999. *Le cinema en histoire. Institutions cinematographiques, reception filmique et reconstitution historique.* Quebec/ Paris: Nota bene/Meridiens Klincksieck

Gauvreau, Michael. 2005. *The Catholic Origins of Quebec's Quiet Revolution, 1931–1970.* Montreal and Kingston: McGill–Queen's University Press.

Gendron, Nicolas. 2015. "RVCQ / Sophie Deraspe / *Les loups*: À marée haute." *Voir,* 17 February. https://voir.ca/cinema/2015/02/17/rvcq-sophie-deraspe-les-loups-a -maree-haute/. Accessed 23 September 2016.

Germain, Louis. 1966. "Un sujet de conversation à la mode... la Pilule." *L'Action populaire,* 9 November, 4.

Gilmore, David D. 2010. *Misogyny: The Male Malady.* Philadelphia: University of Pennsylvania Press.

Gilroy, Paul. *Postcolonial Melancholia.* New York: Columbia University Press, 2005.

Gingold, Michael. 2014. "Dys-" (Fantasia Movie Review). *Fangoria.com.* 20 August. http://www.fangoria.com/new/dys-fantasia-movie-review/. Accessed 13 July 2016.

Gittings, Christopher E. 2002. *Canadian National Cinema.* London: Routledge.

Gledhill, Christine. 1987. "The Melodramatic Field: An Investigation." In *Home Is Where the Heart Is: Studies in Melodrama and the Woman's Film,* edited by Christine Gledhill, 14–22. London: British Film Institute.

———. 1991. "Signs of Melodrama." In *Stardom: Industry of Desire,* edited by Christine Gledhill, 207–29. London and New York: Routledge.

Gobert, Céline. 2015. "*Les Loups,* Sophie Deraspe. La Jeune Fille et la mer." *Critiques, 24 Images,* 26 February. http://revue24images.com/critics-article-detail/2390. Accessed 26 July 2016.

Godin, Pierre. 1997. *René Lévesque, héros malgré lui.* Montréal: Éditions du Boréal.

Gray, Elizabeth. 1966. "Quebec Swallows the Pill." *Maclean's,* 2 May, 2.

Green, Amy M. 2011. "The French Horror Film *Martyrs* and the Destruction, Defilement, and Neutering of the Female Form." *Journal of Popular Film and Television* 39, no. 1: 20–28.

Green, Mary Jean. 2003. "Toward Defining A Postcolonial Quebec Cinema: The Films of Claude Jutra." *Quebec Studies* 35 (Spring–Summer): 89–98.

Grugeau, Gérard. 2014. "*Ressac* de Pascale Ferland. La chambre ardente." *24 images* 166 (March-April): 60.

Guy, Chantal. 2002a. "La modestie qui étouffe." *La Presse,* 13 October, F1–F2.

Haïm, Monica. 2005a. "Bernard Émond. Concevoir le sermon sur la montagne comme un programme social." *Séquences* 240 (November–December): 43–45.

———. 2005b. "*La Neuvaine.* Faire le bien." *Séquences* 240 (November–December): 42.

Hanson, Helen. 2007. *Hollywood Heroines: Women in Film Noir and the Female Gothic Film.* London: I.B. Tauris.

Harcourt, Peter. 2006. "Images of the Rural: The Cinema of Quebec." *CinéAction* 69: 2–11.

Hardy, René. 2015. *Charivari et justice populaire au Québec.* Quebec: Septentrion.

Harvey, David. 1990. *The Condition of Postmodernity: An Enquiry into the Origins of Cultural Change.* Oxford: Blackwell.

Hébert, Anne. 2012. *Le Torrent.* Montréal: Bibliothèque québécoise.

Helfield, Gillian. 2006. "*Cultivateur d'images:* Albert Tessier and the Rural Tradition in Québécois Cinema." In *Representing the Rural: Space, Place, and Identity in Films about the Land,* edited by C. Fowler, and G. Helfield, 48–64. Detroit: Wayne State University Press.

Higson, Andrew. 2006. "Re-presenting the National Past: Nostalgia and Pastiche in the Heritage Film." In *Fires Were Started: British Cinema and Thatcherism,* 2nd ed., edited by Lester D. Freidman, 91–109. London: Wallflower Press.

Hirsch, Marianne. 2008. "The Generation of Postmemory." *Poetics Today* 29, no. 1: 103–28.

Holland, Patricia, and Georgia Eglezou. 2010. "'There is no such thing!': On Public Service, Broadcasting, and the National Health Service and 'People' in the 1980s." In *Thatcher and After: Margaret Thatcher and Her Afterlife in Contemporary Culture*, edited by Louisa Hadley and Elizabeth Ho, 29–52. Basingstoke: Palgrave Macmillan.

Houdassine, Ismaël. 2015. "*Les Loups* de Sophie Deraspe. Les Madelinots à la vie à la mort." *Huffington Post*, 3 February. http://quebec.huffingtonpost.ca/2015/03/02/les-loups -sophie-deraspe-entrevue-photos-video_n_6784006.html. Accessed 23 September 2016.

Huffer, Lynne. 1998. *Maternal Pasts, Feminist Futures: Nostalgia, Ethics, and the Question of Difference*. Stanford: Stanford University Press.

Jameson, Fredric. 1984. "Postmodernism or the Cultural Logic of Late Capitalism." *New Left Review* 146: 53–92.

Jean, Bruno, et al. 2014. *Comprendre le Québec rural*. Rimouski: Université du Québec à Rimouski, GRIDEQ, et Chaire de recherche du Canada en développement rural.

Khanna, Ranjana. 2003. *Dark Continents: Psychoanalysis and Colonialism*. Durham: Duke University Press.

King, Barry. 1991. "Articulating Stardom." In *Stardom: Industry of Desire*, edited by Christine Gledhill, 167–82. London and New York: Routledge.

Kristeva, Julia. 1982. *Powers of Horror: An Essay on Abjection*. New York: Columbia University Press.

Kuhn, Annette. [1984]1987. "Women's Genres: Melodramas, Soap Opera, and Theory." In *Home Is Where the Heart Is: Studies in Melodrama and the Woman's Film*, edited by Christine Gledhill, 339–49. London: British Film Institute. Originally published in *Screen* 25, no. 1 (1984): 18–28.

La Rochelle, Réal. 2004. *Denys Arcand. L'ange exterminateur*. Montréal: Leméac.

———. *Denys Arcand: A Life in Film*, translated by Alison Strayer. Toronto: McArthur and Company.

Lajoie, Mark. 2001. "Imagining the City in Québécois Cinema." In *Cinéma. Imaginaire de la ville*, edited by Charles Perraton, 35–54. Montréal: UQAM Press.

Lamonde, Yvan, and Pierre-François Hébert. 1981. *Le cinéma au Québec. Essai de statistique historique (1896 à nos jours)*. Québec: Institut québécois de recherche.

Lamontage, Jeanne. 1966. "Conte de… sorcière! L'Enfant martyr." *L'Action nationale* 56. 4 December 1966, 349–50.

Lamoureux, Diane. 2011. "The Paradoxes of Quebec Feminism." In *Quebec Questions: Quebec Studies for the Twenty-First Century*, edited by Stéphan Gervais, Christopher Kirkey, and Jarrett Rudy, 307–23. Toronto: Oxford University Press.

Landry, Isabelle. 2003. "Révolution paternelle." *La Presse*, 14 June, A21–22.

Laplante, Robert. 1987. "La colonisation de l'Abitibi/Témiscamingue. Un bilan de la recherche." *Recherches sociographiques* 28, nos. 2–3: 415–33.

Larivière, Claude. 1996. "La voix des jeunes. La continuité entre les générations." *L'Action nationale*, 5 January, 590–93.

Larue, Johanne. 1995. "Lepage/Hitchcock. Leçons d'histoire(s)." *Séquences* 180 (September–October): 28–31.

Lavoie, Simon. 2017. Personal interview with the author, July.

Lê, Linda. 2005. *Le Complexe de Caliban*. Paris: Bourgeois.

Leach, Jim. 2002. "Double Vision: *Mon oncle Antoine* and the Cinema of Fable." In *Canada's Best Features: Critical Essays on 15 Canadian films*, edited by Eugene P. Walz, 27–50. Amsterdam and New York: Rodopi.

———. 2010. "The Landscape of Canada's Features: Articulating Nation and Nature." In *Cinema and Landscape*, edited by Graeme Harper and Jonathan Rayner, 271–80. Bristol and Chicago: Intellect.

Leduc, Louise. 2002. "La naissance d'un dilemme." *La Presse*, 14 March, A12.

———. 2003. "Quand la cigogne s'invite." *La Presse*, "Dossier Plus," 29 November, Plus-4.

Lefebvre, Martin. 1998. "A Sense of Time and Place: The Chronotope in *I Confess* and *Le Confessionnal*." *Quebec Studies* 26 (Fall–Winter): 88–98.

Lemaire, Anika. 2014. *Jacques Lacan* [1977]. London and New York: Routledge.

Lepage-Boily, Elizabeth. "Dix anecdotes sur *Les 3 P'tits cochons*." *ShowBizz.net*, 30 June 2016. http://showbizz.net/2016/06/30/dix-anecdotes-sur-les-3-ptits-cochons-2.

Létourneau, Jocelyn. 2004a. *A History for the Future: Rewriting Memory and Identity in Quebec*, translated by Phyllis Aronoff and Howard Scott. Montreal and Kingston: McGill–Queen's University Press.

———. 2004b. *Le Québec, les Québécois : Un parours historique*. Montréal: Fides.

Létourneau, Jocelyn. 2006. "Mythistoires de Losers: introduction au roman historial des Québécois d'héritage canadiens-français." *Histoire sociale / Social History* 39, no. 77: 157–80.

Létourneau, Yvonne. 1966. "Mariage civil. Oeuvre de la Franc-Maçonnerie." *L'Avenir du nord*, 23 November, 4.

Lever, Yves. 1991. *Le Cinéma de la Révolution tranquille. De Panoramique à Valérie*. Montréal: Yves Lever.

———. 1995. *Histoire générale du cinéma au Québec*, rev. ed. Montréal: Boréal.

Lewis, Charlton T. 1889. *An Elementary Latin Dictionary*. New York: Oxford University Press.

Liddell, Henry George, and Robert Scott. 1940. "xlo/h." *A Greek-English Lexicon*, revised by Sir Henry Stuart Jones with Roderick McKenzie. Oxford: Clarendon Press. Perseus Digital Library. http://www.perseus.tufts.edu/hopper/text?doc=Perseus:text: 1999.04.0057:entry=xlo/h&highlight=shoot%2Cyoung. Accessed 20 September 2016.

Linteau, Paul-André, et al. 1989. *Histoire du Québec contemporain*, vol. 2: *Le Québec depuis 1930*. Montréal: Boréal.

Linteau, Pierre-André, René Durocher, Jean-Claude Robert, and François Ricard. 1991. *Quebec since 1930*, translated by Robert Chodos and Ellen Garmaise. Toronto: James Lorimer.

Liotta, Elena. 2009. *On Soul and Earth: The Psychic Value of Place*. London: Routledge.

Lobos, Teresa. 2014. "Thanatomorphose and Halley: Sex, Death, and the Emptiness of Being." *Off/Screen* 18, no. 5 (May). http://offscreen.com/view/thanatomorphose-halley. Accessed 26 July 2016.

Lockerbie, Ian. 2005. "The Spiritual Sense in the New Auteur Cinema of Québec." *Nouvelles vues sur le cinéma québécois* 4 (Fall): 7–25.

Loiselle, André. 1999. "Subtly Subversive or Simply Stupid?: Notes on Popular Quebec Cinema." *Post Script* 18, no. 2: 75–84.

———. 2003. *Stage-Bound: Feature Film Adaptation of Canada and Québécois Drama.* Montreal and Kingston: McGill–Queen's University Press.

———. 2007. *Cinema as History: Michel Brault and Modern Quebec.* Toronto: TIFF.

———. 2008a. *Denys Arcand's "Le Déclin de l'empire américain" and "Les Invasions barbares."* Toronto: University of Toronto Press.

———. 2008b. "Horreur et dépaysement. L'altérité géographique et médiatique comme source de terreur dans trois adaptations cinématographiques de romans d'épouvante québécois—*Le Collectionneur, La Peau blanche* et *Sur le seuil.*" In *Littérature et Cinéma au Québec, 1995–2005*, edited by Carla Fratta and Jean-François Plamondon, 81–92. Bologna: Pendragon.

———. 2015. "Pure Laine Evil: The Horrifying Normality of Quebec's Ordinary Hell in the Film Adaptations of Patrick Senécal's 'Romans d'épouvante.'" *The Canadian Horror Film: Terror of the Soul*, edited by Freitag and Loiselle, 67–88. Toronto: University of Toronto Press.

Loiselle, Marie-Claude. 2005. "Rencontre: Bernard Émond—Pierre Vadeboncoeur." *24 Images* 123 (September): 28–35.

———. 2010. "Chercher sa place." In *La Donation. Un film de Bernard Émond. Scénario et regards croisés*, edited by Renaud Plante, 143–49. Montréal: Les 400 coups.

Lowenstein, Adam. 2005. *Shocking Representation: Historical Trauma, National Cinema, and the Modern Horror Film.* New York: Columbia University Press.

"L'U.C.F.R. réclame une politique familiale." 1996. *L'Action nationale*, 16 April, 1.

Lussier, Marc-André. 2015. "*Le bruit des arbres*. Chronique d'un été décisif." *La Presse*, 9 July. http://www.lapresse.ca/cinema/201506/03/49-6842-le-bruit-des-arbres.php. Accessed 20 September 2016.

Mackenzie, Scott. 2004. *Screening Québec: Québécois Moving Images, National Identity, and the Public Sphere.* Manchester: Manchester University Press.

Maclure, Jocelyn. 2003. *Quebec Identity: The Challenge of Pluralism*, translated by Peter Feldstein. Montreal: McGill–Queen's University Press.

Maigret, Éric. 2013. "Ce que les *cultural studies* font aux savoirs disciplinaires." *Questions de communication* 24: 145–67.

Manning, Erin. 1998. "The Haunted Home: Colour Spectrums in Robert Lepage's *Le Confessionnal.*" *Canadian Journal of Film Studies* 7, no. 2: 49–65.

Marcil, Olivier. 2002. *La Raison et l'Équilibre. Libéralisme, nationalisme et catholicisme dans la pensée de Claude Ryan au Devoir, 1962–1978.* Montréal: Éditions Varia.

Marcotte, Marcel. 1966. "Les évêques canadiens et la contraception." *Relations*, December, 325–27.

Marshall, Bill. 2001. *Quebec National Cinema*. Montreal and Kingston: McGill–Queen's University Press.

Marsolais, Gilles. 2011 *Cinéma québécois. De l'artisanat à l'industrie*, Montréal: Triptyque.

Massicotte, Claudie. 2012. "Hantise et architecture cryptique. Transmission du passé dans *Le Confessionnal* de Robert Lepage." *Canadian Journal of Film Studies* 21, no. 2: 93–114.

McQueen, Rob. 2011. "The Remembrance of Things Past and Present: An Introduction to GLR/IPCS Symposia on Nostalgia and Colonial Melancholia." *Griffith Law Review* 20, no. 2: 247–51.

Melançon, Benoît. 2009. *The Rocket: A Cultural History of Maurice Richard*, translated by Fred A. Reed. Vancouver: Greystone Books.

Mercer, John, and Martin Shingler. 2004. *Melodrama: Genre, Style, Sensibility*. London and New York: Wallflower Press. Short Cuts series.

Meunier, Hugo. 2016. Review of Les 3 P'tits Cochons 2: Des petits cochons moins cochons. *La Presse.ca*, 1 July. http://www.lapresse.ca/cinema/critiques/201606/30/01 -4996967-les-3-ptits-cochons-2-des-petits-cochons-moins-cochons-12.php.

Michaud, Jacques. 2006. "Le royaume suspendu." In *Le Cinéma au Québec. Tradition et modernité*, edited by Stéphane-Albert Boulais, 167–82. Montréal: Fides.

Modleski, Tania. [1984]1987. "Time and Desire in the Woman's Film." In *Home Is Where the Heart Is: Studies in Melodrama and the Woman's Film*, edited by Christine Gledhill, 326–38. London: British Film Institute. Originally published in *Cinema Journal* 21, no. 3 (Spring 1984): 19–30.

Moers, Ellen. 1997. *Literary Women: The Great Writers*. Oxford: Oxford University Press.

Moine, Raphaëlle. 2014. "The Contemporary French Biopic in National and International Contexts." In *The Biopic in Contemporary Film Culture*, edited by Tom Brown and Bélen Vidal, 52–67. New York: Routledge.

Morissette, Nathaëlle. 2001. "Société québécoise. Le choc démographique." *La Presse*, 5 October 2003, A7.

Morissonneau, Christian, and Maurice Asselin. 1980. "La colonisation au Québec. Une décolonisation manquée." *Cahiers de géographie du Québec* 24, no. 61: 145–55.

Mulvey, Laura. [1977–78]1987. "Notes on Sirk and Melodrama." In *Home Is Where the Heart Is: Studies in Melodrama and the Woman's Film*, edited by Christine Gledhill, 75–79. London: British Film Institute. Originally published in *Movie* 25 (Winter 1977–78): 53–56.

"Munro aurait dû se taire—Lévesque." 1981. *Le soleil*, 23 June, 1.

Murphy, Bernice M. 2009. *The Suburban Gothic in American Popular Culture*. New York: Palgrave Macmillan.

Neale, Steve. 1993. "Melo Talk: On the Meaning and Use of the Term 'Melodrama' in the American Trade Press." *The Velvet Light Trap* 32: 66–89.

———. 1999. *Genre and Hollywood*. New York: Routledge.

Ouimet, Michèle. 2002. "Les Malheurs des garçons." *La Presse*, 26 October, A18.

Pallister, Janis L. 1995. *The Cinema of Québec: Masters in Their Own House*. Cranbury: Fairleigh Dickinson University Press.

Patriquin, Martin. 2018. "Quebec's cultural milieu demonstrates its utter hypocrisy in defending SLAV." *CBC News Online*, 15 July 2018. https://www.cbc.ca/news/opinion/quebec-slav-production-1.4740587.

Paul, Daniel N. 2006. *We Were Not the Savages: Collision Between European and Native American Civilizations*. Third Edition. Halifax: Fernwood.

Pellerin, Jean. 1966. "Autopsie du 5 juin." *Cité Libre*, July–August, 5–7.

Péloquin, François. 2015. "Mot du réalisateur." Dossier de presse pour *Le Bruit des arbres*. http://www.kfilmsamerique.com/telechargements/dossier-de-presse/dossier-de-presse-le-bruit-des-arbres.pdf.

Perron, Bernard. 1994. "Les Aveux de Québec." *Ciné-Bulles* 13, no. 4: 46–49.

Pierce, Sally. 2009. "Gothic Style: A Personal and National Taste." In *Picturing Victorian America: Prints by the Kellogg Brothers of Hartford, Connecticut, 1830–1880*, edited by Nancy Finlay. 49–60. Middletown: Wesleyan University Press.

"La Pilule : on est marié mes on veut quant même vivre sa vie de célibataire." 1966. *La Vallée de la Petite Nation*, 15 December, 14.

Poirier, Christian. 2004. *Le Cinéma québécois. À la recherche d'une identité?* Tome 1: *L'Imaginaire filmique*. Sainte-Foy: Presses de l'Université du Québec.

Pontalis, J.-B. 2012. *Avant*. Paris: Gallimard.

"Pour la révolution violente." 1966. *L'Avenir du nord*, 1 June, 2.

"Pour les jeunes : des succédanés à la violence." 1966. *La Vallée de la Petite Nation*, 1 September, 10.

Pratt, Geraldine, and Rose Marie San Juan. *Film and Urban Space: Critical Possibilities*. Edinburgh: Edinburgh University Press, 2014.

"QPF off reserve—Levesque [*sic*]." 1981. *The Record*, 26 June.

Quignard, Pascal. 2015. *Critique du jugement*. Paris: Galilée.

Rabanne, Paco. 1999. *Journey: From One Life to Another*. Shaftesbury: Element.

Ransom, Amy J. 2019. "Forgiving the Horrible Mother: Children's Needs and Women's Desires in Twenty-First Century Québécois Film." In *Horrible Mothers: Representations across Francophone North America*, edited by Loic Bourdeau, 149–67. Lincoln: University of Nebraska Press.

———. 2014a. "Portraits of the Artist as a Young (Mad)man: The Musical Biopic in Quebec." Paper presented at the Biennial Conference of the American Council for Québec Studies.

———. 2014b. *Hockey, PQ: Canada's Game in Quebec's Popular Culture*. Toronto: University of Toronto Press.

Ravary, Julie. 2016. "The Exportability of National Specificities on the International Circuit: A Case Study of Quebec National Cinema and the Emergence of Its Historical Frescoes in the 2000s." Paper presented at the Society for Cinema and Media Studies Conference, Atlanta, March.

"La rencontre avec Lessard 'déçoit.'" 1981. *Le devoir*, 25 June, 6.

"Rencontre infructueuse avec les Micmacs. Lessard remet l'affaire à Lévesque." 1981. *La Presse*, 24 June, A12.

"Restigouche : Lévesque engage la SQ à ne plus intervenir sur la reserve." 1981. *Le devoir*, 26 June, 1.

Ricard, François. 1994. *La Génération lyrique. Essai sur la vie et l'œuvre des premiers-nés du baby-boom*. Montréal: Boréal.

Rioux, Christian. 2010. "Les grands mythes de la Révolution tranquille – 2 – S'habituer à réussir," *Le Devoir*, 20 September.

Robert, Marc-André. 2013. *Dans la caméra de l'abbé Proulx. La Société agricole et rurale de Duplessis*. Québec: Septentrion.

Roberts, Katherine Ann. 2017. "Under the Aegis of Saint Anne: Faith and Home in Bernard Émond's *La neuvaine*. *French Review* 91, no. 2: 100–12.

Rondeau, Yves. 2002. "Féminisme revanchard." *La Presse*, 29 April A12.

Routledge, Clay. 2016. *Nostalgia: A Psychological Resource*. New York: Routledge.

Royer, Carl, and Diana Royer. 2005. *The Spectacle of Isolation in Horror Films: Dark Parades*. New York: Haworth Press.

Sable, Trudy, and Bernie Francis. 2012. *The Language of This Land, Mi'kma'ki*. Sydney: Cape Breton University Press.

Salée, Daniel. 2003. "L'État québécois et la question autochtone." *Québec. État et société*, tome 2, edited by Alain-G. Gagnon, 117–47. Québec Amérique, 2003.

Santoro, Miléna. 2011. 'Policing Genre Films, or, How American Are Quebec *Polars?*' *French Review* 84, no. 6: 1232–44.

Santoro, Miléna, Denis Bachand, Vincent Desroches, and André Loiselle. 2013. "Introduction: Quebec Cinema in the 21st Century." *American Review of Canadian Studies* 43, no. 2: 157–62.

Schwartz, Ronald. 2005. *Neo-Noir: A New Film Noir Style from Psycho to Collateral*. Lanham: Scarecrow Press.

Shek, Ben-Z. 2010. Review of "Denys Arcand's *Le Déclin de l'Empire américain* and *Les Invasions barbares*." *University of Toronto Quarterly* 79, no. 1: 475–76.

Smith, Greg M. 2003. *Film Structure and the Emotion System*. Cambridge: Cambridge University Press.

Sprengler, Christine. 2009. *Screening Nostalgia: Populuxe Props and Technicolor Aesthetics in Contemporary American Film*. New York and Oxford: Berghahn Books.

Staiger, Janet. 2008. "Film Noir as Male Melodrama: The Politics of Film Genre Labeling." In *The Shifting Definitions of Genre: Essays on Labeling Films, Television Shows, and Media*, edited by Lincoln Geraghty and Mark Jancovich, 71–91. Jefferson: McFarland.

Straram, Patrick. 1966. "Foutre! la 'pilule' gratuite aux épouses des militaires américains." *Parti Pris* 4, no. 3: 129.

Swidler, Leonard J. 1979. *Biblical Affirmations of Woman*. Philadelphia: Westminster Press.

Tétu de Labsade, Françoise. 1990. *Le Québec, un pays, une culture*. Montréal: Boréal/ Seuil.

"Thanatomorphose." 2016. *Internet Movie Database*. http://www.imdb.com/title/tt2385074. Accessed 18 September 2016.

Thériault, Mélissa. 2012. "Heureux les hérétiques. Patrimoine et transmission." *Tout ce que tu possèdes. Scénario et regards croisés. Suivi de contributions de de Gilles McMillan, Jean-François Nadeau, Lucien Pelletier et Melissa Thériault.* 129–39. Montréal: Lux.

Totaro, Donato. 2014. "When Women Kill: Recent North American Horror Films." *Off/Screen* 18, no. 8. http://offscreen.com/view/when-women-kill.

Tremblay, Gaëtan. 1966. "Le peuple contre le peuple." *Parti Pris* 4, no. 1: 19–23.

Tremblay-Daviault, Christiane. 1981. *Un cinéma orphelin. Structures mentales et sociales du cinéma québécois (1942–1953).* Montréal: Québec/Amérique.

Tschofen, Monique. 2006. "*Le Confessionnal / The Confessional.*" In *The Cinema of Canada*, edited by Jerry White, 205–23. London: Wallflower Press.

Vacante, Jeffery. 2006. "Liberal Nationalism and the Challenge of Masculinity Studies in Quebec." *New Left History* 11, no. 2: 96–117.

———. 2017. *National Manhood and the Creation of Modern Quebec.* Vancouver: UBC Press.

van Elferen, Isabella, ed. 2009. "Introduction: Nostalgia and Perversion in Gothic Rewriting." In *Nostalgia or Perversion? Gothic Rewriting from the Eighteenth Century until the Present Day.* Newcastle: Cambridge Scholars.

Varma, Devendra P. 1957. *The Gothic Flame.* London: Arthur Barker.

Vennat, Pierre J.-A. 1966. "La famille, propriété exclusive des femmes?" *Cité Libre*, February, 1–4.

Véronneau, Pierre. 2006. "En Pays Neufs." In *The Cinema of Canada*, edited by Jerry White, 13–22. London and New York: Wallflower Press.

Vidal, Bélen. 2012. *Heritage Film: Nation, Genre, and Representation.* London and New York: Wallflower Press.

Vidler, Anthony. 1996. *The Architectural Uncanny: Essays in the Modern Unhomely.* Cambridge, MA: MIT Press.

Weinmann, Heinz. 1990. *Cinéma de l'imaginaire québécois. De la petite Aurore à Jésus de Montréal.* Montréal: Hexagone.

———. 1997. "Cinéma québécois à l'ombre de la mélancolie." *Cinémas* 8, nos. 1–2: 35–46.

White, Jerry. 2002. "Alanis Obomsawin, Documentary Form, and the Canadian Nation(s)." In *North of Everything: English-Canadian Cinema since 1980*, edited by William Beard and Jerry White, 364–75. Edmonton: University of Alberta Press.

Williams, Linda. 1991. "Film Bodies: Genre, Genre, and Excess." *Film Quarterly* 44, no. 4: 2–13.

Wilson, Janelle L. 2005. *Nostalgia: Sanctuary of Meaning.* Lewisburg: Bucknell University Press.

Wood, Robin. 1979. "An Introduction to the American Horror Film." *American Nightmare: Essays on the Horror Film*, edited by Andrew Britton et al., 7–28. Toronto: Festival of Festivals.

Wright, Angela. 2007. *Gothic Fiction.* New York: Palgrave Macmillan.

FILMOGRAPHY

Arcand, Denys, dir. 1986. *Le Déclin de l'empire américain*. Montréal: Les Films Séville. DVD.

Arcand, Denys, dir. 1989. *Jésus de Montréal*. Montréal: Max Films. DVD.

Arcand, Denys, dir. 2003 *Les Invasions barbares*. Montréal: Cinémaginaire/Astral Films; Paris: Le Studio Canal+. DVD.

Aubert, Robin, dir. 2011. *À l'origine d'un cri*, 2010. Montréal: Max Films/TVA. DVD.

Aubert, Robin, dir. 2017. *Les Affamés*. Montréal: La maison de prod. DVD.

Barbeau-Lavallette, *Anaïs*, dir. 2007. *Le Ring*. Montréal: Christal Films. DVD.

Barnaby, Jeff, dir. 2004. *From Cherry English*. Montréal: Nutaak Média. DVD.

Barnaby, Jeff, dir. 2007. *The Colony*. Montréal: EyeSteelFilm. DVD.

Barnaby, Jeff, dir. 2010. *File Under Miscellaneous*. Montréal: Prospector Films. https://www.youtube.com/watch?v=Zi3B2V_e8fY.

Barnaby, Jeff, dir. 2013. *Rhymes for Young Ghouls*. Montréal: Prospector Films. DVD.

Beaudin, Jean, dir. 1972. *Le Diable est parmi nous*. Montréal: Cinépix. VHS.

Beaudin, Jean, dir. 1977. *J.A. Martin, photographe*. Montréal: National Film Board of Canada. DVD.

Beaudin, Jean, dir. 2004. *Nouvelle-France*. Montréal: Lions Gate Entertainment. DVD.

Bigras, Jean-Yves, dir. 1952. *La petit Aurore, l'enfant martyre*. Montréal: Renaissance Films. DVD.

Binamé, Charles, dir. 2002. *Séraphin. Un homme et son péché*. Montréal: Alliance Atlantis Vivafilm. DVD.

Binamé, Charles, dir. 2005. *Maurice Richard*. Montréal: Cinémaginaire/Film Richard, 2005. DVD.

Brault, Michel, dir. 1967. *Entre la mer et l'eau douce*. Montréal: Coopératio DVD.

Brault, Michel, and Gilles Groulx, dirs. 1958. *Les Raquetteurs*. Montréal: National Film Board of Canada. DVD

Brault, Michel, and Pierre Perrault, dirs. 1963. *Pour la suite du monde*. Montréal: National Film Board of Canada. DVD.

Brault, Michel, Marcel Carrière, Claude Fournier, and Claude Jutra, dirs. 1961. *La Lutte*. Montréal: National Film Board of Canada. Online: onf.ca.

Canuel, Érik, dir. 2005. *Le Survenant*. Montréal: Films Vision 4/Alliance Atlantis Vivafilm. DVD.

Canuel, Érik, dir. 2013. *Lac Mystère*. Montréal: Christal Films. DVD.

Carle, Gilles, dir. 1971. *Les Mâles*. Montréal: France Film and Onyx Films. DVD.

Carrier, Mélanie, and Olivier Higgins, dirs. 2014. *Québékoisie*. Québec: MÖ Films. DVD.

Choquette, Louis, dir. 2008. *La Ligne brisée*. Montréal: Alliance Atlantis Vivafilm. DVD.

Ciupka, Richard, dir. 1998. *Le Dernier Souffle*. Montréal: Films Vision 4/Lions Gate. DVD.

Cohen, Sheldon, dir. 1980. *The Sweater.* Montréal: National Film Board of Canada. www.nfb.ca

Cronenberg, David, dir. 1975. *Shivers.* Montréal: Cinépix. DVD.

Cronenberg, David, dir. 1977. *Rabid.* Montréal: Dunning/Link/Reitman. DVD

Delacroix, René, dir. 1949. *Le Gros Bill.* Montréal: Prod. Renaissance Film. 16mm.

Denis, Mathieu, and Simon Lavoie, dirs. 2011. *Laurentie.* Montréal. Métafilms/Funfilm. DVD.

Denis, Mathieu, and Simon Lavoie, dirs. 2016. *Ceux qui font les revolutions à moitié n'ont fait que se creuser un tombeau.* Montréal: K-Films Amérique, 2017. DVD.

Deraspe, Sophie, dir. 2014. *Les Loups.* Montréal: ACPAV. DVD.

Desrochers, Alain, dir. 2007. *Nitro.* Montréal: Alliance Atlantis Vivafilm. DVD.

Dionne, Luc, dir. 2005. *Aurore.* Montréal: Alliance Atlantis Vivafilm. DVD.

Dolan, Xavier, dir. 2014. *Mommy.* Montréal: Seville Films/Entertainment One. DVD.

Dolan, Xavier, dir. 2013. *Tom à la ferme.* Paris: MK2; Montreal: Sons of Manual. DVD.

Dolan, Xavier, dir. 2016 *Juste la fin du monde.* Montréal: Les Films Séville, 2017. DVD.

Dubuc, Yvan, and Carole Poliquin, dirs. 2015. *L'Empreinte.* Montréal: Les productions ISCA. DVD.

Édoin, Guy, dir. 2011. *Marécages.* Montréal: Max Films Productions. DVD.

Émond, Bernard, dir. 2003. *20h17, rue Darling.* Montréal: Christal Films. DVD.

Émond, Bernard, dir. 2005. *La Neuvaine.* Montréal: ACPAV. DVD.

Émond, Bernard, dir. 2009. *La Donation.* Montréal: ACPAV. DVD.

Émond, Bernard, dir. 2012. *Tout ce que tu possèdes.* Montréal: Association Coopérative des Productions Audio-Visuelles (ACPAV). DVD.

Émond, Bernard, dir. 2015. *Le Journal d'un vieil homme.* Montréal: Association Coopérative des Productions Audio-Visuelles (ACPAV). DVD.

Falardeau, Éric, dir. 2012. *Thanatomorphose.* Montréal: Black Flag Pictures, ThanatoFilms. DVD.

Falardeau, Philippe, dir. 2008. *C'est pas moi, je le jure.* Montréal: Christal Films/eOne Entertainment, 2008. DVD.

Falardeau, Philippe, dir. 2011. *Monsieur Lazhar,* Chicago: Music Box Films, 2012. DVD.

Falardeau, Pierre, dir. 1994. *Octobre,* 1994. Montréal: ACPAV/ONF.

Falardeau, Pierre, dir. 2002. *Le 15 février 1839,* 2001. Montréal: Christal Films. DVD.

Favreau, Robert, dir. 2006. *Un dimanche à Kigali.* Montréal: Equinoxe. DVD.

Ferland, Pascale, dir. 2013. *Ressac.* Montréal: Les Films de l'autre. DVD.

Filiatrault, Denise, dir. 2004. *Ma vie en cinémascope.* Montréal: Alliance Atlantis Vivafilm. DVD.

Grou, Daniel, dir. 2005–2006. *Minuit, le soir.* Montréal: Société Radio-Canada. DVD.

Grou, Daniel, dir. 2010. *Les 7 Jours du talion.* Montréal: Go Films/Alliance Vivafilm. DVD.

Grou, Daniel, dir. 2011–2015. *19-2.* Montréal: Société Radio-Canada. DVD.

Groulx, Gilles, dir. 1961. *Golden Gloves.* Montréal: National Film Board. Online: nfb.ca.

Groulx, Gilles, dir. 1964. *Le Chat dans le sac.* Montréal: National Film Board of Canada. DVD.

Gury, Paul, dir. 1949. *Le Curé de village*. Montréal: Quebec Productions. 16mm

Gury, Paul, dir. 1949. *Un homme et son péché*. Montréal: Quebec Productions. VHS.

Gury, Paul, dir. 1950. *Séraphin*. Montréal: Quebec Productions. VHS.

Guy, Sylvain, dir. 2009. *Détour*. Montréal: Seville Films/Entertainment One. DVD.

Harris, Damian, dir. 1991. *Deceived*. Burbank: Touchstone Pictures. DVD.

Hitchcock, Alfred, dir. 1941. *Suspicion*. Los Angeles: RKO Radio Pictures. DVD.

Hitchcock, Alfred, dir. 1940. *Rebecca*. Los Angeles: Selznick International Pictures. DVD.

Hitchcock, Alfred, dir. 1952. *I Confess*. Los Angeles: Warner Bros. DVD.

Houle, Pierre. 1996. *Omertá, la loi du silence*. Montréal: Société Radio-Canada/TVA. DVD.

Huard, Patrick, dir. 2007. *Les 3 P'tits Cochons*. Montréal: Zoofilms/Christal Films. DVD.

Huard, Patrick, dir. 2010. *Filière 13*. Montréal: Zoofilms/Alliance Vivafilm. DVD.

Ivory, James, dir. 1985. *Room With a View*. New York: BBC Video, 2004. DVD.

Ivory, James, dir. 1992. *Howard's End*. New York: Criterion Collection, 2010. DVD.

Jetté, Michel, dir. 2000. *Hochelaga*. Montréal: Baliverna Films/Lions Gate. DVD.

Jetté, Michel, dir. 2001. *Histoires de pen*. Montréal: Baliverna Films/ Maple Pictures. DVD.

Jutra, Claude, dir. 1963. À tout prendre. Montréal: Les Films Cassiopée. VHS.

Jutra, Claude, dir. 1971. *Mon oncle Antoine*. Montréal: National Film Board of Canada. DVD.

Larouche, Jimmy, dir. 2012. *La Cicatrice*. Montréal: Alma Films. DVD.

Laugier, Pascal, dir. 2008. *Martyrs*. Paris: Canal+. DVD.

Lavoie, Simon, dir. 2012. *Le Torrent*. Montréal: Métafilms. DVD

Lean, David, dir. 1984. *A Passage to India*. Culver City: Columbia Tristar Home Video, 2000. DVD.

Lebrun, Thierry, dir. 2002. *Je me souviens /A License to Remember*. Montréal: National Film Board of Canada, 2002. DVD.

Leclerc, Francis, dir. 2008. *Un été sans point ni coup sûr*. Montréal: Alliance Vivafilm. DVD.

Lefebvre, Jean Pierre, dir. 1965. *Le Révolutionnaire*. Montréal: Faroun Films, 1965. VHS.

Lepage, Robert, dir. 1995. *Le Confessionnal*. Montréal: Cinémaginaire. DVD.

Lepage, Robert, dir. 1998. *Nô*. Montréal: Alliance Atlantis Vivafilm. 2007. DVD.

Mankiewicz, Francis, dir. 1980. *Les Bons Débarras*. Montréal: National Film Board of Canada. DVD.

March, Jane, dir. 1943. *Terre de nos aïeux*. Montréal: National Film Board of Canada. www.nfb.ca.

Martin, Catherine, dir. 2006. *L'Esprit des lieux*. Montréal: Les Films du 3 mars. Online: Vimeo.

Martin, Catherine, dir. 2010. *Trois temps après la mort d'Anna*. Montréal: Association Coopérative des Productions Audio-Visuelles. DVD.

Martin, Catherine, dir. 2013. *Une jeune fille*. Montréal: Coop Vidéo de Montréal and Films 53/12. DVD.

Michaud, Maude, dir. 2014. *Dys-*. Montréal: Quirk Films. DVD.

Miljevic, Stefan, dir. 2013. *Amsterdam*. Montréal: Seville/eOne. DVD.

Nguyen, Kim, dir. 2012. *Rebelle*. Toronto: Mongrel Media, 2012. DVD.

Obomsawin, Alanis, dir. 1984. *Incident at Restigouche*. Montréal: National Film Board of Canada.

Obomsawin, Alanis, dir. 1993. *Kanehsatake: 270 Years of Resistance*. Montréal: National Film Board of Canada.

Ouellette, Rafael, dir. 2012. *Camion*. Montréal: Coop Vidéo de Montréal/K Films Amérique. DVD.

Ozep, Fédor dir. 1944. *Le Père Chopin*. Montréal: Renaissance Films. 16mm.

Péloquin, François, dir. 2015. *Le Bruit des arbres*. Montréal: Ziad Touma and Couzin Films. DVD.

Picard, Luc, dir. 2005. *L'Audition*. Montréal: Christal Films. DVD.

Pilon, Benoît, dir. 2011. *Décharge*. Montréal: Entertainment One/Remstar. DVD.

Pilote, Sebastien, dir. 2011. *Le Vendeur*. Montréal: Seville Films/Entertainment One. DVD.

Pilote, Sébastien, dir. 2014. *Le Démantèlement*. Montréal: Association Coopérative des Productions Audio-Visuelles. DVD.

Pool, Léa, dir. 2008. *Maman est chez le coiffeur*. Montréal: Universal/Equinoxe Films. DVD.

Pouliot, Jean-François, dir. 2003. *Seducing Dr. Lewis/La Grande Séduction*. Montréal: Max Films/Alliance Vivafilm. DVD.

Pouliot, Jean-François, dir. 2016. *Les 3 P'tits Cochons 2: Des cochons un peu moins cochons*. Montréal: Christal Films. DVD.

Roby, Daniel, dir. 2013. *Louis Cyr. L'homme le plus fort du monde*. Montréal: Seville Films/ eOne Entertainment. Blu-ray.

Romero, A. George, dir. 1868. *Night of the Living Dead*. Pittsburgh: Image Ten Productions. DVD.

Roy, Mathieu, dir. 2013. *L'Autre Maison*. Montréal: Max Films/TVA. DVD.

Ruben, Joseph, dir. 1991. *Sleeping with the Enemy*. Los Angeles: Twentieth Century Fox. DVD.

Stevenson, Robert, dir. 1943. *Jane Eyre*. Los Angeles: Twentieth Century Fox. DVD.

Tessier, Éric, dir. 2003. *Sur le seuil*. Montréal: Alliance Atlantis Vivafilm. DVD.

Tessier, Éric, dir. 2009. *5150 Rue des ormes*. Montréal: Cirrus Communications. DVD.

Trogi, Ricardo, dir. 2002. *Québec-Montréal*. Montréal: Go Films. DVD.

Vallée, Jean-Marc, dir. 2005. *C.R.A.Z.Y.* Montréal: TVA Films. DVD.

Villeneuve, Denis, dir. 2010. *Incendies*. Montréal: Films Séville, 2011. DVD.

Zemeckis, Robert, dir. 2000. *What Lies Beneath*. Los Angeles: DreamWorks, Twentieth Century Fox, ImageMovers. DVD.

CONTRIBUTORS

Liz Czach is Associate Professor in the Department of English and Film Studies at the University of Alberta in Edmonton. She publishes on Canadian and Québécois film, film festivals, and amateur films and home movies. She is a former programmer of Canadian film at the Toronto International Film Festival (1995-2005) and past president of the Film Studies Association of Canada.

Kester Dyer teaches in the Department of Humanities at Dawson College in Montreal. He received his PhD in Film and Moving Image Studies from Concordia University, where he completed a thesis examining intercultural tensions expressed through the supernatural in the cinema of Quebec, with a particular focus on Quebec's relationship to Indigenous Peoples. In addition to Indigenous and Québécois film and media, his areas of interest include nationalism, postcolonial theory, Irish film, and genre theory.

Gina Freitag is a horror enthusiast with an MA in Film Studies. She co-edited *The Canadian Horror Film: Terror of the Soul* (2015), alongside André Loiselle. After serving as a coordinator with the Cellar Door Film Festival, the Eve Film Festival, TIFF, and the NFB, Gina has taken on a curator role for The Black Museum, a horror lecture and screening series based in Toronto. Follow her on Twitter: @smalldarkthings.

Jim Leach is Professor Emeritus in the Department of Communication, Popular Culture, and Film at Brock University, St. Catharines, Ontario. He is the author of books on Alain Tanner and Claude Jutra, as well as *British Film*, *Film in Canada*, and *Doctor Who*, and has co-edited books on Canadian documentary films and heist films. His latest book is *The Films of Denys Arcand* (forthcoming in 2020).

André Loiselle is Dean of Humanities and teaches film studies at St. Thomas University in Fredericton, New Brunswick. His main areas of research are Canadian and Québécois cinema, theatricality on screen, and the horror film. He has published more than forty refereed articles and anthology chapters, as well as a dozen books, including *Theatricality in the Horror Film* (2019), *The Canadian Horror Film: Terror of the Soul* (2015, with Gina Freitag), and *Cinema as History: Michel Brault and Modern Quebec* (2007).

Alessandra Pires, PhD, is an independent scholar. She holds a doctorate in Romance Languages and Literatures from the University of Georgia and a *Diplôme d'Études Approfondies* in European Literatures and Cultures from the Université de Nice, France. Her publications explore the interface between francophone and lusophone literatures, the visual arts, and psychoanalysis.

Amy J. Ransom is Professor of French and chair of the World Languages and Cultures Department at Central Michigan University, as well as editor of the scholarly journal *Québec Studies*. Her books on Québécois film, literature, and popular culture include *Hockey P.Q.: Canada's Game in Québec's Popular Culture* (U of Toronto P, 2014) and *Science Fiction from Québec: A Postcolonial Study* (McFarland, 2009).

Katherine Ann Roberts is Associate Professor of French and North American Studies at Wilfrid Laurier University in Waterloo, Ontario. She is the author of *West/Border/Road: Nation and Genre in Contemporary Canadian Narrative* (Montreal: McGill–Queen's University Press, 2018). Her work has appeared in *Quebec Studies*, *The French Review*, the *Journal of Borderland Studies*, the *European Journal of American Studies*, the *Journal of Canadian Studies*, and the *International Journal of Canadian Studies*, and in other collected volumes.

Miléna Santoro is a Professor of French and Francophone Studies at Georgetown University. She has authored or co-edited three books and has published numerous articles on Quebec literature, cinema, and culture, on women writers, and on Canadian Indigenous filmmaking. She was awarded the Ordre des francophones d'Amérique in 2019 and holds the 2018 Prix du Québec, a Certificate of Merit in Canadian Studies from the ICCS, and one of only 50 Médailles Hommage 50e offered worldwide by Quebec's Ministry of International Relations.

INDEX

Quebec culture: erosion of, 184;
depiction of evil in, 85, 88; "male
under siege" mentality in, 96; presence
of sexuality in, 89
Quebec heritage films: *vs.* British
counterpart, 47; characteristics of,
42–44, 47, 48; funding of, 5, 44–45;
heritage bio-pics subgenre of, 50–51,
53; identity crisis and, 22, 48; local
stars, 5–6; myth of collective suffering
in, 50; presentation of the past in, 47,
58; production of, 42; rise of, 5, 21,
43, 49
Quebec horror cinema: construction of
identity and space in, 104; emergence
of, 104; female characters in, 106,
107, 109, 110; image of unsettled
home in, 105–106; literary source of,
109; ordinary men in, 105; prevailing
themes in, 109; representation of
women's body in, 110
Québec-Montréal (Trogi, 2002), 201
Québécois identity: Catholic
roots of, 218; characteristic of
contemporary, 23; crisis of, 1, 204,
205; historical trauma and, 28;
mythology of rural, 150; perceive
decline of, 46; transformation of,
84–85; "ungraspable" nature of, 26;
victimhood, 48–49
Québécois loser, 47, 140
Québécois man, 93, 94, 95
Québékoisie (Carrier and Higgins, 2013),
23, 24
Quiet Revolution: and break with the
past, 202–203; Catholicism and, 92;
cinematic portrayals of, 16; cultural
impact of, 25, 202, 203, 204, 205;
decolonization project of, 30; end
of, 85; modernity and, 12n1; as
movement from childhood into
adulthood, 203–204; Québécois

identity and, 24; roots of, 88–89, 153,
208; socio-economic changes of, 5, 151
Quignard, Pascal, 68
15 février 1839, Le (Falardeau, 2002), 128

Rabid (Cronenberg, 1977), 104
Ransom, Amy, 7, 53, 54, 94, 119
Raquetteurs, Les (Brault and Groulx,
1958), 151, 176n2
Rassemblement pour l'indépendance
nationale (RIN), 87
Ravary, Julie, 21
Rebecca (Hitchcock, 1940), 107
Ressac (Ferland, 2013): depiction of
countryside, 8, 149; depiction
of women's experiences, 196;
intergenerational conflict, 161–162;
landscape shots, 162; motif of escape,
161; plot, 160–162; portrait of remote
life, 159; suicide motif, 160, 162;
young protagonists, 160
Retour à la terre, Le (Perrault, 1976), 9,
182, 188, 189–190
Rhymes for Young Ghouls (Barnaby, 2013),
28, 29, 34
Richard, Maurice, 53–54, 55, 146n8
Richard Riot, 54
Rioux, Christian, 93
Robert, Marc-André, 11
Roberts, Katherine Ann, 9, 65, 216
Robi, Alys, 50, 51
Roby, Daniel, 21, 50
Romero, George A., 117
Room with a View, A (Ivory, 1985), 45
Rose, Kayden, 106
Royer, Carl, 122
Royer, Diana, 122
rural films: audience of, 150; corpus
of, 149–151; depiction of natural
wilderness in, 174; history of, 150–155;
intergenerational relationships in,
173; motif of escape, 175; motif of